Papua New Guinea

Its Economic Situation
and Prospects for Development

A WORLD BANK COUNTRY ECONOMIC REPORT

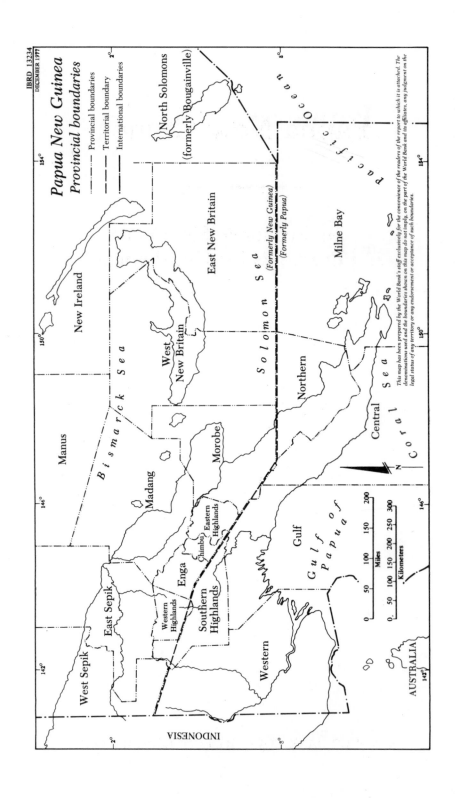

IBRD 13234

DECEMBER 1977

Papua New Guinea
Provincial boundaries

Provincial boundaries
Territorial boundary
International boundaries

North Solomons
(formerly Bougainville)

East New Britain

(Formerly New Guinea)

(Formerly Papua)

Milne Bay

New Ireland

West
New Britain

Bismarck Sea

Solomon Sea

Manus

Madang

Morobe

Northern

Pacific Ocean

Central Sea

Coral Sea

Eastern
Highlands

Chimbu

Enga

Western
Highlands

Southern
Highlands

Gulf

Gulf of Papua

Western

East Sepik

West Sepik

INDONESIA

AUSTRALIA

N

200
150
100
50
0
Miles

300
250
200
150
100
50
0
Kilometers

This map has been prepared by the World Bank's staff exclusively for the convenience of the readers of the report to which it is attached. The denominations used and the boundaries shown on this map do not imply, on the part of the World Bank and its affiliates, any judgment on the legal status of any territory or any endorsement or acceptance of such boundaries.

154°
150°
146°
142°
2°
0°
2°
8°
154°
150°
146°
142°

Papua New Guinea

Its Economic Situation
and Prospects for Development

REPORT OF A MISSION SENT TO PAPUA NEW GUINEA
BY THE WORLD BANK

CHIEF OF MISSION AND PRINCIPAL AUTHOR
GEORGE B. BALDWIN

WITH THE ASSISTANCE OF
SWADESH R. BOSE
ALICE C. GALENSON
PAUL C. MOULIN

The World Bank : *Washington, D.C.*

The views and interpretations in this book are those of the authors
and should not be attributed to the World Bank, to its affiliated
organizations, or to any individual acting in their behalf.

Library of Congress Cataloging in Publication Data

Baldwin, George Benedict.
  Papua New Guinea, its economic situation and
prospects for development.

  (World Bank country economic report)
  1. Papua New Guinea—Economic conditions.
2. Papua New Guinea—Economic policy. I. International Bank for Reconstruction and Development.
II. Title. III. Series: World Bank country
economic reports.

HC687.P3B323   330.9′95′3   77-17242
ISBN 0-8018-2091-X

Foreword

THIS IS THE FOURTEENTH IN THE CURRENT SERIES OF World Bank country economic reports, all of which are listed on the following page. They are published, in response to a desire expressed by scholars and practitioners in the field of economic and social development, to aid and encourage research and the interchange of knowledge.

Economic reports on borrowing countries are prepared regularly by the Bank in support of its own operations. These surveys provide a basis for discussions with the governments and for decisions on Bank policy and operations. Many of these reports are also used by the governments themselves as an aid to their economic planning and by consortia and consultative groups of governments and institutions providing assistance in development. All Bank country reports are subject to the agreement of—and several have been published by—the governments concerned.

HOLLIS CHENERY
Vice President for Development Policy
The World Bank

Washington, D.C.
December 1977

v

WORLD BANK COUNTRY ECONOMIC REPORTS

Published for the Bank by The Johns Hopkins University Press

Korea: Problems and Issues in a Rapidly Growing Economy
Kenya: Into the Second Decade
Yugoslavia: Development with Decentralization
Nigeria: Options for Long-Term Development
Economic Growth of Colombia

Published by the World Bank

Papua New Guinea: Its Economic Situation and Prospects for Development
The Philippines: Priorities and Prospects for Development
Lesotho: A Development Challenge
Turkey: Prospects and Problems of an Expanding Economy
Senegal: Tradition, Diversification, and Economic Development (also published in French)
Chad: Development Potential and Constraints (also published in French as *Le Développement du Tchad: Possibilités et Limites*)
Current Economic Position and Prospects of Peru
Current Economic Position and Prospects of Ecuador
Employment in Trinidad and Tobago

Contents

List of Tables

Preface

THE WORLD BANK, BETWEEN 1963 and 1976, sent a number of economic missions to Papua New Guinea.[1] This short span of time saw a country that was an economically and politically fragmented, primitive protectorate of Australia evolve—peacefully and amicably—into a self-governing and finally independent nation. Although Papua New Guinea has become politically independent of Australia, its economic dependence persists and is likely to do so for several years to come. Nevertheless, the prospects for self-reliance—which is not the same as self-sufficiency—are promising. The analysis of these prospects is the central theme of this book. An important secondary theme, one treated more explicitly in some of the documentary appendixes than in the text, is Papua New Guinea's unusually clear set of development policies, policies that are remarkable for their attempt to reconcile objectives of growth and quality of life.

Until Papua New Guinea is able to carry through an economic transformation that will make it fully self-reliant, the country will continue to be highly dependent on external grant aid, which comes primarily from Australia. This dependence is found in (a) Papua New Guinea's continuing reliance on Australia's annual budgetary grant, without which Papua New Guinea's central government budget and its balance of payments would not be viable, and (b) the dominant role foreigners (mainly Australians) play in a number of modern activities in the public and private sectors requiring skilled or high-level manpower. An important task of the World Bank's

1. The report of the first World Bank mission, in 1963, was the basis of a comprehensive economic survey, published as *The Economic Development of the Territory of Papua and New Guinea* (Baltimore: Johns Hopkins Press, 1965). Although the political and economic context has changed drastically since this time, the book still provides highly useful background information on the country. The report of the mission which visited Papua New Guinea in mid-1974 was not published, but it has provided considerable material for the present book. Other references on the country are listed in Appendix G.

economic mission in 1976 was to assess the prospects for a progressive reduction and an eventual ending of this historical dependence on Australia, that is, for Papua New Guinea's prospects for self-reliance. A Bank mission headed by Guenter H. Reif, which visited the country in 1974, eighteen months before independence, identified this issue as crucial for future assistance to the country. In studying this issue after independence, the 1976 mission concluded that the prospects for self-reliance were promising and that there were good grounds for believing that the country would eventually be able to "earn its own living" without grant assistance. Of conceptual and technical interest is the book's treatment of this problem—what "self-reliance" consists of and how to judge the prospects for it. While the discussion inevitably makes use of standard economic terms and concepts, an effort has been made to avoid language that would be understood only by specialists.

The prospects for self-reliance are central to the World Bank's ability to extend development loans to Papua New Guinea. The Bank had made loans to Papua New Guinea before independence, but always with the guarantee of the colonial power. With independence, the Australian guarantee was no longer available. Consequently, the Bank had to decide if it could lend to Papua New Guinea on the basis of that country's own creditworthiness. This judgment turned primarily on whether the country could become self-supporting, a term that implies an ability to service foreign debt on commercial or semicommercial terms. The World Bank's soft-loan affiliate, the International Development Association (IDA), was already prepared to extend its highly concessional credits to Papua New Guinea, but adding regular World Bank loans, which would expand the total volume of assistance the World Bank could extend to the country, was another matter. A favorable Bank judgment on this point would also affect the country's access to other sources of external assistance and the terms on which that assistance would be offered. A primary purpose of the 1976 economic mission was to assemble the evidence and conduct the analyses needed to make that judgment.

This book is an edited version of the Bank's economic report of July 1976 on Papua New Guinea; that report has not been changed in any substantial way. A few annexes and tables were dropped as being of only minor general interest; others have been retained substantially as they appeared in the original report. A decision was made not to attempt any complete updating of data but to do only as much as could be done from data readily available in the Bank.

Bank officials made a return visit to the country in November 1976, and the memorandum on that visit, plus more recent materials received in the Bank, form the basis for the one chapter which did not appear in the original report—Chapter 8, "Postscript." That chapter summarizes the main economic and political events that have occurred since early 1976.

The economic mission responsible for the study consisted of George B. Baldwin, chief of mission, Swadesh R. Bose, Alice C. Galenson, and Paul C. Moulin. They were in the field for about one month in February and March of 1976. Mr. Bose covered agriculture and rural development; Ms. Galenson, wage and manpower issues, industry, and balance-of-payments projections (she also wrote the postscript chapter); Mr. Moulin, forestry, fisheries, and balance-of-payments statistics. Mr. Baldwin covered all other topics and was the principal author of the report. Gregory B. Votaw, director of the Country Programs department in the Bank's East Asia and Pacific regional office, was instrumental in organizing and guiding the Bank's review of Papua New Guinea's creditworthiness. Other staff in the Bank's East Asia and Pacific regional office who made important contributions to the final report were Kevin Young, who helped with the balance-of-payments projections; F. L. C. H. Helmers, division chief; Edward K. Hawkins, senior economist; and Parvez Hasan, chief economist for the region. The present text was edited by Charlene Semer.

Acronyms

ASAG	Australian Staff Assistance Group
BCL	Bougainville Copper Ltd.
BHP	Broken Hill Proprietary Ltd.
BPC	Budget Priorities Committee
BPNG	Bank of Papua New Guinea
BRT	Bougainville Royalty Trust
CPI	Consumer price index
CPO	Central Planning Office
CRA	Conzinc Riotinto of Australia Ltd.
DASF	Department of Agriculture, Stock and Fisheries
ELCOM	Electricity Commission
FAO	Food and Agricultural Organization
GDP	Gross domestic product
GNP	Gross national product
IDA	International Development Association
IMF	International Monetary Fund
LGC	Local Government Council
MRSF	Mineral Resources Stabilization Fund
NI	National income
NIDA	National Investment and Development Authority
NIPS	National Investment Priorities Schedule
NORAD	Norwegian International Aid Agency
PAYE	Pay as you earn
PDC	Provincial Development Corporation
PNGDB	Papua New Guinea Development Bank
PSA	Public Servants Association
P&T	Department of Posts and Telegraphs

RIP   Rural Improvement Program

SITC   Standard industrial trade classification
SRI   Self-reliance index

VEDF   Village Economic Development Fund

Section I

Background

1

Introduction and Summary

THE RECENT HISTORY OF PAPUA NEW GUINEA offers a rich study re-source for economists and political and social scientists. For many years the country's only national institutional structures were provided externally by Australia. In late 1975, shortly before the preparation of the World Bank's report upon which this book is based, Papua New Guinea became politically independent, gaining its own identity as a nation. Now it must face the problems that will arise in gaining its economic identity and independence as well. The transition, thus far, has been remarkably well managed.

This book fixes on one aspect of this transition process. The book's time span is largely confined to the 1970s, although some projections are made into Papua New Guinea's next decade. The analysis revolves around the country's present and prospective economic position; the theme is Papua New Guinea's financial self-reliance. The book touches on history and politics only peripherally, and it reports on the government's first steps to establish its own unique institutions and to guide its own development only insofar as these will affect the country's ability to be self-sustaining.

The first section of the book presents the background material the Bank considers relevant to its economic and financial analysis. Following this chapter's summary of the entire book, Chapter 2 places in historical context the salient characteristics of Papua New Guinea's land, its people, its history, and its political environment. Chapter 3 focuses on the country's economic structure; it traces the evolution of this structure, describes the changes that are emerging along with political independence, and explores the likely direction of future changes.

Papua New Guinea is a newly independent country of 2.8 million people who live in an area slightly larger than the Republic of the Philippines. It is a land of mountainous terrain scattered over a mainland and several large and small islands. The land is endowed with good soils, abundant rainfall, considerable mineral resources (mainly copper but also gold and silver), and forestry and fishery resources of good commercial potential. The capital city, Port Moresby, is the largest urban settlement in what remains an overwhelmingly rural society. Only seven towns have more than 10,000 inhabitants. Of the arable land, 90 percent is still under subsistence agriculture, and 60 to 70 percent of the population are subsistence farmers, many of whom have only recently emerged from neolithic culture.

At the present time, about a third of Papua New Guinea's domestic production comes from agriculture, forestry, and fishing. Two-thirds of that sector's output comes from households that are either wholly or primarily subsistence based. Another 20 to 25 percent of domestic output comes from one copper mine, an opencast mine at Panguna on Bougainville Island; an additional 20 to 25 percent of domestic output is generated by the activities of the central government; and the remaining 20 to 25 percent comes from a miscellany of sectors that are still small: manufacturing, wholesale and retail trade, hotels and tourism, finance and insurance, nongovernment construction, and personal services. Within this structure, a relatively abundant subsistence agriculture is slowly being converted into a subsistence-plus-cash-crop agriculture; cash-crop farming is predominantly export oriented, and the 500 to 600 plantations in Papua New Guinea are completely export oriented. The country's main agricultural exports are coffee, cocoa, and copra.

Papua New Guinea's per capita income was estimated at US$460 in 1976. This falls to about US$410 if the incomes of the 35,000 expatriate residents of the country are excluded. The distribution of income is such that probably half the population has an average income of only about US$150. This wide difference occurs because such a large proportion of Papua New Guinea's people are only partially, if at all, involved in cash-earning pursuits. The strikingly primitive state of much of the economy and society contrasts with the surprisingly well-developed status of the central government and many of its services. Education and health care and some of the country's infrastructure—harbors, electricity supply, telecommunications, and air services—are comparatively advanced.

Before its independence, Papua New Guinea was administered for more than half a century by Australia. The ties between the two countries have been and remain extremely close. In the 1960s, Australian policy changed, and Canberra began to prepare the country for independence. Papua New Guinea's first House of Assembly (parliament) was elected in 1964; local political parties were formed; and indigenes (as the local inhabitants were then called) were admitted to the administration. After the third national election, in 1972, a national coalition was formed from three minority parties in the House, with Michael Somare, the present prime minister, as its leader. Papua New Guinea became self-governing on December 1, 1973, and full independence was achieved on September 16, 1975. The transfer of power was peaceful, amicable, and orderly. Today, relations between Australia and Papua New Guinea are excellent. Some 2,000 Australians continue to work for the government of Papua New Guinea.

The Somare government inherited a Westminster-type structure, with a cabinet composed of ministers who are members of the national parliament and who preside over ministries run by strong civil service staffs. These staffs are still heavily expatriate, although they are now headed by an able cadre of nationals. In the four years after its election, the Somare government showed an impressive ability to deal with the young country's financial, economic, and political problems. An effective set of institutions for economic and financial management has been created. These include a strong ministry of finance that has developed a tight system of budget controls, operating through a budget priorities committee; a planning office; and a central bank that, with International Monetary Fund assistance, has organized a set of international accounts. The new country's banking system has been successfully disentangled from that of Australia. A new national currency, the kina, has been introduced and fully accepted. By agreement with Australia, a clear reserve position has been established. A set of exchange regulations has been formulated and introduced. The cabinet has approved a set of principles to govern development policy and foreign investment, and Papua New Guinea's National Investment and Development Authority (NIDA) has published a set of investment priorities. A major five-year aid agreement with Australia was negotiated in March 1976. No one can say how sturdy or fragile Papua New Guinea's policy or administration will prove to be, but the short-run record provides strong grounds for optimism and few for anxiety.

Before its independence, Papua New Guinea relied heavily on budgetary transfers from Canberra to pay the costs of government. Because it was part of the Australian monetary system, Papua New Guinea had no balance-of-payments or foreign-exchange requirements of its own. Independence did not end the country's dependence on Australian budgetary aid, and it created a balance-of-payments problem that had not previously existed. A central objective of the government is to develop the country's economic independence by progressively reducing its continuing dependence on large Australian grants for financing its budget and for providing a large proportion of its foreign-exchange needs. At present, Australian aid provides 40 to 45 percent of the government's budgetary resources and 45 to 50 percent of its foreign-exchange requirements. There are reasonable grounds, however, for believing that the country's dependence on Australian grant aid might end entirely within the next 20 to 25 years.

Section II of this volume outlines the government's attitudes toward economic development and the policies it is pursuing to achieve its stated development goals. The likely course of Papua New Guinea's development is assessed along two lines: Chapter 4 deals with the government's strategies for self-development, and Chapter 5 reviews the role that foreign investment may play in Papua New Guinea's economic future.

The government feels that development strategy must aim at, first, increasing internal and external financial viability and, second, using the growing resources of financial viability to pay for the substantive programs needed to increase productivity on a wide front. The government is sensibly cautious about the speed and directions of economic growth it will try to stimulate. It hopes to guide economic and social development along lines that reflect its clearly expressed social and cultural values. These values include the need for increasing national production; this increase is expected to come from a small number of highly productive enclave projects and from a broader range of output in agriculture and industry.[1] The government's objectives include as much concern for income distribution (both horizontal and vertical) and for quality-of-life objectives (notably environmental protection) as for growth in itself. These goals have been clearly stated in recent policy documents.

---

1. An enclave project is defined as any very large foreign-owned project involved in exploitation of natural resources.

The government has made a modest start toward introducing cash crops for domestic consumption; these include fruits, vegetables, poultry, and livestock. Domestic production of the three main imported food staples—rice, sugar, and tinned fish—is insignificant. Prospects for the latter two appear good; prospects for rice are uncertain. Immediate, vigorous growth of indigenous production outside the enclaves is unlikely, however. Entrepreneurship is weak, markets are small and scattered over difficult terrain, and transport costs are high. The expected rapid growth of towns will create needs for construction and for the production of marketed foods. Translating human needs into effective demand will tax government ingenuity and resources. Increasing urbanization and a growing pool of unemployed, educated young people are likely to be among the most worrisome social problems by the mid-1980s. A program of sites-and-services housing and a direct approach to generating employment appear to be high-priority objectives.

The government's attitude toward foreign investment has been well defined. It realizes that a small number of large-scale natural resource projects will be the key to greater internal and external financial viability for many years and that such projects will depend on foreign managerial, technical, and financial resources. Foreign investors will be assured attractive returns, but Papua New Guinea, rather than the foreign investor, is to be the main beneficiary of above-average returns. The government will insist on the training of nationals and the progressive localization of technical and administrative positions.[2] A 1967 agreement between the country's largest enterprise, Bougainville Copper Ltd. (BCL), and the Australian administration, then governing Papua New Guinea, did not reflect these standards, and the agreement was renegotiated in 1974. Relations between the company and the new, independent government are now very good.

Although enclave projects will provide most of the additional domestic revenues and foreign exchange needed to pay for development, the government must devise and carry out the program activities that will set the pace and determine the directions of growth. In this sense, the government is the "lead sector" in the economy. There is not yet any central development plan, but in 1976 a decision was made to prepare a public expenditure plan by the end of 1977. In view of the government's crucial role, the quali-

2. "Localization" is the term used to describe the replacement in various jobs of expatriates by Papua New Guineans.

ty of staffing of government departments will largely determine the economy's ability to put growing financial revenues to effective use. At present the government is unusually well staffed, although the great majority of nonpolicy posts—the technical-professional cadre—are held by expatriates. Output from the well-developed educational system, which includes two young universities, is providing the manpower for a systematic program of localization. In the early 1970s a somewhat aggressive approach to localization, plus the anxieties surrounding the introduction of self-government at the end of 1973, led to a heavy exodus of Australian staff; that drain has now ended, anxieties seem largely to have been removed, and localization is now being pursued at a rate that seems about optimal.

Fully realizing the contribution additional large enclave projects can make to Papua New Guinea's financial and external viability, the government is actively pursuing four major possibilities—the Ok Tedi and Frieda River copper projects, the Vanimo forestry—pulp mill complex, and oil and gas exploration. The present judgment is that Ok Tedi has relatively good prospects, but Vanimo appears more doubtful; Frieda River is still in the early stages of investigation; and a modest oil and gas drilling program hangs between the encouragement of highly favorable structures and the discouragement of having made no commercial finds to date.

Foreign investment is also being welcomed in many lesser activities, including housing construction, certain types of plantation agriculture, manufacturing, and coastal shipping. In only a few well-defined cases will local participation be required. The government is not using fiscal incentives to attract large foreign investments; it is relying instead on the commercial attractiveness of its resource endowment, which it has begun to bring to world attention by a modest promotional effort. New investment in the private sector has been severely slowed by events of the past three or four years, but output from existing firms and plantations has not suffered. There is some evidence of a modest revival of foreign investors' interest in new projects.

The last section of this book, Chapters 6 to 8, is concerned with the important question of whether Papua New Guinea's successful transition into self-government and independence can eventually be matched by economic self-reliance—and if so, how soon. Both the Papua New Guinean and Australian governments are fully aware that the country's public finances, its government structure, and its economy would collapse were it not for the annual

Australian grant-in-aid of about A$200 million. This grant amounts to nearly US$80 per capita, giving Papua New Guinea one of the highest per capita aid figures of any country in the world. In March 1976 the Australian government signed a five-year aid agreeemnt that will provide a minimum of A$180 million (US$198 million) a year, with supplements likely; in fact, supplements of A$10 million (US$11 million) and A$20 million (US$22 million) have already been agreed upon for the first two years of the agreement.[3]

Chapter 6 considers the problems Papua New Guinea faces in meeting from its own domestic revenues the public expenditure requirements of a developing country. The strength of Australia's long-term aid commitment and the large role that tax revenues from enclave projects play in the thinking of government policymakers have until very recently kept the Papua New Guinea government from giving equal attention to its own ability to finance a growing proportion of its expenditures from domestic revenues. In the last two years, however, good progress has been made in finding new sources of tax revenue and raising rates on existing sources and in resolving to reduce the very high cost of government, part of the Australian legacy. In early 1976 a technical assistance mission from the International Monetary Fund (IMF) made a study of the situation of Papua New Guinea's domestic revenue and public expenditure. If implemented, the IMF's recommendations might increase domestic revenues from existing tax sources by about 10 percent in the next three years. In 1977, the government was studying these proposals to determine their net impact and their feasibility.

On the expenditure side, the key problem is containing pressures for wage and salary increases from the 50,000 heavily unionized government employees. The real wages of a majority of government employees appear to have been maintained or even improved despite the fact that as of March 1977 the consumer price index had risen more than 70 percent since it was first calculated in 1971. Over the longer run, it appears that only if revenues grow nearly twice as fast as expenditures will the government be able within the next 20 years to end its dependence on Australian grants.

Papua New Guinea's balance-of-payments prospects are discussed in Chapter 7. The outlook depends on Papua New Guinea's ability to sustain the level of imports it will require and to service foreign equity and debt capital without depending on the foreign

---

3. U.S. dollar equivalents used here are based on the April 1977 exchange rate. For rates in previous years, see Table SA12 in the Statistical Appendix.

exchange provided by foreign grants. This prospect appears promising if—but only if—the real growth of imports can be held to about 4 to 5 percent a year. Thus, the greatest constraint on economic growth will be the volume of imports the country can afford.

The World Bank's balance-of-payments projections through fiscal 1985[4] show relatively small deficits on current account for most of this period, but these deficits would become very large were it not for an assumed level of Australian aid of US$250 million through 1981 and of US$200 million through 1985. The government could not expect to borrow abroad on anything like the scale needed to replace a loss of Australian aid. Thus, only large amounts of Australian aid can prevent an unmanageable loss of exchange reserves, and such aid will be essential to maintain Papua New Guinea's external viability during the next decade. On the (realistic) assumption that Australian aid will continue on a large scale, the present fairly low reserves are likely to stabilize and to start slowly rebuilding within the next year; by the mid-1980s reserves would cover about four months' import requirements instead of the slightly lower level on hand in May 1976.[5]

The expected gradual improvement in external self-reliance will be strongly assisted by increasingly better terms of trade for primary commodities. The World Bank expects this improvement to occur by the end of this decade, but this optimistic prospect will come to nothing if the government proves unable to confine the real growth of imports to a level that is compatible with growing self-reliance. The performance of the economy will be very sensitive to the growth rate of imports; considerable import growth must be expected and will be essential, but too rapid a growth will be fatally disruptive.

It is unlikely that domestic production of goods now imported can be developed to any significant extent within the next decade, although a start should certainly be made on the relatively few such activities that look especially promising. In an effort to contain nonessential imports, customs duties on luxuries were increased rather sharply in the budget for fiscal 1976; it is doubtful that further use of this intervention would have any additional effect on these imports. The most important contributions to limiting import growth

4. The fiscal year here and throughout this book is dated from July 1 of the preceding calendar year to June 30 of the year cited.

5. Early projections for fiscal 1977 indicate that reserves are already above the level of four months' worth of imports.

will come from incomes and monetary policies that firmly limit the growth of demand for imports and from an investment program that is neither too ambitious nor too biased in favor of projects with high import requirements.

Concern for import growth must become a much more central objective of government economic and financial management than it is now. Informed policymaking, aimed at controlling import growth, will require better knowledge than is now available of how imports respond to changes in monetized activities of various kinds. How much will imports change as expatriate incomes increase or decrease, as the cash incomes of nationals grow, as various types of investment activities develop, and as government expenditures expand? Finding answers to these questions should be among the highest priorities for government economic research and policymaking.

The World Bank's balance-of-payments projections yield a public debt-service ratio of almost 3 percent by the mid-1980s (it is now about 6 percent). The broader ratio of gross factor payments (public and private debt service plus expected dividend payments) to total export earnings, including earnings from nonfactor services, is misleading because factor-service payments of enclave projects are self-financing. If the copper sector's factor payments are netted out, the gross ratio falls to a level very close to the public debt-service ratio. Because of the favorable outlook for these key ratios, the decreasing need for external borrowing, and the reasonable prospects for political viability, the World Bank concluded that Papua New Guinea could manage additional modest amounts of medium- or long-term loans, provided that they be obtained on terms comparable to those of the World Bank and, preferably, that they include some concessional element.

More than a year has passed since the Bank's 1976 economic mission returned from Papua New Guinea and wrote its report. A Postscript chapter has been added to cover the main events of this period. The chapter is intended merely to update the account presented in the earlier chapters; it does not in any way alter the basic analysis or conclusions of the 1976 report.

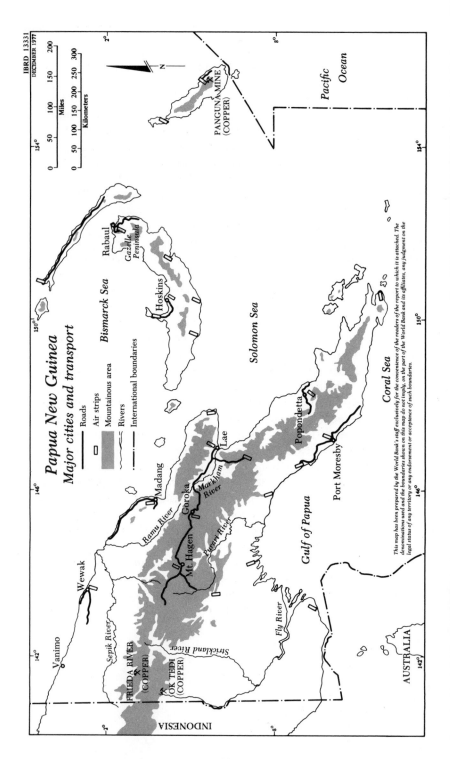

Papua New Guinea
Major cities and transport

Roads
Air strips
Mountainous area
Rivers
International boundaries

IBRD 13331
DECEMBER 1977

Miles
Kilometers

Pacific Ocean

PANGUNA MINE
(COPPER)

Rabaul
Gazelle Peninsula
Bismarck Sea
Hoskins

Solomon Sea

Madang
Ramu River
Goroka
Markham River
Lae
Mt. Hagen
Purari River
Popondetta

Coral Sea

Port Moresby

Gulf of Papua

Fly River

Strickland River

Sepik River

Wewak

Vanimo

FRIEDA RIVER
(COPPER)

OK TEDI
(COPPER)

INDONESIA

AUSTRALIA

This map has been prepared by the World Bank's staff exclusively for the convenience of the readers of the report to which it is attached. The denominations used and the boundaries shown on this map do not imply, on the part of the World Bank and its affiliates, any judgment on the legal status of any territory or any endorsement or acceptance of such boundaries.

12

2

A Sketch of Papua New Guinea

T HE MAINLAND OF PAPUA NEW GUINEA lies about 100 miles north of the eastern half of Australia. The mainland lies on the eastern portion of the island of New Guinea; the remainder of the island is the Indonesian province of West Irian. Although 85 percent of Papua New Guinea's land area is on the mainland, the country also encompasses about 600 islands. The largest of these are New Britain, New Ireland, and Manus in the Bismarck Archipelago, Bougainville and Buka in the northern Solomons, and the Trobriand, Woodlark, D'Entrecasteaux, and Louisiade island groups to the east of mainland Papua New Guinea. In all, the country extends nearly 1,300 miles from east to west and about 800 miles from north to south. Its total land area is 178,000 square miles— slightly less than that of Thailand but substantially more than that of New Zealand or the Philippines.

The Land

The topography of Papua New Guinea is rugged. Much of the land area of both the mainland and the islands is characterized by steep mountains, some peaking at more than 15,000 feet. In contrast, the basins of the Fly and Purari rivers in the west and the Sepik River in the north are vast, swampy plains. Several other large rivers cut through the mountain ranges, but only the Fly and the Sepik are even partially navigable; the rest serve to obstruct rather than to aid movement and communication. (See map page 12.)

Because of these formidable geographic barriers, Papua New Guinea is culturally and economically fragmented. The airplane was introduced much earlier and has penetrated much farther than the automobile or truck; there are no railroads at all. Papua New Guinea is said to have more airstrips per capita than any other country in the world. The early growth of air transport was associated with gold mining activities, and it is used for much of Papua New Guinea's internal shipping and most of its domestic passenger traffic. Small charter flights account for the largest part of air traffic, but a national airline—Air Niugini—ties together the main towns with regular service, albeit at very high cost.

Roads are in early stages of development, and the difficult climate and terrain of Papua New Guinea make their construction and maintenance expensive. At present the two principal mainland towns—the administrative capital of Port Moresby and the commercial, light-manufacturing town of Lae—are not linked by road. The country's only major long-distance highway connects Lae with the central highlands. This road evolved from a rugged track built during World War II, and it is still unpaved. Its use is relatively light but growing.

There is some interisland coastal shipping, but this is presently a relatively weak mode of transport, with considerably greater potential than has yet been developed. Ocean shipping is more important in overseas cargo traffic than in coastal shipping, but most external passenger traffic is carried by airlines.

In contrast with its transport facilities, Papua New Guinea's communications system is quite modern. The telecommunications network has been significantly improved in recent years; the posts and telegraphs organization, a government-owned enterprise, has built a trunk telephone system that compares favorably with those in many developed countries. The principal means of mass communication in Papua New Guinea is radio broadcasting, which is also a government activity.

The people of Papua New Guinea occupy a part of the world that is rich in natural resources but difficult to shape into an integrated national network of production and distribution except at great cost. The many regions with good soils and a variety of climatic conditions at different elevations allow a wide spectrum of agricultural possibilities. Subsistence agriculture occupies 90 percent of the cultivated land and engages from 60 to 70 percent of the population. Forest cover is extensive and of considerable commercial potential, but access to many forest areas is difficult and expensive. A combination of heavy rainfall and extensive mountain ranges provides one of the world's richest hydroelectric potentials, although demand for electricity will probably develop only slowly.

Mineral resources are also good. Gold was once the country's primary export, but because of declining production after World War II it was surpassed by various agricultural exports. With the opening of the large opencast mine on Bougainville in 1972, copper has assumed first place among exports, now accounting for roughly half of the country's total exports and 20 to 30 percent of its gross domestic product. Oil and gas drilling by some international companies has resulted in encouraging, but not yet commercially exploitable gas finds and no oil. The fisheries potential is promising, but the four foreign firms that operate from Papua New Guinea ports send their catches to canneries in other countries, and Papua New Guinea's popular tinned fish is all imported.

The People

The 2.8 million indigenous people of Papua New Guinea comprise a variety of distinct ethnic groups, predominantly Melanesian. Insulated by mountains, forests, large rivers, and the sea, the original Stone Age tribes have until very recently lived unto themselves in conditions of primitive isolation. This separation has preserved unique cultural and linguistic differences among the various tribes. Some 700 local languages, most of them mutually unintelligible and none of them written, have been identified. The size of these language groups ranges from 200 to 300 persons to the largest groups of about 100,000. There are, however, three languages that are quite widely spoken—Pidgin, English, and Motu. English is the principal language of instruction in the school system.

The social systems of the various groups are also different. Patrilineal, matrilineal, and ambilineal descent systems occur. The social obligations among kinship groups are complex. Members of the group have an obligation to assist and support others who might be in need—a tribal social security system that makes members reluctant to leave the protection of the tribal environment. Indeed, the institution of *wontok*—pidgin for "One Talk," an individual's primary clan group—has followed the course of urbanization and serves as a basis of settlement in towns. It establishes claims and obligations among members originating from the same clan group, and it both mitigates the problems of urban immigrants and diffuses the earnings of many of those urban dwellers fortunate enough to have paid employment. Land ownership is also a community right, with use granted to individuals or families by agreement among the owning group. About 97 percent of the land in Papua New Guinea is held by local populations under these traditional tenure systems.

Along with the rough terrain of Papua New Guinea, the abundance of the land has helped to preserve tribal isolation. Subsistence production provides a variety of fruits, vegetables, and nuts, as well as materials for houses and clothing. Basic wants are easily satisfied, and as long as the range of demands is limited, there is little incentive to trade with others. Some tenuous trade relations existed for several hundred years between highland and lowland groups and along the coast. Contact was occasionally established with Malay and Chinese traders, but the vast majority of the local populations remained effectively isolated from other Pacific populations, from the Malay and Indonesian civilizations immediately to the west, and from one another.

Only during the past century have contacts gradually widened between these subsistence tribal groups and the outside world. As the original German settlers and missionaries on the northern coasts and islands discovered—and as their British and Australian successors later confirmed—the indigenous culture of the region was a more primitive one than the western world discovered anywhere during the last 300 years. Although the processes of modernization have made giant strides in Papua New Guinea during the past two or three generations, particularly since World War II, they began among a people who had no alphabet, knew neither the knife nor axe nor any form of metal, used only stones for cutting, hunted and killed with bow and arrow and club, had as cloth neither wool nor cotton but only pounded bark, and used neither bullocks, oxen, horses, nor cows in their subsistence agriculture. Against the recent yesterday of this Stone Age background, it is remarkable how rapidly and relatively smoothly the various processes of modernization have begun to take effect.

The present population of Papua New Guinea is nearly the same as that of New Zealand but only about one-fifteenth that of the Philippines or Thailand. Thus, the country has substantial physical size and a population that is still relatively small. About 40 percent of the total population is concentrated in the highlands in the central mainland, a region that remained sheltered from modern influences longer than many others in the country. Only in the Eastern Highlands is any population pressure yet felt. Papua New Guinea's indigenous population is increasing at an annual rate of 2.8 percent, and it is expected to reach about 3.5 million by the mid-1980s. Because of this rapid growth, the age structure of the population is quite young; in 1971, 46 percent of the population was less than 15 years old. Although this does not pose a strain on land resources, except in the highlands, it may in the near future place large demands on health and educational facilities and on employment opportunities.

Until quite recently, the only urban centers were a handful of coastal towns; there are still only seven towns that have more than 10,000 inhabitants. The largest is the capital, Port Moresby, with 76,000 residents, followed by the port town of Lae, with 38,000. This pattern is now being changed rapidly by high rates of rural–urban migration. Overall, urban areas grew at an annual rate of 16 percent between 1966 and 1971, and future urban growth is being projected at 8 to 12 percent a year. Papua New Guinea's National Housing Commission expects the 1975 urban population of 250,000 at least to double during the next decade. Towns are at present growing faster than their ability to employ and house new arrivals, with consequent rapid increases in urban unemployment, squatter housing, dependency, and crime.

Papua New Guinea's school system was pioneered by missionaries as early as 1872, but the role of education did not begin to expand rapidly until about 1960. In that year 95,000 students were enrolled in school, 92,000 of them in primary schools; 80 percent of all primary students were in mission schools. The first Papua New Guinean entered university in Australia in 1960. The colonial government rapidly expanded its efforts in education after that year, strongly emphasizing primary eduation. But even by 1966 less than half of the children who had passed English-language elementary schools entered the secondary level, and only a tiny proportion received tertiary education—there were two college graduates.

By 1975, 69 percent of the boys and 44 percent of the girls in the 7- to 12-year age group were enrolled in primary school. Secondary education is developing, though at a slower pace. In 1975 there were about 30,000 secondary students in 88 high schools, two-thirds of which were boarding schools, and another 10,500 students were in technical, vocational, or teacher training. Still, about 85 percent of all enrollments were in primary schools.

Papua New Guinea now has two universities. The University of

Papua New Guinea in Port Moresby has 1,000 full-time and 500 part-time students, and the University of Technology at Lae has almost 1,000 students. These are exclusively boarding institutions, their staffs are still largely expatriate, and only 35 percent of the entering students complete the course without dropping out at least temporarily.

Despite the rapid advancement of the school system, as recently as 1971 more than 70 percent of all adults were illiterate, and a majority of people ten years of age or older spoke only a vernacular language. Of the minority able to speak one of the three lingua francas, 44 percent spoke Pidgin, 25 percent English, and 9 percent Motu; many spoke at least two of these. Because English is the standard medium of instruction in Papua New Guinea's schools, the percentage of English-speaking Papua New Guineans should increase; this should make an important contribution to national integration.

At all levels of the education system above primary school, a large proportion of teachers are expatriates, and teaching costs are high. The development of indigenous teachers is of crucial importance in reducing the costs of education to levels the country can afford. Other problems may arise if social pressures to continue the expansion of places for secondary students result in more secondary graduates than the economy can find jobs for.

Peripheral health care in Papua New Guinea has been well developed during the past quarter century. As in education, the missions were important in establishing health service posts and still play an important role in providing health care in remote areas. In the 1950s, under Australian administrative control, a rural health care system through village aid posts was set up, and today there are some 1,600 such posts—more than one for every eight villages. These posts are manned by orderlies who are health auxiliaries, not by trained doctors or nurses. The orderlies' work is directed by health extension workers from the district and by 144 subdistrict health centers with about 30 beds each. Hospital cases are referred to one of twenty-one district or base hospitals staffed by expatriate and local medical officers. Training facilities are available locally for aid post personnel and, since 1970, for medical officers in the Faculty of Medicine of the University of Papua New Guinea. Overall, the system provides a network of rural health care that seems well designed for Papua New Guinea's manpower and financial capabilities.

The main diseases prevalent in Papua New Guinea are infectious diseases such as pneumonia, malaria, diarrhea, tuberculosis, and leprosy; malnutrition is a problem in the coastal areas of Papua New Guinea proper and especially in the highlands regions. Most of Papua New Guinea's health problems are caused by, or related to, low environmental standards, and they could be alleviated by immunization programs or relatively simple improvements in food and water supplies. Health conditions are improving, however, and rural infant mortality, which stood at 110 deaths per 1,000 in 1971, had been reduced to 101 by 1974.

History and Political Development

The outside penetration of Papua New Guinea has occurred at different dates in various parts of the country. Although the island of New Guinea was first sighted by Portuguese and Spanish navigators in the early part of the sixteenth century, permanent contact with Europeans did not occur until more than 300 years later. Only after 1870 were missionary, labor recruiting, trading, prospecting, and eventually plantation activities begun. These contacts were limited largely to the coastal fringes of New Guinea and to the accessible parts of the other islands. Not until shortly before World War II did Europeans first encounter the population groups in inland New Guinea. Systematic European penetration and political and economic development of these areas started after World War II.

The western part of New Guinea, now West Irian, was claimed by the Dutch early in the nineteenth century. In 1884, Germany and Great Britain divided the territory that currently constitutes Papua New Guinea along the central watershed of the island of New Guinea and between the two naturally separated groups of smaller islands. Papua, the southern section, became a British protectorate and later a British possession; in 1906, it became an Australian territory. New Guinea, the northern section and its neighboring islands, was under German control until occupied by Australia during World War I. After the war, Australia continued the administration of New Guinea under a mandate from the League of Nations. During this period the Europeans explored the interior of the island, set up administrative posts, built airstrips and roads, organized medical aid posts, and gradually established law and order among the various tribes. Christian missions were set up throughout the territories, and they provided the great majority of schools and medical posts.

Between the wars, Australia was responsible for both Papua and New Guinea, but they were administered separately until World War II, when an Australian military government governed them jointly. After the war, under the United Nations Charter and a Trusteeship Agreement, the Australian government accepted the obligation "to promote the political, social, economic and educational advancement of New Guinea and its progressive development towards self-government and independence in accordance with the freely expressed wishes of its people." Later, Australia unilaterally accepted the same obligation for Papua, and the two territories continued to be jointly administered by Australia as the Territories of Papua and New Guinea, with headquarters at Port Moresby.

AUSTRALIAN ADMINISTRATION

Until the early 1960s, Australian policies in Papua New Guinea were based on the assumption that Australia would remain in administrative control of the territories for a long time to come, and little was done to include the indigenous people in the governmental process. The structure of territorial government was based on the Papua and New Guinea Act of 1949. Executive authority rested with an Australian administrator assisted by an executive council. The Territory Public Service, separate from the Commonwealth Public Service, was established. There was a local court system, with appeals from the Supreme Court going to the High Court of Australia.

The Legislative Council in Papua New Guinea could—with the consent of the Australian administrator or the governor-general—pass certain laws, although the Commonwealth Parliament retained the right to legislate directly. This council did not include indigenous members until 1951, and even then their representation was only token. The Papua and New Guinea Act also provided for native local government councils, the first of which was established in 1950. With administration approval, the councils could pass head taxes, build or maintain roads and bridges, health centers, medical aid posts, schools, markets, wells, and water tanks. In 1963 there were still only 77 local councils, covering about a third of the total population, but by 1975, 95 percent of the population was within the jurisdiction of a local council. Each council's jurisdiction includes several villages. The integration of these councils with the traditional form of village government—by "big men" elected by the males of the villages—still presents some problems in local areas.

Policy decisions and administrative control, even in detail, remained centralized in Canberra as late as 1968. The Australian administrator in Port Moresby was merely a coordinator without the prestige and authority of a British colonial governor. Within Papua New Guinea, the administration did not delegate major responsibilities to the district and local levels. The Papua New Guinea public service was without significant local participation; it was in fact an extension of the Australian public service, dominated by Australian values and methods.

The development of an Australian-type administrative system, staffed almost entirely by Australians, was based on the assumption that the Territories of Papua and New Guinea would one day be integrated into Australia as the country's seventh state. To prevent the emergence of an educated, anticolonial élite that might jeopardize this process, Australia pursued a policy of "uniform development" of the local population. In education, all segments of the local population were intended to advance at the same rate, and almost all effort was devoted to primary education. The paucity of trained local applicants precluded serious efforts to localize public administration or private business until "uniform development" should have proceeded much farther. Consequently, those Papua New Guineans who entered the monetized economy before the 1960s remained mainly plantation laborers, domestic servants, and low-level government employees.

This policy discouraged the evolution of local political leadership and entrepreneurial talents and thus hampered the already difficult process of stimulating active local involvement in a modern society. Land was abundant and population pressure on land resources was low. The fairly reasonable standard of living in the rural subsistence sector provided little incentive for local people to enter the modern cash economy with great speed. In addition, there was virtually no tradition of manufacturing, and hence there were almost no small-scale industries. Traditional trade was also limited. With the expatriate-dominated modern sector of the economy expanding fairly rapidly, Australian policy inevitably widened the gap betweeen the modern sector and Papua New Guinea's traditional society.

Alongside the early neglect of educational policies oriented toward rapid localization and independence was a similar—and equally understandable—neglect of local government structures.

With modernization and the franchise, such structures were needed so that traditional sources of authority could accommodate new functions. In the 1960s, when Australia's political assumptions about Papua New Guinea's future changed, it became clear that Papua New Guinea would have to accelerate its social evolution, particularly in education, in order to provide the trained manpower needed for growing political and economic independence. In the 1970s, when this independence was realized, Papua New Guinea was left with a government administration that was more elaborate than it needed and more costly than it could support from its own resources.

Preparing for Self-Government

An important step in persuading the Australian government to give serious consideration to Papua New Guinea's political and economic future was taken when a U.N. Trusteeship Council mission, headed by Sir Hugh Foot, visited Papua New Guinea in 1962. That mission criticized the Australian government for its lack of a positive policy to encourage political, social, and economic progress in its territories. In response, the Australian government began serious moves to prepare Papua New Guinea for self-government.

In 1963 the auxiliary division of the public service was abolished, and its members were transferred into the third (lowest) division of the regular public service, thus ending second-class status for indigenous employees of the government. In 1964 the first elected parliament in Papua New Guinea took office, and Papua New Guinean members were in the majority; there were also ten nonnative members and ten officials nominated by the territorial administrator. In 1967 this first House of Assembly established a Committee on Constitutional Development, which gave the first serious thought within Papua New Guinea to the country's political future.

In 1968 a second national election was held, and the second House of Assembly was elected; it was to last four years (1968–72). The 1968 election, unlike that of 1964, provided for universal suffrage and resulted in the election of eighty-four members—sixty-four Papua New Guineans and twenty Europeans; in addition, ten official members were appointed by the Australian administrator. The 1968 election was considered an organizational marvel. Voter registration, even in the most remote areas, was almost complete, and two-thirds of those registered voted.

In anticipation of the 1968 election, Papua New Guinea's first domestic political parties were organized. Interest in domestic politics increased considerably during the sitting of the second House of Assembly, when emerging local leaders had to take positions on whether or not to challenge the colonial administration with respect to more rapid development of self-government and eventual independence. Most of the activity surrounding the formation of identifiable interest groups into political parties occurred within the House of Assembly; the political parties were not widely based, with strong local roots and organizations, as are those in the West.

The main party to emerge in the late 1960s and early 1970s was the Pangu Pati, the Papua New Guinea party, which had close associations with the early labor movement. Since Pangu was in favor of early independence, this party assumed the role of the loyal opposition in the House. It was headed by Michael Somare, who subsequently served as chief minister and, after independence, as prime minister. At the other extreme was the United party, composed almost exclusively of leaders from the highlands who were against early self-government and independence and preferred a much slower evolution. Not all highland leaders joined the United party; a group who broke with it formed themselves into the National party. A fourth party, the Peoples Progressive party, led by the present minister of agriculture and deputy prime minister, Julius Chan, had strong representation from some of the major islands.

At the time when local political parties were being formed, the Australian government in Canberra was devolving more and more authority to its representatives in Port Moresby. This reflected a deliberate decision to accelerate the country's evolution toward self-government and independence. In 1971 a National Identity Ordinance was approved, establishing a national flag, a national crest, a national holiday, and a name for the country, "Papua New Guinea." This was an important symbolic milestone in the process of molding a nation from the diverse groups that make up Papua New Guinea.

The 1972 election, for the third House of Assembly, provided a victory for those political forces favoring early self-government. Neither the Pangu Pati, which favored early independence, nor the United party, which opposed it, gained an absolute majority in the new 100-member house. Pangu leaders managed to form a national coalition consisting of Pangu, the Peoples Progressive party, and the National party, and Somare was elected leader of the coalition. The territorial administrator then appointed Somare deputy chairman of the administrator's Executive Council, which put him in line to become Papua New Guinea's first chief minister in what would be a Westminster-type cabinet government. The Australian government then agreed to establish self-government on December 1, 1973. On that date, Australia remained responsible only for defense, foreign affairs, international trade agreements, and internal security.

As the new government assumed its constitutional powers, the central political issue became the timetable for independence. The United party, representing mainly the populous, relatively underdeveloped ethnic groups of the highlands, was the largest single party in the House. It continued to oppose early independence, mainly for fear that the key posts in the country would fall to the more advanced ethnic groups of the coastal areas and the islands. The ruling national coalition made great efforts to win the confidence of the highlanders and to subdue separatist tendencies evident in some other parts of the country, notably in the Gazelle Peninsula in East New Britain. The United Nations had by this time endorsed early independence for Papua New Guinea, and the Australian government itself, after the labor victory in the Australian elections of 1972, was increasingly anxious to see Papua New Guinea become independent as early as possible.

Somare made it clear that he did not want to press for independence until a constitution had been drafted and adopted; this took somewhat longer than had been hoped. The issue of eligibility for citizenship was not successfully resolved until the spring of 1975, and provincial self-government is still at issue.[1] Nevertheless, a constitution was framed, and the date for independence was fixed for September 16, 1975.

Upon independence, Papua New Guinea was admitted immediately to the British Commonwealth; today, the British monarch serves as formal head of state, represented locally by a governor-general, as in Australia and New Zealand. Papua New Guinea joined the United Nations the month after independence and has subsequently joined most of the United Nations' specialized

---

1. Deciding the qualifications for citizenship was a particularly knotty issue. Most Australians wanted a provision permitting dual citizenship. This was rejected. Anyone who had had two of his four grandparents born in the country could immediately apply for citizenship; anyone else could apply for naturalization if he applied within two months of completing eight years of residence in the country. By January 1976, 750 of the 37,000 expatriates in the country had applied for naturalization, a figure well above the number expected by the government.

agencies, in addition to the International Monetary Fund and the World Bank.

Papua New Guinea has also established a modest number of embassies and consulates abroad. It has limited its diplomatic posts to capitals in which it has close commercial, geographic, and strategic ties and in which it feels it important to establish diplomatic representation separate from Australia. In other capitals, Australia continues to provide representation for Papua New Guinea's diplomatic interests on a courtesy basis.

PROVINCIAL AND LOCAL GOVERNMENT

In a young nation as ethnically diverse and geographically scattered as Papua New Guinea, it is not surprising that centrifugal regional forces have presented major challenges to the central government. The question of whether or not the constitution should provide for provincial self-government—the establishment of local executives responsible, not to Port Moresby, but to provincial parliaments—was a major issue in the discussions. The question was resolved by omitting any constitutional formula for provincial government. The pressures for establishing such governments in certain provinces, notably on the island of Bougainville, were so strong, however, that a form of provincial government was in fact established there in 1974.

Other areas in which provincial sentiments have pushed strongly for some form of self-government are Papua and the Gazelle Peninsula. In Papua, a region not particularly well endowed with known natural resources, the Papua Besena movement tried to mobilize support for more self-government and more assistance from the central government. In the Gazelle Peninsula in East New Britain, the aggressive Mataungan Association among the Tolai people stirred up militant protests in the early 1970s. By 1975 the Gazelle situation appeared to have been effectively defused, and Gazelle leaders no longer spoke of secession.

On the island of Bougainville, pressures have continued not only for self-government, but for outright secession. The most recent expression of secessionist sentiment on Bougainville occurred in February 1976, when a series of protests thrust a crisis on the central government. The February protest was directed entirely against property, not persons, and no deaths or injuries were reported; secessionist leaders and the government were able to agree to hold discussions on the future of the island. The crisis over

Bougainville was a major factor in reviving the central government's interest in working out arrangements for provincial self-government, and in February 1977 the Organic Law on Provincial Government was approved by Parliament. By mid-1977, five provincial governments had already been established under this law, and the other fifteen will probably be created by 1979.

The Organic Law distinguishes the powers of the national and provincial governments. Provincial governments may make laws concerning subjects such as local licensing, primary education, and housing, which are primarily provincial in effect. In addition, they may legislate on a long list of other subjects so long as the laws they pass are not inconsistent with an act of the national parliament. This "concurrent" category includes community and rural development, agriculture, public works, secondary and vocational education, transport, marketing, and employment, as well as many other areas that affect the provinces directly but in which national uniformity may eventually be desirable. The national parliament may rule on these subjects only to the extent that they are of national interest. In cases of conflict, national law has precedence, and the national parliament may overrule any provincial law.

Financial relations between the national and provincial governments are also defined in the Organic Law. The new provincial governments will take over the assets of the existing area authorities. Each province is given an unconditional grant based on the expenditures of the national government in fiscal 1977 for those functions handed over to the provincial government. Insofar as the budget allows, this grant will be maintained in real terms over the years and will be increased as the provincial governments take over additional functions. Conditional grants may also be given for specific sectors, such as education. By June 1977, some provincial governments were responsible for their own administrative costs, and one province was responsible for provincial public works and maintenance expenditures. Provinces have the sole power to levy retail sales, land, head, and entertainment taxes, as well as fees for licensing of mobile traders, liquor sales, and gambling establishments. In addition, they receive all royalties from minerals, oil and gas, timber, fish, and hydroelectric power after the central government's collection costs have been deducted, and 1.25 percent of the value of their exports less the value of the royalties. Provinces can borrow on a short-term basis (up to six months), but medium- or long-term loans must be approved by the finance minister, and borrowing is unlikely to take place without a central government guarantee.

Each province will be allowed a six-person secretariat, independent of the national government, but all other staff must be part of the national public service, and in principle one position will be eliminated in the central government for each additional one created at the provincial level. Regular evaluations of individual jobs are to be carried out in order to uncover any unused capacity; in many provinces, sufficient slack exists so that additional responsibility can be absorbed without creating new positions. High staff turnover has been a problem in some provinces, because career opportunities were usually more favorable in Port Moresby. By establishing provincial offices as a regular part of the national public service with equal opportunities for promotion, the new system may reduce the rate of turnover and thus improve services.

The Australian Legacy

The most important modernizing force since the establishment of colonial rule more than fifty years ago has been government. Its policies and objectives, its investment and service programs, its financial resources, and its physical presence at various levels have displaced private influences—the missionary, the planter, and the coastal trader—as the chief agents of modernization. As a colony of Australia, Papua New Guinea was run until the mid-1960s on the basis of outlooks and policies controlled in Canberra; the territorial administrator in Port Moresby was responsible to Canberra. This historical fact is central to understanding a problem central to Papua New Guinea's economic independence: the economy's present high degree of dependence on Australia.

The problems of colonial administration and of territorial development in Papua New Guinea had a much closer resemblance to those of Europe's nineteenth-century penetration of primitive Africa than to the Europeans' earlier penetration of the far more developed civilizations of Asia. The colonial official and his countrymen could not live off the land, for the land produced nothing they needed; nor could they adapt and build on what existed. They found little to eat or wear or build within the neolithic subsistence culture, and everything that needed to be done had to be done "from scratch."

The European found a vacuum and proceeded to fill it, mainly with imports. This applied to building houses; introducing language, writing, and education; building roads, harbors, and airstrips; introducing money and banking institutions; opening stores and stocking them with goods the administrators needed; persuading a few natives to work for wage employment, and giving them models of the things they could buy with their new cash incomes. Eventually, the formation of Australian social institutions was allowed and even encouraged; for example, trade unions, including government employees' unions, were formed, and a system of arbitration machinery was set up for settling public and private wage disputes that, in recent years, has been patterned directly on machinery in use in Australia.

A natural part of this relationship was the growth of close trade and other ties between Australia and Papua New Guinea. From capital goods through almost every type of durable and nondurable consumer good (including most of the foods eaten by the white administrators and by that minority of Papua New Guineans who drifted into the cash economy), the things people saw, came to want, and could buy were things that came from Australia. They were ordered by Australian buyers, supplied by Australian suppliers, carried in Australian ships, and financed through branches of Australian banks. Three large importing and distributing companies, two headquartered in Australia and the third in Port Moresby but owned and run by Australians, distributed most imports.

In the building and repair trades, and in the few local factories that grew up, almost all the skilled labor and supervisors were Australians, as were the owners. In the government, almost all posts, including most of the clerical positions, were filled by Australians, or by the sprinkling of New Zealanders and Britons always present in the expatriate community. The services that were developed, their staffing patterns, the qualifications required for filling posts, the types of activities undertaken, and the forms of documentation produced were all modeled on Australia. Almost everything that had to be printed was printed in Australia. The physical standards that grew up—in post and telegraphs, in government housing, in the design of university buildings or of the modern central government headquarters building in Waigani (Port Moresby), in the manuals and procedures of the Public Works Department—came primarily from what the administrators were familiar with, from Australia.

The administrators themselves and the private expatriate community that served the needs they generated were all Australians; only in the last ten to fifteen years have Papua New Guineans begun to occupy some of the junior positions. The Australian administrators were not part of a separate colonial service, as the British were in Asia and Africa. They were part of the regular Australian civil service and many of them were assigned to Papua or New Guinea for long rather then short tours of duty. Both government servants and private Australians found working in Papua New Guinea attractive because the scale of salaries and allowances was higher than the one which prevailed in Australia, and this allowed them to build up savings for remittance home. Well-paid government service acted as a wagesetter for the monetized parts of the economy. Government workers were represented by trade unions whose cases were pleaded by lawyers recruited from Australia; wage disputes were decided through compulsory arbitration proceedings heard by an Australian public member. It was inevitable that Papua New Guinean wage and salary costs should grow out of Australian costs and consumption standards, not out of the local economy and culture.

One of Papua New Guinea's central problems in its early years of independence is to reorient its economy away from what have been, and remain, essentially Australian standards of investment, consumption, and incomes toward standards more appropriate to what Papua New Guinea will be able to afford now that it has become an independent nation. The only way Papua New Guinea's past cost levels (particularly those of government) could be maintained in the future would be for the Australian government to underwrite them with aid transfer payments from Canberra to Port Moresby. Because Papua New Guinea's government services will inevitably continue to grow during the years ahead, a constantly rising stream of aid would be required to support them under present standards.

Australia is currently providing about 40 to 45 percent of the funds needed to finance the Papua New Guinean budget. Budgetary assistance will have to continue for many years, and there seems no doubt that it will do so. Both the Australian and the Papua New Guinean governments agree that this stream should grow smaller, not larger, as rapidly as possible without disrupting national public finances. Papua New Guinea will be able to achieve increasing fiscal self-reliance partly by developing new sources of domestic revenue, but a large contribution to increasing self-reliance will have to come from cost savings that will only be possible as part of a delicate, but deliberate, effort to reorient domestic standards and costs away from those of Australia. This effort need not be sudden or drastic, and it need not disturb the close ties of trade and assistance and of mutual political interest that have created such close relations between the two countries.

3

The Changing Structure
of the Economy

XCEPT FOR ITS ROAD NETWORK, which is in an early stage of development, Papua New Guinea has a relatively good base of infrastructure facilities and services. Costs are high, however. The telecommunications network is excellent; electricity is expanding rapidly to serve most major centers; harbor facilities are generally adequate for present traffic; truck and local air services are well developed; the water supply is relatively good in most towns but will be strained to keep up with the rapid urbanization that is expected. The greatest needs appear to be for road development, coastal shipping services, and urban housing. As new large enclave projects develop, they will be required to include necessary infrastructure in their own financing and are not expected to be a drain on government resources.

The Private Sector

The largest single occupation, involving more than half the population, remains subsistence agriculture. This is not yet declining in absolute terms, although its relative share in total output is slowly falling. Within the agricultural sector, there are many and widely scattered islands of wage labor on the plantations, which are completely oriented to the production of cash crops for export.

By no means do all agricultural exports come from the plantation sector. Two of the "big six" export crops, coffee and palm oil, depend heavily on smallholders, who have made at least a partial transition from subsistence agriculture to a measure of cash cropping. Smallholder cash cropping for domestic markets is much weaker than smallholder production for export markets. The technical and institutional problems of building up domestic markets for food products are more difficult than those of producing for export. Thus, more smallholders are likely to leave subsistence agriculture for export production than for meeting domestic demands.

Sectors other than agriculture are still relatively small and are unlikely to provide the sources of new demand necessary to lead the economy to higher levels of productivity and income. Manufacturing, construction, and tourism are still of secondary importance as sources of employment and income. Although the growth of export-led agriculture will be a major stimulant to demand, the dominant influence in leading the economy will be the central government, much the largest sector outside agriculture and the primary source for creation of exogenous demand. For at least the next decade or two and perhaps longer, government programs and provision of technical assistance to implement them will be the principal influence on any restructuring of the economy.

The monetized activities of the economy—which account for more than 70 percent of output and incomes but involve less than half the population—are highly dependent on imports. This is true of both consumption and investment activities. Because domestic costs of production and distribution will be higher than the c.i.f. costs of many imports, import substitution is likely to proceed slowly and with great selectivity. The government recognizes this fact; it now needs to develop the cost, marketing, and distribution data needed to select specific agricultural and manufactured products as promising candidates for import substitution.

The expatriate community remains vital, and the economy would face severe problems if this resource were withdrawn. Although nationals now firmly control government policymaking and are gradually moving into the higher nonpolicy jobs, expatriate technical, managerial, entrepreneurial, and advisory contributions remain critical to the functioning and further growth of the economy. Government leaders appear to accept this fact and are not pressing for hasty localization of these positions. The generally good relations between Papua New Guineans and the expatriate community are a national asset of great value.

Government Policies

The government has a fairly clear set of objectives and policies that define the desired kind and pace of development. National development will be a guided development that tries to subordinate growth to a set of social and cultural values emphasizing distributional and environmental objectives and individual and national self-reliance. The influence of market forces and incentives will not be denied, but the government hopes to prevent them from dominating the pace and directions of economic growth.

Achieving self-reliance in public finance and in the economy's external accounts is an explicit long-run aim of government. It underlies the government's approach to investment in major natural resource projects, which it encourages on a selective, controlled basis. The 1970s have seen the opening of one major copper mine that has already improved the country's finances. A second copper mine is likely to be constructed before the end of the decade, with production by the mid-1980s. There is cautious optimism that the favorable geological structures in the Gulf of Papua will yield commercial oil and gas finds in the next few years. These two or three large enclave projects will provide most of the funds the government needs to pay for the expanded service and technical assistance programs necessary for higher levels of productivity and income.

Rapid improvement in financial conditions as a result of two or three major natural resource projects is unlikely to create the same boom conditions in Papua New Guinea that have followed the exploitation of the oil resources in the Middle East. Government policy is likely to be closer to Norway's announced policy of trying to prevent its new oil wealth from disrupting its social structure. If Papua New Guinea's rising domestic revenue is directed largely to replacing transfer income now received from Australian aid, the additional revenue generated by these enclave projects will not become fully available to stimulate additional demand.

From an economic point of view, the government's two most worrisome problems are likely to be uncontrollable urbanization and the urban unemployment that follows. Although rural development understandably enjoys top priority in development planning, it is unlikely that even a successful rural development program will slow urban migration to the point where no special measures need to be taken to deal with the growth of urban slums and urban unemployment. These problems will need to be tackled directly and not left to the hope that vigorous rural development will prevent them from becoming serious.

Domestic Product and Expenditure

National accounting data cannot provide clear outlines of the structure of Papua New Guinea's heavily subsistence economy or of the changes taking place in this structure; too much is concealed in home activities and barter transactions. The coverage and quality of Papua New Guinea's economic statistics are above average for a developing country, however, and they do provide at least an indication of principal trends in recent years.

Gross domestic product (GDP) is a measure of the value of goods and services produced within a country's borders during any given year. Table 3.1 shows the trend of Papua New Guinea's real, or constant-price, domestic output and of its gross expenditure on this output for the seven years ending June 30, 1974. These years include the period of the introduction of self-government and the preparation for independence, as well as the boom years of 1971 and 1972, when the Panguna copper mine on Bougainville was being developed. Total domestic output grew by more than 60 percent during this time, at an average annual rate of 8.4 percent.

Nonmarket production—that originating in the subsistence sector—did not decrease during this six-year period, but it was a declining proportion of GDP. In fiscal 1968 nonmarket production accounted for 28 percent of real GDP, and in fiscal 1974, for about 18 percent. The subsistence sector, then, has been relatively stagnant in recent years, and most growth—on average, about 11 percent a year—took place in the monetized part of Papua New Guinea's economy.

Gross fixed capital formation fluctuated widely between fiscal 1968 and 1974, largely because of construction of the Bougainville mine. Fixed investment more than doubled between the two years preceding 1970, when construction began, and the next three years, when the mine was being developed. During the first period, fixed investment accounted for 16.5 percent of domestic expenditure; it rose to about 30 percent during the construction phase. In the years following completion of the mine, fixed investment declined both

Table 3.1. Expenditure on Gross Domestic Product at Constant Prices,
Fiscal Years 1968-74
(Millions of fiscal 1969 kina)

Item	Fiscal year						
	1968	1969	1970	1971	1972	1973	1974
Consumption	425.7	453.9	488.4	508.4	519.9	494.9	484.6
Government	144.9	150.7	155.0	151.8	162.3	156.4	155.4
Private	280.8	303.2	333.4	356.6	357.6	338.5	329.2
Market	160.2	176.1	207.4	230.2	227.5	209.2	201.3
Nonmarket	120.6	127.1	126.0	126.4	130.1	129.3	127.9
Gross fixed capital formation	86.1	91.4	174.0	250.9	204.9	102.1	74.6
Market	84.9	91.3	171.6	250.8	203.6	99.1	74.4
Nonmarket	1.2	0.1	2.3	0.1	1.3	3.0	0.1
Increase in stocks	7.0	6.7	5.4	14.6	8.4	9.6	−0.3
Gross domestic expenditure	518.8	552.0	667.8	773.9	733.2	606.6	558.9
Exports (goods and services)	77.4	86.8	96.6	110.7	149.9	252.8	363.5
Less imports (goods and services	164.7	184.2	261.6	328.0	309.3	237.3	218.9
Statistical discrepancy	−0.7	−1.3	1.1	0.6	−2.8	−1.5	−7.7
Gross domestic product	430.8	453.3	503.9	557.2	571.0	620.6	695.8
Market	308.9	326.1	375.6	430.7	439.7	488.3	567.8
Nonmarket	121.8	127.3	128.3	126.5	131.4	132.3	128.0

Source: Papua New Guinea Bureau of Statistics, *National Accounts Statistics,*
1960/61–1973/74.

relatively and absolutely, reflecting the rather slow pace of investment during the first years of Papua New Guinea's self-government, when uncertainty affected expatriate confidence.

The mine also had a large impact on Papua New Guinea's external trade. The huge bulge in imports, particularly in fiscal 1971 and 1972, is mainly made up of imports for the Bougainville project and for its 10,000 expatriate employees. The mine's effect on exports after it went into production in April 1972 is also clear: even in real terms, exports were nearly five times greater in 1974 than in 1968. The growth of exports from Bougainville contributed much the largest share of the growth in GDP during this period.

The growth in real consumption has been much smaller than export growth, and within the category of consumption, private consumption as a whole has grown almost three times faster than nonmarket consumption. This occurred despite a 25 percent reduction in the number of expatriate consumers, from a 1971 peak of more than 50,000 to 35,000 in 1976. Expatriates, with their higher incomes and tastes for imported goods, have been a significant force in market expenditures on consumption goods. The declining number of expatriates has apparently been offset by a much larger increase in the number of nationals whose consumption needs are now being wholly or partially met through market transactions—evidence of the fairly rapid spread of monetization among Papua New Guineans.

Distribution of Income

National accounting statistics may be used to derive a per capita income figure for Papua New Guinea, but this figure says nothing about income distribution.[1] The 1976 edition of the *World Bank Atlas* gives a figure of US$450 (K330) as Papua New Guinea's 1975 per capita GNP, placing it 88th in a list of 146 countries. But this simple division of GNP by the population of 2.8 million conceals large distributional differences in income. Personal income levels vary widely among three groups—subsistence farmers, nationals wholly or partly within the cash economy, and expatriates. Per capita incomes for each group must be estimated directly.

It is possible to make a crude estimate of total income earned by the 12,000 to 15,000 expatriates in the labor force and thus to calculate per capita expatriate income. The per capita income of nationals, combining the subsistence and nonsubsistence sectors, can be derived by subtracting estimated expatriate income from national income and dividing this figure by the indigenous population. Using this method, the average per capita income of expatriates for 1975 appears to be on the order of K5,000 to K6,000 (US$6,850–8,220) a year and that of Papua New Guinea nationals would be about K270 (US$370)—about a twentyfold difference. This wide difference in incomes should grow progressively narrower in the future. The spread of the cash economy clearly will raise incomes at the bottom of the distribution, and localization will progressively eliminate high expatriate incomes at the upper end.

There is also a wide variation in income among Papua New Guinea nationals. In 1975 the imputed per capita income of large numbers of subsistence farmers was not more than K100 (US$137) a year. Smallholders on the Hoskins palm oil estate in West New Britain earned about K1,500 (US$2,055); divided among six to eight people (more than one family), this resulted in a per capita income

---

1. Papua New Guinea's national income is discussed in Appendix A.

of K190 to K250 (US$260–342) a year. Government wages generally set the pattern for the rest of the economy, and the average annual salary of the 43,000 nationals employed by government in fiscal 1976 was K1,850 (US$2,350)—about K400 (US$508) per family member.

Papua New Guinea has a minimum wage system that covers unskilled, semiskilled, and skilled occupations. Minimum wages, as well as hours of work and other conditions of employment, are set by minimum wages boards, and cost-of-living reviews are made periodically. The urban minimum wage covers mainly service industries; thus, it has little effect on Papua New Guinea's export competitiveness but does have serious implications for the government budget. The national rural minimum wage applies to workers not covered by the urban minimum wage, mainly those in primary production, and it may directly affect the competitiveness of Papua New Guinea's agricultural exports. On an annual per capita basis, the urban minimum wage was about K260 (US$356) in 1975, and the rural minimum wage, about K90 (US$123).

Wages and salaries in Papua New Guinea have risen rapidly in recent years. For example, the minimum wage in Port Moresby increased from K8 (US$9) weekly in 1971 to K25.80 (US$35) in late 1975; this represents a doubling of real wages. During the same period, the national minimum wage rose from about K5.30 (US$6) a week to K8.90 (US$12) for workers in primary industries and to K10.75 (US$15)for other rural employees.[2] The widening urban-rural wage ratio, from 1.5 to 1 in 1971 to more than 2.4 to 1 in 1975, has contributed to excessive migration from rural to urban areas and to high urban unemployment rates.

Unions are stronger in Papua New Guinea than in many developing countries, a legacy of Australian rule. About 32,000 workers, roughly a quarter of the paid indigenous work force, belonged to unions in 1972. Unions are represented on the minimum wages boards, holding power equal to that of government and employers in wage determination. Disputed wage issues go to conciliation or arbitration, and there have been four arbitration hearings since 1963; the most recent of these, a dispute over what portion of government wages should be tied to the cost-of-living index, was still in progress in 1976. The chairman of all four hearings has been the same person who makes wage determinations in Australia.

---

2. See Table SA4 in the Statistical Appendix for changes in minimum wages since 1960.

Sectoral Origin of Production and Incomes

Table 3.2 shows the proportion of GDP originating in each principal industry group from fiscal 1965 to 1972, the most recent year for which these figures are available. In the early 1970s agriculture, hunting, forestry, and fishing contributed slightly more than a third of GDP. No other industry was even half as large.

Table 3.2. Distribution of Gross Domestic Product by Industrial Origin, Fiscal Years 1968-72
(Percent)

Industry	Fiscal years				
	1968	1969	1970	1971	1972
Agriculture, hunting, forestry and fishing	42	44	40	35	34
Market	15	17	16	13	11
Nonmarket	27	27	24	22	23
Mining and quarrying	0[a]	1	1	0[a]	3
Manufacturing	5	5	5	6	6
Electricity, gas, water, and sanitary services		1	1	1	1
Construction	13	12	13	18	15
Wholesale and retail trade	8	8	8	7	7
Transport, storage, and communications	5	5	6	6	6
Financing, insurance and real estate	4	4	4	4	4
Less imputed bank service charge	−0[a]	−1	−1	−1	−1
Community, social, business and personal services	11	11	11	10	10
Public authority and defense	9	9	10	10	11
Domestic product excluding import duties	98	98	97	96	96
Import duties	3	3	3	4	4
Gross domestic product	100	100	100	100	100

a. 0.5 or less.
Source: Computed from Papua New Guinea Bureau of Statistics, National Accounts Statistics, 1960/61−1973/74, Table 4.

The contribution shown for the public sector is deceptive, because it should—but does not—include almost all the utilities as well as a large part of construction. A number of public services in

Papua New Guinea are provided by statutory corporations whose financial operations are conducted outside the budget of the central government. The three major statutory corporations are the Electricity Commission (ELCOM), the Department of Posts and Telegraphs (only the Telecommunications Service of this department is extrabudgetary), and the Harbours Board. During the period 1970 to 1973 annual revenues from these corporations averaged K14 million—about 2 percent of GDP. If these operations and the government's construction activities are included with the public authority data in Table 3.2, government becomes the largest contributor to GDP after agriculture, although it is still only about two-thirds the size of the agricultural sector.

Another large portion of GDP originates in private construction activities, which grew greatly in importance during fiscal 1971 and 1972, the years of mine construction on Bougainville. Since 1972 the construction phase on Bougainville has given way to copper production, and mining activity from that one source alone accounted for 20 to 25 percent of GDP in 1975. The sudden and large increase in GDP stemming from this source would, of course, reduce somewhat the proportional contributions shown in Table 3.2 for the other sectors in 1971 and 1972.

In spite of the Bougainville mine's great impact, rural activities remain Papua New Guinea's most important productive source. For the most recent years shown in Table 3.2, the community, social, business, and personal services (including hotels and restaurants) category was less than a third the size of agriculture and related activities; wholesale and retail trade was about a fifth the size; manufacturing, a sixth; and real estate, only an eighth. Although the relative contribution of the rural sector to GDP fell during the period covered by the table, the absolute size of this sector did not. Further, nonmarket rural output, a declining proportion of GDP, represented an increasing share of total agricultural output during the 1968-72 period. During those years, however, agricultural export prices fell, reducing the relative importance of market, as compared with nonmarket, agricultural production; since 1972 rising export prices have undoubtedly reversed that trend. For most of the years between 1968 and 1975 the absolute value of nonmarket output—or the nonmonetary sector—was substantially constant.

Table 3.3, showing the recent structure and growth of employment in the various economic sectors, underscores the importance of rural activities in Papua New Guinea's economy. In all the years between 1968 and 1976, about half the total labor force was in primary production other than mining and quarrying. This category is not well defined, but it appears to refer to the plantation sector, to forestry and fishing, and to agricultural smallholders engaged primarily in cash cropping.

Table 3.3. Work Force in Monetized Activities by Industry,
Fiscal Years 1968-76
(Thousands of persons)

Industry	Fiscal years						
	1968	1971	1972	1973	1974	1975	1976
Primary[a]	148.8	160.5	157.8	166.0	171.6	179.6	185.1
Mining and quarrying	3.5	4.7	6.8	6.9	7.0	7.1	7.2
Manufacturing	11.4	14.8	15.5	16.8	17.3	17.7	18.3
Building and construction	16.3	30.4	20.6	14.2	15.3	16.5	18.9
Transport, storage, and communication	10.3	15.4	13.5	11.6	12.2	12.3	13.3
Commerce, finance, and property	14.0	20.8	18.7	14.1	14.9	14.6	15.1
Hotels and amusements	14.5	20.4	19.8	21.2	21.8	21.3	22.3
Public authority and other industries	60.2	71.2	71.7	71.4	71.4	71.6	72.2
Total	279.0	338.2	324.4	322.2	331.5	340.7	352.4

Note: Data include expatriates.
a. Includes people partly in subsistence and partly in cash-cropping activities.
Source: Papua New Guinea Central Planning Office, November 1976.

The overall picture during the period covered by the table is not one of steady growth. The boom years of Bougainville mine development are clearly reflected between 1968 and 1971; they are followed by an actual reduction in the money-sector labor force when the mine was completed and no further major stimulus to the economy had emerged to take its place. The softening of growth after the Bougainville peak is evident in several, but not all, sectors. Construction, transport, and commerce and finance declined, but employment in hotels and recreation and in the large miscellaneous category has remained stable. The sectors that have shown the most vigorous growth are mining and manufacturing. Both are still relatively small, however; mining contributed only 2 percent and manufacturing only 5 percent of total money-sector employment in 1976.

The employment figures shown in Table 3.3 include only workers in the monetized sector of the economy, but most of Papua New

Guinea's families depend upon subsistence agriculture for a living. Although new cash-motivated activity, even outside of Bougainville, is growing in response to new wants being stimulated and satisfied by cash income, there is no reliable estimate of participation in the monetized economy. The money supply has been increasing by about 20 percent a year for the past several years (see Statistical Appendix Tables SA21 and SA22), but this is much faster than the rate of growth of monetary activities. The July 1971 census showed that 45 percent of all males over ten years old who were not in school had not worked or sought work for cash remuneration during the previous twelve months (see Statistical Appendix Table SA2). In spite of the spread of formal education among Papua New Guineans, it is unlikely that many will leave traditional rural life and its agriculture; indeed, in absolute terms, this sector is still growing.

AGRICULTURE

Agricultural activity in Papua New Guinea is carried out in three forms: by traditional subsistence production; by smallholder cash cropping; and on plantations. Many families raise both subsistence and cash crops. Government policy has been to promote cash cropping, largely of export crops. Until recently, little attention has been paid to developing traditional agriculture, because it was considered fairly efficient and adequately productive in terms of its resource endowment. Further, problems in storing, transporting, and marketing traditional crops, such as taro, sweet potatoes, yams, and cassava, made them unsuitable for export. With no significant internal markets for traditional produce, growing cash crops for export seemed the most appropriate means of extending the modern cash economy into the rural sector and gradually lifting the standard of living in the villages.

Today, greater emphasis is placed on improving traditional agriculture in order to raise rural living standards. Although the same transport and marketing constraints apply to enlarging the subsistence sector, the government is experimenting with increasing the yields and nutritional value of traditional crops and with diversifying subsistence production to include more nonroot crops and animals. At the same time, the government has continued to encourage production of export and domestic cash crops along with subsistence crops.

Export crops. In the early period after World War II, the main beneficiary of the government's policy favoring cash crops was the expatriate plantation sector, which grew rapidly. The government purchased land from Papua New Guineans for lease to expatriates, who had easy access to favorable credit terms. Fiscal incentives available to the plantations included virtually duty-free import of, and accelerated depreciation on, machinery and equipment. The government also helped mobilize the local labor supply for the plantations. The introduction of the head tax forced the local population to earn cash, usually by working on the plantations. Often, male workers under long-term (one- to three-year) contracts were airlifted from their villages to distant plantations, leaving their families behind; the cost was often serious disruption to family and clan life and neglect of village farms.

Papua New Guinea's 500 to 600 plantations are mostly on the New Guinea part of the mainland and on the larger islands. Almost all are owned by expatriates, but increasingly they are being acquired by nationals. They are worked by some 35,000 paid laborers. The annual productivity of, and value produced by, plantation agriculture are many times those of subsistence farming, and the output of the main plantation crops—coffee, cocoa, copra, coconut oil, and palm oil—has until recently been the mainstay of the country's exports.

Government extension programs in recent years, designed to encourage Papua New Guineans to cultivate cash crops, have met with varying degrees of success from crop to crop and also from region to region. The most success has been with export crops. Coffee, introduced on a large scale in the highlands in the late 1950s and early 1960s, has proved the most successful crop involving local village participation. In fact, it is now produced mainly by smallholders, not plantations. The acreage of coconut lands owned by Papua New Guineans has also gradually increased during the last decade or so, and the expatriate share in total acreage and production has declined. In 1972 and 1973 almost 60 percent of the crop area devoted to coconuts was planted by Papua New Guineans, who accounted for 40 percent of coconut production. About two-thirds of the most promising new crop, palm oil, is produced by smallholders; this apparently will become a major export commodity.

Attempts at developing other smallholder cash crops have met with only limited success. Cocoa and rubber planting have remained largely plantation activities, and tea cultivation has not been readily accepted by smallholders. Although tea can be grown well in the highlands, it cannot compete with that produced in most of the traditional tea-growing countries, and the world market outlook for this crop is not encouraging.

Import substitutes. With a relatively large expatriate sector, growing urbanization, and changing consumption habits among Papua New Guineans, the import bill for such food products as rice, sugar, and European vegetables and fruits has been rising steadily. In response, the government has put considerable emphasis on developing import substitutes in agriculture. A notable feature of Papua New Guinea's agricultural sector, however, is its lack of response to domestic demand, partly because present transport and storage facilities preclude the development of national markets. Fairly rapid progress seems possible in certain food products, and some has already been made, but progress in others will probably be slow. The most promising products are livestock (cattle and pigs), poultry, vegetables, and fruits.

Most pigs are still raised in the village traditional system and used in ceremonial feasting and barter. Commercial pig production by smallholders in rural and semiurban areas is making some progress, but overall production is not increasing significantly. Poultry production is growing rapidly, despite difficulty in obtaining cheap feed. A prospective feed grain project, if realized, may reduce the cost of feed for pig and poultry production.

Government extension services presently are devoting nearly a third of their time to livestock production, and the cattle population is increasing rapidly. In 1976 expatriate-owned ranches had about 150,000 head of cattle, and smallholdings about 47,000; by 1985 herds are expected to reach 300,000 on ranches and 150,000 on smallholdings. The recent drop in world livestock prices discouraged farmers from investing in the animals available from the basic breeding herds built up with World Bank assistance. Although Papua New Guinea's cattle are for meat production, dairies have been established in Lae and Port Moresby to reconstitute imported dried milk.

Considerable extension time is also going into promoting fruit and vegetable production, and response has been quite good in several areas to growing new types of vegetables, both for home use and for the market. Problems of marketing and transport are major obstacles at present. A national market for perishables will not exist for many years, so specific programs will have to be worked out on a local and regional basis. There is some prospect that fresh fruit and vegetable imports may be eliminated by the early 1980s.

Domestic production of rice, an increasingly popular food item, has been less successful. Unless domestic production is increased or imports restricted, rice imports are likely to reach more than

100,000 tons a year by the early 1980s. Although rice growing may never be economic in Papua New Guinea, the government has made efforts to increase rice production and processing; it has also, in effect, limited imports and attempted to shift demand away from rice and toward traditional foods. The demand for sugar is also increasing rapidly, and imports of refined sugar were around 20,000 tons in 1976. Sugar cane is indigenous, however, and could be commercially produced in several areas. Potentially, sugar could become an export commodity for Papua New Guinea.

The outlook for cash crops. The prospects for improving traditional agriculture by adding cash crops or by diversifying subsistence production are difficult to assess. Characteristic of Papua New Guinea's subsistence agriculture is its relative richness; over much of the country, nature's bounty produces enough to eat with relatively little effort. The root crops that dominate subsistence farming are "plant-and-wait" crops, requiring little disciplined cultivation. This is true also of smallholder coffee, cocoa, and oil palms, which is one reason these have done so well. Until enough subsistence farmers have their life styles changed by the development of new consumption wants, the relative ease of producing traditional foods may discourage experimentation with new ones.

It is difficult to judge the seriousness of this problem. It is inconsistent with the willingness of highland farmers to go to the islands for cash employment, although this may involve much higher wages for not very much more work than they are accustomed to. It is also inconsistent with the frequent, favorable comments from expatriate employers in mining, manufacturing, and many service trades that Papua New Guineans, including many recruited from traditional village society, are easily trainable and make good employees in modern occupations.

OTHER RURAL ACTIVITIES

Fishing and fish processing. Fish exports have become an important source of foreign exchange in Papua New Guinea. Increasingly, fishing provides cash income to persons in the subsistence sector, and in some areas it contributes significantly to employment. The development of Papua New Guinea's rich potential of freshwater fish and better marketing of saltwater fish caught in Papua New Guinea waters not only would be an import substitution measure, but at the same time it would improve nutrition by helping to alleviate the serious protein and fat deficiencies, especially among population groups in the interior of Papua New Guinea.

Fresh fish now is consumed only by the population in coastal settlements or by freshwater fishermen. The habit has not spread inland largely because of storage, transport, and marketing difficulties. Tinned fish, most imported from Japan, is increasingly popular in the highland areas and the towns. As yet there are no domestic fish canneries, and such canneries, if established, might not be able to compete with low, marginal-cost prices offered by Japan.

Until recently, fishing in Papua New Guinea was confined to coastal waters, to the Sepik River basin, and to the Fly River estuary. In the late 1960s exports of marine products began, and since then the industry has expanded fairly rapidly. The value of fish exports increased from K0.9 (US$1) million in fiscal 1970 to an estimated K10 (US$13.7) million in 1975. Tuna and prawn have been the main varieties exported, with crayfish and barramundi, caught in the inshore and estuary waters, becoming increasingly significant. Deep-sea fishing for tuna is done by four foreign-controlled companies. As a result of government negotiations, the tuna fleets will be progressively brought under local registration. Prawn fishing is carried out in large-scale operations, with a greater degree of participation by domestic interests; there is substantial scope for the expansion of prawn fisheries. Barramundi and crayfish exports are of special importance because of the direct benefits derived by local fishermen, who handle most of the operation, including both catching and processing. A further field for development lies in freshwater fisheries, particularly in the Sepik and Fly river basins.

Forestry. About 85 percent of Papua New Guinea's land area is covered by forests, and forest resources are among the country's most promising economic prospects. They could be used both to expand the supply of local building materials and to earn foreign exchange. Although much of this forest land is economically inaccessible at present, government studies indicate that the areas that potentially could be developed under existing conditions cover about 20 million acres. The forestry industry is expected to show much growth during the next decade. This will have a significant effect on the balance of payments, a relatively minor effect on the generation of additional domestic revenue, and very important effects on local economies, employment, and societies.

Papua New Guinea's forest resources are varied in composition, even within given tracts. Of some 200 species with economic potential, only a few are now used commercially, and yields per hectare of extraction are low. The handling of such a heterogeneous mix, combined with the absence of infrastructure to support such operations, raises the unit cost of production and places the country at a competitive disadvantage with respect to other Southeast Asian timber producers. Better acceptance of the lesser-known species, encouraged through information on possible end uses, and improved treatment processes will narrow this disadvantage.

The level of Papua New Guinea's log harvest in 1976 was slightly under 1 million cubic meters. More than 60 percent of this volume is exported, and the rate of growth of exports is expected to exceed that of local consumption. The composition of exports will shift with the development of new integrated projects. Log exports will be negligible by 1980, when the emphasis will be on sawn timber, veneer, plywood, and woodchips. The export value is expected to increase considerably with the shift to more domestic processing.

The traditional form of land tenure in Papua New Guinea causes problems in forestry development. The establishment of large blocks of timberland for further development has sometimes been hindered by ownership disputes and reluctance to lease or sell to persons outside the tribes. The release of any area usually requires the consensus of a number of ownership units that must negotiate individually. The usual pattern of release of an area is by selling timber rights to the government, which then arranges disposal of these rights. A new system for purchase of timber rights, under which the owners receive a small down payment and are given 25 percent of the royalties paid to the government, has proved satisfactory; the system is being applied throughout the country.

INSTITUTIONS AFFECTING RURAL DEVELOPMENT

Land tenure. Most land in Papua New Guinea—about 97 percent—is held under traditional tenure systems in which possession is usually vested in a local group, with individual members holding use rights for varying periods. The government controls only about 2 percent of the land, and another 1 percent is owned under freehold title by foreign interests. Under the Land Acquisition Act the government can acquire land owned by nonnationals (mainly plantations) in order to transfer it to Papua New Guineans; provision is made for compensation of the former owners. Customary owners may dispose of an interest in land to the government or in accordance with custom. Urban land already in use or required for use in the foreseeable future is held by the government.

The Australian administration had hoped in the course of time to replace the traditional group land tenure system by western-type individual ownership patterns, but conflicts emerged between Australian legal norms and local tenure systems. The problem of reconciling traditional land customs and western practices persists and has delayed productive use of some areas of land.

Rural credit. Availability of credit is currently not a large constraint on the expansion of agricultural production. In general, Papua New Guineans have been cautious in accepting agricultural credit, and the experience with those who have has been encouraging.

The Papua New Guinea Development Bank (PNGDB) is almost the only institution that lends for small-scale village operations. Its role has been essentially a pioneering one, using new approaches and systems to suit conditions in the country. The fact that credit institutions generally lend to individuals rather then to groups has limited the use of credit for production purposes, because individual credit does not conform to traditional group ownership forms.

The PNGDB was established in 1967, and it has shown an impressive record of lending to Papua New Guineans, particularly those living in rural areas. In fiscal 1975, 51 percent of the agricultural loans to Papua New Guineans, representing 80 percent of the value of such loans, was for cattle, pigs, poultry, and oil palm projects financed mainly through International Development Association (IDA) credits. Although the PNGDB is a major credit source for rural areas, the largest part of the money it lends goes to commercial and industrial activities. Only a third of the value of loans it has made since its inception has gone into agricultural activities, and the government is encouraging the PNGDB to extend its operations in rural areas.

The Rural Improvement Program. The Rural Improvement Program (RIP) is one of the government's principal rural development programs. Part of the National Works Program in the Ministry of Finance, it is designed to encourage and foster development projects using local initiative, local planning, and self-help. The government sees it as a vehicle for bringing about social and economic development in rural areas and for promoting local government institutions. The program provides assistance for small-scale public works, such as local roads, bridges, culverts, and water supplies; in some cases, projects such as community centers, educational facilities, airstrips, irrigation and drainage, animal husbandry, and coastal transport projects are also included.

The RIP, an outgrowth of the Rural Development Fund established in 1968, took its present form in 1972. In the budget for fiscal 1976 it was the second-largest item in the National Works Program budget. RIP grants must be matched by equivalent local contributions in cash and kind, but these have not come up to expectations in many areas; in some provinces, actual expenditures on the program fell considerably short of those budgeted in fiscal 1974 and 1975. (See Statistical Appendix Table SA25.) Despite geographic variation in performance, the program appears to be working fairly well and to be capable of further expansion. The program has important political and administrative aspects in addition to its role as a source of stimulation for the construction of local infrastructure.

The Public Works Department of the central government is not involved in the selection of projects under the RIP, although it can assist in their preparation, supply, and supervision. Projects are initiated by local government councils (LGCs), by community groups in the few remaining noncouncil areas, and by area authorities.[3]

The major problems of the RIP in regard to project implementation are shortages of materials, poor planning, and lack of technical and supervisory staff. The Public Works Department has a unit for providing technical assistance to the RIP and other projects; it also carries the main responsibility for delivering necessary supplies to RIP sites. The Central Planning Office provides courses in project planning and management for LGC functionaries working with RIP projects, and members of the administrative staff of the LGCs receive some training through the Administrative College in Port Moresby.

Village Economic Development Fund. As one of the means to facilitate participation of the rural population in business enterprises, the government in fiscal 1975 established the Village Economic Development Fund (VEDF) with a grant of K1.5 million. It is aimed at overcoming shortages of risk capital available to villagers for commercial projects. Many village groups that cannot raise the capital necessary to qualify for a PNGDB loan for commercial enterprises can obtain from the VEDF grants of up to 40 percent of the cost of a project. The remainder is supplied through a PNGDB loan and the groups' own resources. The PNGDB acts as a point of contact for

3. In 1977, area authorities began to be replaced by provincial governments.

groups wishing grants and makes application for grants on their behalf to the Ministry of Finance, which administers the fund. The PNGDB has a special projects section to handle enquiries for the fund. In fiscal 1975, 26 loans of K0.4 million were made by the PNGDB to match government grant money of K0.5 million, which together financed village projects costing about K1 million. Villagers' demand for such grant money is reportedly very high, but it is too early to judge the prospects of the fund's operation.

DASF extension service. More than half the staff of Papua New Guinea's Department of Agriculture, Stock and Fisheries (DASF) is engaged in agricultural extension work.[4] The extension service works with local rural populations on agricultural improvement and innovation projects. The service also provides technical assistance to LGCs in preparing RIP projects and supervises the execution of these projects. It was feared that independence might bring an outflow of expatriate staff in sufficient numbers to impair seriously the efficiency of the extension service. The DASF did lose—and is still losing—valuable experienced expatriates who had been employed and financed by the Australian government, but the effect of this loss has been less serious than was anticipated.

GOVERNMENT

The central government in Papua New Guinea is by far the largest employer, the largest source of demand for investment activity, the largest mobilizer and provider of capital, and the largest source of funds spent at local government levels. In the long run no sector of the economy will have nearly as great an effect on the pace, direction, and quality of development as the central government. It may be called the leading sector in Papua New Guinea development—the exogenous source of new effective demand in the economy. It is response to this demand that mobilizes and rearranges resources, drawing them into new higher-productivity, higher-income activities. The main role of the enclave projects, which some observers might consider the leading sector in this country's development, is more properly seen as providing the government with the revenues needed to play its leading-sector role.

The government continues to depend heavily on Australian expatriates for staffing in both the public and the private sectors. Ex-

4. The DASF is now the Department of Primary Industry.

patriates still supply needed administrative and technical skills that are not yet available among the local population. But the coming of self-government in 1973 and independence two years later meant that Papua New Guinea must eventually weaken its ties to Australia and its reliance on expatriates in general. The arguments for administrative self-reliance are financial as well as political: although Australia left behind an impressive standard of public administration, the cost of maintaining this standard will remain high until the country is able to produce an adequate supply of trained manpower to staff existing organizations.

Even before self-government, the territorial administration had taken steps to replace Australians with nationals. At the time self-government was realized, the Somare government set a target of cutting the expatriate staff in half within three years. This created considerable anxiety among expatriates, and in a relatively short time many more left than the government wished. This put a severe strain on government capabilities and led international observers into pessimistic predictions about Papua New Guinea's viability as an independent nation. After eighteen months, the target was dropped and replaced by a more flexible and pragmatic policy: to speed up training in needed fields and to encourage the substitution of local for expatriate staff whenever practicable. The dangerously rapid outflow of expatriates has subsided with this more gradual approach—perhaps aided by the depressed job market in Australia—and localization appears to be moving as quickly as possible, given the supply of trained Papua New Guineans.

As of July 1, 1975, expatriates accounted for 13.5 percent of the total government staff of 49,759. About half these expatriates were of the Australian Staffing Assistance Group (ASAG), which was directly supported by Australia until its termination in mid-1976. Now all expatriate government employees' salaries fall on the Papua New Guinean budget. Many senior administrative offices and almost all professional and higher technical posts are filled by expatriates, but all department heads are now nationals. The need for expatriates in most professional and in many technical grades will continue for several years. The largest single group among the expatriates is teachers, most of them at the secondary level. The next largest group, at least of the ASAG component, comprises middle- and higher-level clerical workers. The replacement of expatriate school teachers and clerical workers should be able to proceed fairly rapidly over the next few years without any great adjustment of the educational or administrative systems.

Table 3.4. Employment of Nationals in the Public Service, 1971-75

Occupational category	1971		1972		1973		1974		1975	
	Total	Percentage nationals	Total	Percentage nationals	Total	Percentage nationals	Total	Percentage nationals	Total	Percentage nationals
Professional	1,169	6.7	1,403	6.7	1,487	7.6	1,530	10.7	1,553	12.6
Subprofessional	5,354	34.1	5,427	35.7	5,704	44.7	5,798	52.2	6,563	50.8
Skilled workers	10,147	77.6	11,145	76.4	12,763	81.1	13,916	86.5	14,429	87.8
Semiskilled workmen	9,894	84.3	9,575	84.5	9,534	88.5	9,914	93.4	8,397	92.6
Unskilled workmen	15,190	99.5	16,570	99.6	17,668	99.8	18,968	100.0	21,142	100.0
Total	41,754	79.6	44,120	79.2	46,975	83.2	50,126	86.6	52,084	86.6
Local	33,236		34,943		39,083		43,409		45,105	
Expatriate	8,518		9,177		7,892		6,717		6,979	

Source: Papua New Guinea Central Planning Office, Programmes and Performance, 1975-76, p. 333. Figures presumably refer to the end of the fiscal year, June 30.

The most pressing need today is to start training people in specific technical and vocational skills, but the educational system is still geared rather heavily to the education of generalists. Technical training is now receiving increased priority, and a National Training Council has been proposed, with responsibility for rationalizing technical courses. The Administrative College, under the Public Service Board, includes short specialized courses in its curriculum. The government also runs a number of specialized colleges. In line with its policy of self-reliance, the government prefers to build up domestic training institutions and to train as many people in Papua New Guinea as possible

Recent progress in localizing the public service is shown in Table 3.4. The public service as a whole was 87 percent localized in 1975, compared with 80 percent in 1971. A senior-executive training program run by the Public Services Commission has turned out from 80 to 100 senior administrators a year for the past two or three years; they now form a young but effective "old boy" network whose members occupy key policy administrative posts in almost all agencies. In the professional category the proportion of Papua New Guineans nearly doubled, although it remains at only 13 percent. Large gains were also made among subprofessional, skilled, and semiskilled workers. The class of unskilled workers was already almost totally localized. The biggest gains were made in 1973 and 1974, when expatriate employment fell sharply during the Australian exodus.

More important than the government's direct economic impact is its role in setting goals, devising policies and programs, and mobilizing the real and financial resources needed to achieve these goals. The government has taken a number of effective steps to make clear its development objectives and policies. Notably, it has established clear, simple aims and has defined—pragmatically and without ideological dogma—the principles that will govern the pace and direction of investment and the terms on which foreign investment will be welcome.

What the government has not yet done with equal effectiveness is, first, to spell out its sector strategies to decide the relative amounts of resources to be allocated to sectors and to major activities, and, second, to concentrate attention on those activities which it regards as priority activities for reaching its development goals. This is not to say that the government must have a detailed development plan, but it does need an outline document that goes beyond anything now in existence. This document should help stimulate further definition of programs, set budget priorities, and achieve greater understanding and coordination among the executing departments.[5]

ENCLAVE PROJECTS

Nothing in Papua New Guinea's history has changed the structure of the country's economy so rapidly and radically as the construction of the Panguna copper mine on Bougainville Island. Figure 1 shows the impressive size of the project and its relative weight within the country's monetized GDP, fixed investment, imports, and exports. During the construction period, from 1970 to 1972, the project accounted for more than 60 percent of gross fixed investment and a third of imports. As the mine came into production in 1973 and 1974, it contributed about a third of the country's GDP and more than half of its exports. The main contributions of the project to the economy are financial, particularly in domestic revenue and foreign exchange earnings. The project's contribution to employment or to the stimulation of service and feeder activities on Bougainville appear relatively modest.

The Bougainville mine belongs to Bougainville Copper Ltd. (BCL), a Papua New Guinean company, 53 percent of which is owned by Conzinc Riotinto of Australia Ltd. (CRA), a subsidiary of Rio Tinto-Zinc Corporation of London. The existence of low-grade copper ore on Bougainville had been known since the 1920s, but it was only in 1964 that a feasibility study was undertaken. Early results were sufficiently encouraging to justify an agreement between the company and the Australian territorial administration. The agreement was patterned closely on existing Australian mining law: to minimize the risks of the shareholders and creditors financing the project, a three-year tax holiday was provided, followed by five years of accelerated depreciation and the subsequent exemption of 20 percent of net revenue earned from copper sales (but not from gold and silver sales) from the normal company tax (33.3 percent), which was expected to be enforced from the eighth year. The agreement was to be nonopenable for forty-two years.[6]

The decision to proceed with the project was made in late 1969. Financing arrangements provided for paid-in capital of A$133 mil-

5. A discussion of development strategy was issued by the government in 1976, and a four-year government expenditure plan is now being prepared (see Chapter 8).

6. The estimated mine life from presently available reserves is 30 years, using an annual extraction rate of about 180,000 metric tons of metal equivalent.

Figure 1. Impact of Bougainville Mine on Papua New Guinea's Economy

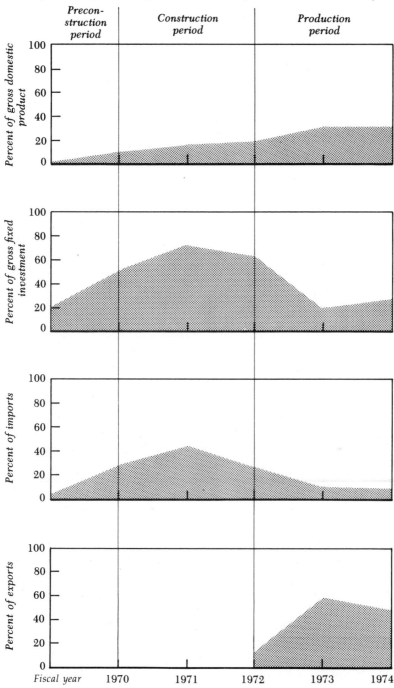

Source: Adapted from Department of Statistics and World Bank estimates.

lion (US$150 million); the government's share was A$25 million (US$28 million), which it borrowed in Australia. An additional A$277 million (US$310 million) was raised through a mixture of bank loans and suppliers' credits. Credit terms provided for most of this debt to be repaid by the end of 1978. Site development and construction began immediately, a construction force of 10,000 (mostly expatriate) workers was assembled, and the mine was brought into production in April 1972, slightly ahead of schedule and within its final cost estimate of A$400 million (just over US$500 million). There were no serious production problems, and BCL was able to meet its delivery target at a time of strongly rising world copper prices.

The mine reached production at a time when the political context within which this huge project would operate had completely changed. Papua New Guinea was about to be self-governing and would cease to be an Australian colony as soon as a constitution could be approved and a date set for independence. The combination of rising political consciousness and the knowledge that BCL would earn extraordinarily high profits in its early years led to demands for renegotiation of the 1967 agreement. During 1974 renegotiations were successful in making the agreement fit the drastically different political and economic conditions. The agreement advanced the stream of tax benefits that the tax holiday and accelerated depreciation would have deferred, and it defined a minimum fair rate of return on total investment. On returns in excess of this rate, the normal national company tax of 33.3 percent would be replaced by a progressive tax designed to assure that the government, not the company, would be the main beneficiary of high earnings resulting from favorable swings in world copper prices. It was also agreed that the revised agreement could be reopened by either party after seven years. Both parties are reported to be satisfied with the agreement, and their relations are good.

One additional mining project of approximately the same size as the Bougainville mine is likely to go forward during the next decade: the copper mine at Ok Tedi, on the mainland not far from the Indonesian border. Its impact on the economy would be roughly similar to that of the Bougainville project. The government recently signed a concession agreement with a consortium of mining companies headed by Broken Hill Proprietary Ltd. for engineering feasibility studies. The proven reserves have exceeded the minimum needed for further investigation, but the potential profitability of a mine depends on its construction costs. The companies are required by the agreement to complete their feasibility studies by early 1979 and to decide within the following year whether to proceed with construction. The earliest year in which copper production could be expected is 1985.

Other large enclave projects are in the offing, but none has advanced as far as has the Ok Tedi project. The two most likely to be developed in the near future are the Purari hydroelectric power project and offshore drilling for oil and gas. Studies for the Purari power scheme are under way, but no further steps will be taken unless adequate use can be ensured. A concession agreement regarding oil and gas development in the Gulf of Papua has been completed between the government and a consortium headed by Exxon, and drilling has resumed; an onshore well will soon be drilled.

OTHER INDUSTRY

Manufacturing accounted for about 8 percent of GDP in 1974. The number of establishments registered as factories increased from 123 in fiscal 1956 to 331 in 1963, then to 556 in 1968 and 729 in 1971; as Table 3.5 shows, there has been no significant change since then. In 1974 about half of Papua New Guinea's factories were in engineering industries, 17 percent were in food, drink, and tobacco; and 18 percent were in sawmilling and joinery. Less than 15 percent of the factory labor force was expatriate, although a large majority of the establishments were undoubtedly owned by foreigners, primarily Australians. Coffee, coconut oil, plywood, sawlogs, bottles, cigarettes, and tobacco are among Papua New Guinea's principal manufactures. Other manufacturing activities include beer brewing, soft drink bottling, baking, slaughtering, tire recapping, furnituremaking, some agricultural processing, and manufacture of light consumer goods. There is no textile mill, no cement mill, no sugar mill, no refining of metal or oil, and no manufacture or assembly of any kind of metal consumer durables.

Another notable feature of Papua New Guinea's private, nonagricultural economy is the almost total absence of handicraft workers and the small-scale traders, shopkeepers, and service-repair establishments that provide such a large volume of employment, especially urban employment, in many other countries. Partly this reflects the fact that Papua New Guinea's urban growth is quite recent. It also reflects the restrictive effects of the large number of registration and licensing requirements that the Australian adminis-

Table 3.5. Summary of Factory Operations, Fiscal Years 1968-74

Industry	Fiscal years						
	1968	1969	1970[a]	1971	1972	1973	1974
Engineering industries							
Factories (number)	256	281	328	359	354	342	379
Employment (number)[b]	3,794	4,273	4,858	5,399	5,659	5,402	6,075
Salaries and wages (thousands of kina)[c]	5,794.1	6,901.7	8,539.7	9,883	12,124	12,139	14,316
Value of output (thousands of kina)	18,068.4	21,605.3	27,322.8	33,339	39,777	40,118	53,025
Gross value added (thousands of kina)[d]	9,992.7	11,679.6	14,919.3	18,000	21,580	22,152	27,082
Food, drink, and tobacco							
Factories (number)	83	94	100	117	126	124	129
Employment (number)[b]	2,332	3,225	3,304	3,785	4,086	4,114	4,278
Salaries and wages (thousands of kina)[c]	1,626.2	1,878.6	2,217.2	2,760	3,470	3,897	4,784
Value of output (thousands of kina)	17,735.6	22,496.7	24,972.4	33,291	36,224	42,554	54,816
Gross value added (thousands of kina)[d]	6,645.0	8,359.3	9,315.8	11,877	13,572	17,227	19,719
Sawmills, joinery, and the like							
Factories (number)	143	152	153	155	144	135	133
Employment (number)[b]	3,794	3,932	3,958	4,026	4,276	4,182	4,489
Salaries and wages (thousands of kina)[c]	2,984.5	3,146.9	3,110.8	3,671	4,295	4,354	5,135
Value of output (thousands of kina)	13,350.7	14,882.6	15,426.2	17,496	19,072	18,929	22,387
Gross value added (thousands of kina)[d]	7,137.6	8,000.4	8,104.0	9,339	10,083	10,013	12,282

All other industries							
Factories (number)	74	82	88	98	98	101	97
Employment (number)[b]	1,500	1,857	1,719	2,073	2,315	2,500	2,479
Salaries and wages (thousands of kina)[c]	1,860.2	2,088.5	2,122.3	2,881	3,708	4,453	4,827
Value of output (thousands of kina)	16,665.8	16,246.0	18,522.2	22,855	26,465	36,597	53,074
Gross value added (thousands of kina)[d]	6,190.4	7,003.5	7,600.3	10,018	13,176	20,041	19,985
Total all industries							
Factories (number)	556	609	669	729	722	702	738
Employment (number)[b]	11,420	13,287	13,839	15,283	16,336	16,198	17,321
Indigenous	9,338	10,957	11,375	12,640	13,556	13,680	14,896
Nonindigenous	2,082	2,330	2,464	2,643	2,780	2,518	2,425
Salaries and wages (millions of kina)[c]	12.3	14.0	16.0	19.2	23.6	24.8	29.1
Value of output (millions of kina)	65.8	75.2	86.2	107.0	121.5	138.2	183.3
Gross value added (millions of kina)[d]	30.0	35.0	39.9	49.2	58.4	69.4	79.1
Materials used (millions of kina)[e]	34.2	38.4	44.3	54.9	58.2	62.1	95.7
Power, fuel, and light (millions of kina)[f]	1.7	1.8	2.0	2.8	4.9	6.6	8.5
Land and buildings (millions of kina)[g]	17.2	19.9	22.9	30.6	46.2[h]	46.7	53.5
Plant and machinery (millions of kina)[g]	20.8	24.2	25.5	29.0	73.3[h]	72.7	79.2

a. Some of the apparent increase from fiscal 1970 to 1971 was the result of the inclusion in 1971 of sixteen factories that were already operating before June 1970 and that reported their activities for the first time in fiscal 1971. These factories employed 287 persons in 1972; salaries and wages were A$429,486; value of output was A$1,717,902; value of land and buildings was A$479,842; and value of plant and machinery was US$408,253.

b. Average over whole year including working proprietors.

c. Excludes drawings of working proprietors.

d. Value added to materials by manufacture or processing.

e. Includes repairs, replacements, and cost of containers.

f. Includes lubricating oil and water.

g. Includes estimated value for rented premises and machinery.

h. Large increase is the result of inclusion for the first time of power-generation establishment for Bougainville Copper Company Ltd.

Source: Papua New Guinea Bureau of Statistics.

tration introduced to enforce Australian standards of public health, to prevent the development of too much competition for existing (largely expatriate) establishments, and (perhaps) to discourage urban migration. In any event, these past limitations on entry to urban occupations seem outdated in terms of health and amenity standards appropriate for an independent Papua New Guinea, especially in view of the need to generate many more employment opportunities in the fast-growing towns. The government is currently reviewing some sixty laws and ordinances to determine whether they deserve repeal or relaxation in the interest of stimulating employment growth.

FINANCIAL INSTITUTIONS

Before 1973, Papua New Guinea's financial arrangements were basically an extension of the Australian monetary and banking system, governed by Australian legislation and supervised by the Reserve Bank of Australia. As a first step towards creating an independent Papua New Guinean banking system, the Bank of Papua New Guinea was established on November 1, 1973, as the country's central bank. Simultaneously, the Banks and Financial Institutions Act was promulgated, providing the basis for the control of banks and financial institutions by the central government through the central bank. On April 19, 1975, a separate national currency—the kina—was introduced. For the first time, the government had its own instruments of economic management and could exercise independent monetary, fiscal, and foreign-exchange policies.

Commercial banks. The Australian distinction between savings and trading banking no longer exists in Papua New Guinea; the commercial banks are organized along the lines of the European mixed banks. Institutions that were formerly branches of Australian banks, finance companies, and life insurance companies were registered under the 1973 Banks and Financial Institutions Act as Papua New Guinean institutions. In April 1974, the Papua New Guinea Banking Corporation took over the largest Australian commercial bank, the Commonwealth Trading Bank and Commonwealth Savings Bank of Australia; it has been a leader in developing the banking system to meet the needs of Papua New Guineans. The commercial banks had formerly catered largely to the expatriate sector, and Papua New Guineans were often unable to borrow because they lacked acceptable collateral, usually in the form of individual land titles. Now a growing number of Papua New Guineans have opened savings accounts, and as a means of improving bank services for local people, the banks are being urged to open more branches in the countryside and to organize mobile bank offices.

Papua New Guinea Development Bank. The principal source of development finance and a major vehicle for increasing the proportion of the economy under domestic control, the Papua New Guinea Development Bank has as its primary aim to promote economic development, particularly in rural areas, through provision of loans. To earn, as required by law, sufficient income at least to cover operating costs, the bank extends large, more profitable loans, mainly to expatriates, which subsidize the costs of the smaller loans to Papua New Guineans. Applications from Papua New Guinean borrowers have priority and are granted concessionary rates of interest. (See Statistical Appendix Table SA24.)

Aside from rural lending, loans to businesses wholly owned by Papua New Guineans have risen steadily, particularly for transport and building and construction firms. Loans to expatriates—larger in amount and fewer in number—were mainly for shipping, air transport, and forestry enterprises (see Statistical Appendix Table SA24). Recently the Development Bank introduced a new guideline for lending to companies that are substantially foreign owned. Under this rule the bank will lend no more than 25 percent of subscribed capital to foreign-owned companies, although exceptions will be made in special cases. The bank has continued to help establish local businesses by appointing nationals as managers, gradually converting ownership and full control over management to the Papua New Guinean manager but bearing the risk until the project is clearly profitable under Papua New Guinean management. The bank also makes special efforts to help less developed districts. The bank's laws have been changed to enable it to finance the purchase of expatriate-owned enterprises by Papua New Guineans. Such takeovers now represent an increasing proportion of the bank's business, and demand for such finance is expected to increase.

Savings and loan societies. Savings and loan societies have played a useful role in educating and guiding Papua New Guineans in monetary matters. They are designed to mobilize small savings as sources for small loans to the local people and to teach them to handle money and keep simple accounts. Although the number of societies has increased rapidly over the years, membership and funds have remained stagnant at levels far below those of the Papua New Guinean savings bank accounts.

Papua New Guinea Investment Corporation. The Papua New Guinea Investment Corporation was established in 1972 to acquire a significant share of local ownership in large foreign-owned enterprises for eventual sale to Papua New Guineans. The corporation is intended to allow a substantial inflow of foreign capital without an excessive degree of foreign ownership. Participation by the corporation is also expected to give foreign investors some assurance against possible future expropriation.

The corporation buys portions of operating companies and holds these portions for sale at market prices through a mutual fund. Resale to Papua New Guineans of equity held by the corporation has been minimal, but resale to domestic groups, such as cooperatives or savings and loan societies, has been increasing.

Provincial Development Corporations. Along with the recent shift toward greater provincial government responsibility will come a new, government-supported institution designed to play a major role in promoting local saving and development. Provincial Development Corporations (PDCs) will be financed initially by an interest-free government loan of K100,000 (US$125,000) plus a grant of K0.05 (US$0.06) per capita. The loan will be repayable five years after the beginning of provincial government but may then be extended at commercial interest rates. The only other central government role in PDCs will be the provision of advisory services. PDCs may also raise money through share issues, joint ventures, or borrowing, although they are unlikely to borrow without the guarantee of the central government.

Three of the PDCs already in existence demonstrate the great variety of functions these agencies can assume. In the Eastern Highlands, the PDC will be used to raise revenue for the provincial government through investments. The East New Britain PDC is negotiating to buy a plantation jointly with a village that has been unable to raise all the necessary funds. This PDC would like eventually to be able to provide management services for the entire plantation industry of the Gazelle Peninsula. Other activities under consideration in East New Britain include a poultry farm and cocoa marketing. The PDC would operate as a holding company, without becoming directly involved in the businesses.

The Bougainville Development Corporation (BDC) enters into joint ventures, serving as a management bureau for its subsidiaries in such diverse activities as transport services, a restaurant, and a steel company. The controlling shareholder of the BDC is the Bougainville Royalty Trust (BRT), which in turn is controlled by the provincial government. Dividends are passed on by the BRT as shares to village governments, so that BDC profits are being spread throughout the island.

Possible sources of finance for PDCs, beyond the central government grant, are the PNGDB, the VEDF, the Papua New Guinea Banking Corporation, various banks and savings and loan companies, foreign companies and governments, and international institutions; foreign borrowing can be done only with the approval of Papua New Guinea's finance minister and is unlikely to take place without a central government guarantee. PDCs could provide foreign companies the local partner needed to meet the requirements of Papua New Guinean participation in many types of ventures.

Section II

Development Policy and Outlook

4

Goals for Internal Development

THERE ARE AMPLE GROUNDS FOR OPTIMISM about the long-run outlook for economic development in Papua New Guinea. Although it is unlikely that the country can become completely independent of Australian aid during the next decade, or even two, the real amount of such aid is likely to grow progressively smaller as Papua New Guinea becomes increasingly self-reliant in the critical areas of public budget financing and of the balance of payments. Progress toward self-reliance will depend on bringing into production one or two large new enclave projects, on limiting the real growth of imports, and on raising additional domestic revenue from the new enclave projects and from other sources as well. The realization of these objectives will depend on continued economic management of a high order; this, in turn, will depend on continuing the present use of expatriate technical assistance in the government service for several years, although in declining amounts.

The government did not work out a development plan immediately upon independence. By late 1976, however, there was a growing feeling that the steps taken so far to define its development objectives and the means of attaining them were inadequate, and the government issued two statements (the *National Development Strategy* and the *National Investment Strategy*) that set forth the goals and priorities to be followed in the preparation of a long-term plan.

The postponement of long-range development planning reflected some indecision as to what kind of plan would, in fact, be useful. Trying to produce a comprehensive integrated national plan of the kind developed by many countries in the 1950s and 1960s seemed of questionable utility. Too often, the preparation of these plans was a rather academic exercise that failed to engage decision-makers in the planning process or planners in basic decisionmaking, and the resulting plans were often too long to be read. In addition, many of these plans assumed that governments have effective control over far more of the economy than is realistically the case. For these reasons, the government decided that its plan should concentrate on government expenditure, focusing on crucial target areas, department by department. A major aim would be to force departments to identify their priorities and to establish goals. In Papua New Guinea's circumstances, this modest approach to planning makes excellent sense.

The Government's Development Goals

The most explicit statement of the Somare government's development objectives is the Eight Aims, announced by the new national coalition government in December 1972. This statement of principles is used by the Central Planning Office (CPO) and the Budget Priorities Committee (BPC) as a criterion for reviewing spending proposals by government departments and for making budget recommendations to the cabinet.[1]

THE EIGHT AIMS

The Eight Aims specify the following national goals:

1. *Larger proportion of the economy controlled by Papua New Guinea.*
   Rapid increase in the proportion of the economy controlled by Papua New Guineans and in the proportion of personal and property income that goes to Papua New Guineans.

2. *More equal distribution of benefits.*
   More equal distribution of economic benefits, including movement toward equalization of incomes among people and toward equalization of services among different areas of the country.

3. *Decentralization.*
   Decentralization of economic activity, planning, and government spending, with emphasis on agricultural development,

1. The Central Planning Office now has become the National Planning Office.

village industry, internal trade, and the channeling of more spending through local and area bodies.

4. *Small-scale artisan activity.*
An emphasis on small-scale artisan, service, and business activity, relying on typically Papua New Guinean forms of organization wherever possible.

5. *Self-reliance.*
An economy less dependent for its needs on imported goods and services and better able to meet the needs of its people through local production.

6. *Locally raised revenue.*
An increasing capacity to meet government spending requirements from locally raised revenue.

7. *Equal participation by women.*
A rapid increase in the active and equal participation of women in all types of economic and social activity.

8. *Necessary government control and involvement.*
Government control and involvement in those sectors of the economy where control is necessary to assure the desired kind of employment.

Thus, the Eight Aims provide the goal statements that might be found in a conventional long-term plan. The budgeting machinery, developed to serve the needs of an independent government, provides the mechanism for implementing these goals.

THE ROLE OF BUDGETMAKING INSTITUTIONS AND PROCEDURES

Since November 1973, Papua New Guinea has developed an effective set of budgetmaking institutions, procedures, and documents. This evolution began with the establishment of the CPO, responsible to a committee of the cabinet (the National Planning Committee) for which the CPO serves as a secretariat. The CPO has been well staffed, initially with expatriates only, but recently with increasing numbers of nationals, including, as of early 1976, the director.

The central task of the CPO has been to see that the annual budget allocations reflect the Eight Aims. In performing this function, the CPO, working closely with the budget division of the Ministry of Finance, has helped to create a set of procedures that makes it all but impossible for either ministers or department heads to submit spending requests or program proposals to the cabinet without having them pass through a review of CPO staff and the Budget Priorities Committee (BPC) of the Ministry of Finance, which advises the minister of finance on the allocation of expenditures. In addition to its traditional annual spending request, each department is now required to prepare policy statements justifying its activities in terms of the government's Eight Aims. These statements and the budget requests that accompany them involve CPO assistance and review in varying degrees. The material that emerges from this process provides the CPO with the raw material for the annual budget document, *Programmes and Performance.* This is published at the time the minister of finance presents his proposed budget to the House of Assembly (in September).

The present budget process involves a considerable amount of planning and review in addition to the normal negotiating of departmental allocations. One result is to establish a highly effective correspondence between the government's policy objectives and its budget allocations. Equally important are (a) the high degree of expenditure control the new procedures give to the authorities responsible for central economic management and (b) the use of the procedures to educate ministers and department heads on the country's overall fiscal situation and on national political and economic objectives. Thus, a climate of opinion and pressure is created that works strongly in favor of responsible budgeting.

SPECIFIC DEVELOPMENT GOALS

The Eight Aims and the 1976 strategy statements do not exhaust the government's development goals. Additional statements that translate these aims into specific objectives in certain sectors are the *Framework for Industrial Development in Papua New Guinea* (see Appendix C); the *Second National Investment Priorities Schedule* (see Chapter 5 and Appendix D); and the government statement on *Petroleum Policy and Legislation,* March 1976 (see Appendix E).

The *Framework* spells out a strategy for the growth of industrial activities that is consistent with the overall development objectives of the government. The document makes clear the government's concern for spreading development more widely, for asserting the nation's right to be the prime beneficiary of the exploitation of its natural endowment, for protecting highly prized environmental and cultural values, and for avoiding, as far as possible, the blight of un-controlled urban industrialization. These goals are not opposed to the growth of productive capacity; they help define the government's concept of development and establish the broad terms on which the government will permit it to occur. A notable feature of this specification of ends is the government's clear and positive attitude toward foreign investment, which is regarded as one of the principal means for realizing development objectives.

The somewhat qualified and cautious attitude of government spokesmen toward economic growth does not reflect any basic doubt about the need for substantial growth in productive capacity as the basis for social development and self-reliance. Some voices have been raised against even the present modest pace of development, as being too fast and disruptive, and against the wisdom of inviting foreigners to exploit the country's natural resources. Even so, there is no significant sentiment at all for freezing the Papua New Guinean society in its present condition out of respect for traditional culture. There is, however, widespread sentiment for trying to preserve what is good in traditional society and for avoiding some of the negative aspects of unselective and poorly controlled development in other countries. The relatively early stage of development is a great advantage in achieving these quality-of-life objectives.

In a report on its 1976 economic mission to Papua New Guinea, the World Bank suggested two goals that it believes should be given an important place in a national development plan: first, a continuing improvement in the country's fiscal viability (measured by a rise in the self-reliance index)[2] and, second, a gradual reorientation of the economy toward expectations, standards, and cost levels that can be sustained with the country's own resources. These two objectives are related; a determination to increase fiscal independence will involve a determined and persistent effort to raise additional domestic revenue and to economize in expenditure. These objectives can be attained only if political leaders, the expatriate community, and other present and potential taxpayers understand and accept the need to reorient Papua New Guinea's living standards.

An appropriate development strategy might be characterized as a combination of "leveling-up" and "leveling-down" measures.

2. The self-reliance index is the proportion of the government's total budgetary expenditure financed from domestic revenues plus foreign loans.

Leveling-up programs are designed to increase productivity and incomes, actions that will involve more spending; leveling-down actions are taken to reorient the country's expectations and costs to levels more consistent with its future as an independent nation—actions implying lower spending. The development plan should be as specific as possible in identifying potential sources of new revenue and areas of expenditure in which it will be important to achieve economies. The special role of enclave projects in the economic future will deserve explicit attention.

The central development strategy for Papua New Guinea in the foreseeable future must be to use a very small number of enclave projects based on natural resources to generate the financial resources needed to carry out the government's development objectives. Without the enclave projects, there can be no prospect of financial viability, no prospect of a healthy inflow of external capital, and no prospect of a development plan any larger than the small surpluses generated by Australian aid can support. Thus, enclave projects are a vital, but certainly not a sufficient, basis for a national development program.

Possible Size of a Development Plan

One of the first tasks the planners will face is estimating the size of a development plan. This will define the amount of resources available for "development." The World Bank, for its own purposes, made estimates of the overall dimensions of a plan, given certain assumptions. The most important of the Bank's assumptions is that government current expenditures would not be allowed to expand by more than 4 percent a year in real terms. This assumption reflects the emphasis the Bank places on keeping the growth of those government expenditures not financed by borrowing slightly below the growth of internal revenues. This rule of thumb is designed both to increase fiscal self-reliance and to limit the pressure on imports generated by the country's great propensity to import. Other, less important assumptions are that (a) the plan might be a four-year plan (mainly to coincide with the last four years of the current five-year Australian aid agreement, which ends in fiscal 1981), and (b) total government expenditures will be classified into current and capital expenditures, and all capital expenditures would be considered "development expenditures."

It is entirely possible, perhaps even likely, that the government will use another way of classifying plan expenditures. The government might define "development expenditures" as a mixture of selected recurrent and selected capital expenditures, both based on identifying activities defined as "development activities," and classify all other expenditures as "nondevelopment." Another possibility is to leave the budget as it is at present, with current expenditures and capital works shown separately, and to concentrate on program objectives and targets without any change in the existing way of presenting or financing government expenditures. Whichever alternative is used, the total level of government expenditures and the methods of financing them would be the same.

Table 4.1 presents one possible starting point for estimating the size of a four-year plan. It begins with the assumption that current expenditures will be allowed to grow at not more than 4 percent a year; capital expenditures will be allowed to grow more rapidly, because their present weight in total expenditures seems unduly low and because they can be financed by sources other than internal revenues. The assumption used is that government capital expenditures on average might grow at slightly more than 20 percent a year (but only for the next few years) in order to raise them from their recent, unusually low level.[3] Under these two assumptions, total government expenditures would increase by an average of 6 percent a year.

It is too early in the development of the planning effort for the government to know whether it will agree with the Bank's (highly tentative) judgment that the investment component in total expenditures should be substantially increased. The result may well be affected by rather arbitrary decisions on how various budget expenditures should be classified; for example, a substantial part of the present Rural Improvement Program consists of small-scale investment activities that are carried in the budget under "current expenditures" rather than "capital works."

Government spokesmen responsible for organizing the planning effort are unquestionably correct in wanting to begin with identifying program priorities in the ministries and then to derive expenditure classifications from the types of resources and activities these programs are found to require. A major concern of the planners is likely to be designing an appropriate classification system for plan expenditures and developing corresponding classifications in the annual budget, so that the plan and the budget can be directly re-

3. In fact, the budget for fiscal 1977 shows a 19 percent increase in capital expenditures over the previous year.

lated. This can probably be done by the use of explanatory notes and supplementary tables in the budget estimates; in this case, the introduction of planning concepts and expenditure classifications is unlikely to require any extensive reorganization of the traditional budget accounts.

Table 4.1. Possible Size and Financing of a Four-Year Development Plan, Fiscal Years 1978–81
(Millions of fiscal 1977 kina unless otherwise noted)

Item	Fiscal years				
	1977	1978	1979	1980	1981
Government expenditures					
Current	425	442	460	478	497
Capital	40	54	64	76	90
(Percent of total)	(9)	(11)	(12)	(14)	(15)
Total	465	496	524	554	587
Plan financing					
Current account	175	175	170	165	160
Australian aid[a]	190	200	190	190	180
Difference—current account savings	15	25	20	25	20
Borrowing, foreign plus domestic[b]	25	29	44	61	70

a. The figures for Australian aid are based on the minimum figure of K180 million for each of the five years starting July 1, 1976, plus supplements that are to be negotiated annually and are to reflect both inflation and unspecified other considerations. The supplements for fiscal 1977 and 1978 have already been agreed upon and are reflected in the figures used. The figures for the subsequent three years are World Bank mission estimates of what the total figures might be.

b. The breakdown of financing between foreign and domestic sources will depend upon the availability of domestic sources and the government's foreign borrowing strategy. One possible foreign borrowing strategy is demonstrated in the balance of payments projections in Table 7.4. This alternative requires substantial dependence on domestic sources during fiscal 1978 and 1979. If domestic funds are not sufficient during the next few years, the government may want to borrow additional short-term funds from foreign sources.

Source: World Bank estimates.

Table 4.1 also suggests how government investment might be financed. A notional estimate of the gap between revenues and current expenditures is shown, followed by estimates of Australian aid during the fiscal 1977–81 period—a fairly firm figure in the light of the March 1976 aid agreement. The amount by which Australian aid exceeds the gap provides a measure of government savings on current account, one important source of financing for capital expenditures. Some of the remaining capital funds will have to come from a combination of foreign borrowing, the reinvestment of earnings of revenue-earning statutory bodies, and one or two other sources.[4] Two such sources might be (1) a proposed national provident fund, which may become operational by 1978 and is expected rapidly to become the largest pool of domestic savings available for government borrowing, and (2) an expansion of agricultural stabilization funds which is also under discussion.

The final—and largest—domestic source of investment financing would be private domestic savings, which are outside the public savings available directly from the budget. The World Bank mission did not study the feasibility of mobilizing this volume of nonbudget domestic savings; because this figure is little more than a residual, it is far from firm. Table 4.1 is only a starting point for estimating plan size and financing, but the construction of macroestimates of this sort will be essential at the outset of plan preparation to help define spending limits for the ministries and statutory agencies that will draw up the specific investment proposals.

Program Emphases

The 1976 World Bank mission endorsed the approach to development planning recommended by the Bank's 1964 general survey mission: adding slightly to the existing planning organization, assigning program planning responsibilities to the operating ministries, and focusing the development effort on operational programs that reflect centrally defined priorities and financial constraints. The national plan document itself should be as brief as possible, with sectoral details left to separate sector plans.

At least four or five government agencies have already prepared their own development plans. These documents reflect the strong technical capacity of many agencies and represent an excellent start on the "bottom-up" process of defining specific development programs and investment requirements. These plans have been drawn up principally on the basis of what agency technicians would like to see their agencies do; they have not been harmonized with the priorities and financial constraints central authorities must provide. Existing plans give a running start to preparation of an overall development plan, but not all sectors are represented by these

4. Foreign borrowing, which is included as a source of plan financing, represents estimated draw-downs of development loans made in earlier years, primarily World Bank loans, International Development Association credits, and Asian Development Bank loans. A small volume of supplier credits is also assumed.

plans, not all of the plans are sectorwide in coverage, and each is largely uncoordinated with the others.

AGRICULTURE AND RURAL DEVELOPMENT

In an overwhelmingly rural society that still has a large subsistence sector and limited internal markets for manufactured products, the main target of development activities must be the rural population. The main avenue for increasing the welfare of rural groups is to provide them with opportunities, knowledge, motivation, and means to become more productive. In general, higher productivity requires progressive extension of the cash economy, either to supplement or to replace traditional subsistence activity. The spread of cash-cropping has been given much attention in recent years, and this effort has met with considerable success. Diversifying subsistence production for nutritional reasons is likely to be more important and more feasible than improving yields on traditional subsistence crops.

Two sets of rural programs will be crucial for achieving rural development objectives—the production programs of the DASF and the RIP programs aimed at extending rural infrastructure. The priority areas for work on agriculture are: undertaking the more specialized studies needed to mount more effective attacks on specific problems such as growing of rice, sugar, livestock, oil palms, fruits, and vegetables, as well as expansion of fisheries; improving extension services, farm and crop financing, and marketing and storage; adding cash income possibilities to subsistence farming; reducing dependence on long-fallow rotations to restore soil fertility; and reducing land pressure in the more densely populated highlands districts.

Three of the most important agricultural products that deserve a closer look are rice, sugar, and tinned fish. All are major imports which have been growing fairly vigorously and can be expected to continue growing as monetization proceeds. A valid case exists on the demand side, and on the supply side as well, for looking for import-substitution projects that will help slow the growth in these already large imports.

There are clear differences of opinion as to whether rice can best be grown as a smallholder crop or whether it could be developed on a nucleus-estate basis. Proponents of the former view cite two failures of large-scale rice projects on the Guadalcanal plains of the Solomon Islands in recent years. The feasibility of producing tinned fish is also questionable. It is not known whether a major cannery would produce the type of fish for which the domestic market has developed a taste; even if it should have the right output, it might not be able to produce at the relatively low costs necessary to meet the marginal-cost pricing reportedly used by Japanese producers, who are the main suppliers.

The great difficulty in mounting any kind of integrated rural development program is organizational and administrative, because responsibility is spread over many independent agencies, each charged with developing sector programs appropriate for its own rural target population. A common understanding and some spirit of coordination among the many agencies concerned might be further cultivated if a rural development workshop could be held early in the planning period. If productive, the workshop could be repeated, perhaps annually. Participants should include representatives from the DASF, the Ministries of Education and Health, the PNGDB, the Public Works Department, the RIP, the Summer Institute of Linguistics (whose members have much useful experience in rural development), and church and missionary societies. The CPO and other agencies have already begun team-building activities: in late 1975, they initiated a series of area planning seminars, which will contribute to the growth of the interagency understanding and cooperation that is needed for successful rural programs. More needs to be done, however, with a more explicit focus on rural programs.

INDUSTRY

Papua New Guinea's industrial investment policy was outlined in late 1976 in the *National Investment Strategy*. In the main, small-scale—and mostly private—investment will be encouraged through ensuring that credit will be available. It will be difficult to find opportunities to build plants large enough to avoid the high unit costs that small plants entail. In general, little attention is being given to specific industrial possibilities, and more intensive study will be needed to identify industries for which feasibility studies will be justified.

The production of import substitutes appears to be feasible in some industries, and the National Industrial Development Agency (NIDA) has set up a priority schedule for development of these industries. Internal transport costs are a major factor determining the feasibility of import substitutions. It would seem wise to schedule import-substitution studies in industry to follow, rather than to precede, the proposed study on internal transport costs, since estimating the size of a national market or of regional markets will depend heavily on knowing what internal transport costs are likely to be.

INVESTMENT IN INFRASTRUCTURE

This area of investment is inherently costly, and even modest programs will require large resources. For the next few years, the top priorities are likely to be regional roads, coastal shipping, and electricity. The telecommunications network and harbor facilities do not appear to need large expansion in the near term. Increasing urbanization will clearly require considerable investment in water and sewerage, in systems designed to meet modest standards.

Transport. In view of the rugged terrain in many parts of Papua New Guinea, the relatively thin population densities, and the early stage of production and distribution activities, there is a high premium on holding investment in highway construction to a minimum. In addition to not building many such roads, "minimizing investment" means using the lowest possible design standards and the cheapest acceptable construction methods for those that are undertaken.

It may make more sense to plan the type of roads used in military or forestry operations, rather than the first-stage standards that were used in the highlands highway construction. At least as much effort should be put into identifying low-cost design standards and construction methods as on the priorities of road selection.

Interisland and coastal shipping. The important shipping sector is beginning to get the attention it needs. A World Bank expert visited the country in April 1976 to conduct a reconnaissance and to recommend steps the government might take. The Norwegian International Aid Agency (NORAD) also offered a technical assistance grant to Papua New Guinea to conduct a survey of the sector in order to identify feasible projects. It is hoped that the government will propose including in this survey attention to costs and tariffs in the industry in view of their importance to future investment decisions in industry and agriculture. The size of domestic markets will depend largely on the extent to which the present high internal transport costs can be overcome.

Air services. Air freight is almost as important in Papua New Guinea as coastal shipping. Little is known about the volumes, cargo routes, costs, equipment used, and ownership of operations that now characterize this industry, nor is there much understanding of its potential contribution under the rugged and costly transport conditions in much of the country. This deserves examination, and, as in the case of first-stage trunkroad construction, there may be military experience worth canvassing before any firm proposals are developed.

Air Niugini, Papua New Guinea's principal scheduled airline, has the unenviable distinction of having one of the highest cost and fare structures of any carrier in the world. This is anything but healthy for a country that depends so heavily on air transport. There are many inefficiencies in the company's operations, and there is undoubtedly room for cost reduction despite the high-cost conditions within which the company must operate.

Telecommunications. Telecommunications is particularly important in Papua New Guinea, because other forms of communications and travel are difficult and expensive. The Posts and Telegraphs Department is one of the better-staffed technical departments of the government. It has created a first-class telecommunications network that is profitable and has shown a strong growth of both internal and external traffic. Although additional telecommunications investment might be justified on financial grounds alone, it may or may not have a convincing economic basis.

Electricity. There has been considerable talk and study of a large multipurpose hydroelectric project, costing an estimated 2 billion kina, to exploit the enormous hydro potential of the Purari River in the Gulf province. A feasibility study has been prepared by outside consultants, working with a Japanese group interested in the project and with the government of Papua New Guinea. Although the project might be viable in the long run, its short-term prospects appear dim, both because costs have escalated rapidly and because there are grave doubts about the market prospects for proposed outputs, about the intentions of the foreign investors, and about the wisdom of taxing Papua New Guinea's capacity to support a project of this scale, even if the investment were spread over a fairly long period.

HOUSING AND URBAN LAND USE

The rapid growth of towns, which has now started in Papua New Guinea, can lead only to squalid conditions unless the government decides to take firm measures. These measures should include land-use planning, the provision of minimum-cost housing for the urban poor, and the promotion of an urban housing industry capable of building houses that the growing middle class can afford to rent or buy.

The National Housing Commission has already done some interesting work on prospective urbanization and on how to deal with it.[5] The urban environment is still relatively unspoiled, but it is strongly threatened by an expected explosion of urban growth over the next decade or two. Strengthening the Housing Commission and developing specific patterns of urban land use and of appropriate investment, including a substantial expansion of existing proposals for sites-and-services housing, is highly desirable.

The government is fortunate in having a leasehold tradition that largely eliminates land speculation. It has also experimented quite successfully with the one form of low-cost housing that holds promise of providing housing for the poor at minimum acceptable standards—minimum-service self-help housing built on sites provided by government. This activity appears to deserve a reasonably high priority. The expansion of government services may require more investment in housing for government servants; housing is now tight in many places, especially outside Port Moresby. Before the Housing Commission is entrusted with the responsibility for an expanded program of rental housing, it must improve drastically the rent collections from its present tenants.

One way of preventing the growing towns from being scarred by industrial growth is to segregate industry into specific areas supplied with special services or, in effect, to build industrial estates. The desirability and feasibility of adopting such an industrial zoning policy in the few towns where industry is likely to become important should be reviewed—perhaps by a joint task force of the Ministry of Industries and the National Housing Commission.

The urban construction industry is not well developed and depends heavily on expatriate companies, although a few local entrepreneurs are now beginning to enter the industry. The inclusion of housing construction as a priority field for foreign investment reflects this state of affairs. The industry itself must expand substantially in response to the expected rapid growth of urbanization. It may therefore be useful to extend the projection work of the National Housing Commission by looking more closely at the expected volume of different types of building materials to be needed, ar-

5. *National Housing Plan*, part I, October 1975.

rangements for developing planning and administrative machinery in the principal urban centers, the number of skilled laborers likely to be needed, and perhaps the financing of construction enterprises and of house purchase and rental. Some individuals in the Housing Commission are interested in the role of the construction industry, and particularly of home construction, as a lead sector in the monetized part of the economy.

EDUCATION AND HEALTH

Education and health are the most costly of the government's service activities, and both are already relatively well developed. Although some minor investment in both of these areas can doubtless be justified, it should be held to a minimum during the next few years in deference to other government sectors with greater potential for increasing production and employment.

Everything possible should be done to try to reduce the present high costs of the country's two universities, which claim a disproportionate share of the government's educational funds. Localization of teaching staffs, especially at the secondary level, has a long way to go and can eventually save substantial sums. Investment needs in education are minimal. They consist almost exclusively of expanding existing institutions that supply manpower in high-priority occupations; there is little or no need to build completely new schools or colleges. The only possible exception would arise if there were no other way of overcoming the inequalities in educational opportunity that now exist in some parts of the country.

Papua New Guinea's health delivery system is notable for its extensive use of health auxiliaries in peripheral units, a low-cost solution well adapted to the country's needs and resources. The main health service needs are (a) a modest expansion of aid posts, mainly in districts in the highlands and in West New Britain, which are not yet well served; (b) expansion of the health center network—the proposed standard of 1:10,000 population appears too generous, however, and 1:15,000 seems more appropriate to the country's resources; and (c) the remodeling or rebuilding of the College of Allied Health Sciences at Madang—the main center for training key health extension officers and health inspectors—and possibly the construction of one additional such college to overcome the saturation of clinical training opportunities in the Madang area.

EMPLOYMENT

With a rapidly growing stream of young people completing

school and a high rate of rural–urban migration, an urban unemployment problem is beginning to emerge; it threatens to become serious in the next five to ten years. It is not at all clear what can be done to reduce the impact of this problem, but the first development plan should include whatever ideas can be identified and should attempt to suggest some programs. Perhaps an urban improvement program, parallel to the RIP, could be organized, although it should not have to pay anything like the current official minimum wage. A national service corps, often suggested but not acted upon, might provide twelve to eighteen months of useful service for educated youth, who would thereby repay society for their highly subsidized educations. The crucial problem is to find useful things for young persons to do and to organize a program without creating a costly administrative establishment. An apparently important influence on urban employment is the elaborate system of ordinances and regulations that now governs entry into many urban occupations and trades; ways to reduce these constraints are being reviewed.

The Measurement of Development Progress

In a development strategy that surrounds the growth of GDP with a number of conditions and qualifications, the measurement of progress will not be reflected very satisfactorily in the conventional national accounting measures. Although such measures are indeed relevant and useful, they are less suitable than other indicators for measuring the country's progress toward the wider goals of development.

A more satisfactory basis for judging progress is to supplement the conventional economic measures with an appropriate set of social indicators. The government has recognized this fact and has already taken steps to develop such a set of indicators. In June 1975 a United Nations Development Programme consultant submitted a report entitled *Social Planning Indicators and Social Reporting for Papua New Guinea*. The government has used this document as the basis for technical discussions on the possibility of constructing a meaningful series of indicators that can be incorporated into its regular statistical series to supplement existing economic indicators. This effort is a timely and logical expression of the government's determination to link economic growth to a wider set of social and cultural objectives.

5

The Role of Foreign Investment

FOREIGN CAPITAL AND EXPATRIATE entrepreneurial and technical skills have historically been the dominant forces in bringing Papua New Guinea into the stream of modern economic and social development. It seems clear that for many years to come foreign entrepreneurship, management, and capital will continue to play a more important role in Papua New Guinea than in many developing countries. The terms and conditions on which foreign resources will henceforth make their contribution to Papua New Guinea's further development have been fundamentally altered, however, by the political events of the past decade. The government of Papua New Guinea has moved rapidly and effectively to define its attitudes and policies toward eligibility of expatriates for citizenship and their employment in both the public and private sectors and toward foreign investment—existing and new, small and large. The government has actually relied heavily on the foreigners in government service, plus a number of foreign consultants, to work out the policies, laws, and administrative procedures that now govern the terms and conditions upon which foreign skills and capital will be welcomed.

Basic Principles Underlying Government Policy

Present national policy is to welcome both foreign investment and the expatriate skills necessary to make it effective, so long as the foreign investors abide by the basic policies of the government. The principles guiding government policy are clear, and the government hopes they are sufficiently clear to discourage certain types of foreign investment it does not wish to have. The main ground rules are the following:

—A moderate amount of large-scale foreign investment in natural resource industries is being actively sought.
—Foreign investors will be assured of opportunities to recover their investments and to make reasonable profits on them, but the largest part of profits that exceed normal industry profits will be expected to go to the government through taxation; because natural resources belong to Papua New Guinea, the government, not the foreign investor, is to be the main beneficiary of the exploitation of resources.
—If additional infrastructure must be built to ensure viability of a resource investment, project financing must include the infrastructure component; foreign investors must not expect the government to provide infrastructure investment necessary only to a single project—that is, "captive infrastructure."
—The government will expect foreign investors to do as much processing of domestically produced raw materials within Papua New Guinea as is reasonable, with standards to be worked out as each project is negotiated.
—Foreign investors must propose specific plans for the training of domestic staff and for the progressive localization of their work forces.
—The government has a deep-seated concern for environmental impact; foreign investors must be prepared to show sensitivity for this and to incur reasonable costs for keeping adverse effects to a minimum.

The principles underlying the government's policy toward foreign investment bear a strong resemblance to some of those underlying the drive for a new economic order by many Third World countries—especially the insistence on better terms of trade for poorer countries in their relations with richer ones. The similarity is largely coincidental, because the policy of Papua New Guinea has developed at home, independent of the political discussions and alliances that have marked the growth of pressures elsewhere for a new economic order.

The government intends to gear the volume of major foreign investments to its expected needs for increased domestic revenue and for foreign exchange. It is not interested in maximizing the number of major foreign investment projects for other purposes; it does not put a high premium on growth of GDP for its own sake, doubts that such projects can make a major contribution to the growth of employment opportunities, and is wary of introducing more disruption of the environment and of local cultures than is needed to meet the financial objective of increasing self-reliance.

Policy Implementation

The National Investment and Development Authority (NIDA) was established under the National Investment and Development Act of 1974 to coordinate government policies toward foreign investment and to serve as the registration authority for foreign enterprises. NIDA participates along with other branches of the government in general planning and policymaking with respect to investment, especially foreign investment, and it can recommend special measures to attract desired investments or to establish government corporations in areas where private investment is unlikely or undesirable.

The first task of NIDA was to survey all existing foreign business operations. These will be required to register and will be subject to certain terms and conditions. All new foreign enterprises, as well as existing ones wishing to engage in new activities, also will be required to register. They will be accepted only if the activity is one in which foreign investment is desired and if the enterprise accepts the conditions proposed by the minister for labor, commerce, and industry in the *Second National Investment Priorities Schedule* (NIPS—see Appendix D). Since its creation, NIDA has coordinated evaluations and negotiations for a wide variety of proposals with a total investment of over K150 million (excluding large mining projects); these have included cement production, flour and stock feed milling, oil palm estate development, and timber production. NIDA supervises investors to ensure that they carry out the mutually agreed terms of their registration.

NIDA, after consulting with other departments, is also responsible for recommending the areas in which foreign investment will be promoted, those in which it will and will not be permitted, and those in which it will be restricted to ventures with substantial Papua New Guinean equity. These policies are spelled out clearly in the NIPS. The cabinet has approved a general industrial development policy for Papua New Guinea, the *Framework for Industrial Development in Papua New Guinea* (see Appendix C), and NIDA is studying the role of foreign and government investment to achieve the desired objectives. In addition to its general investment policies, integrated sector programs are being formulated.[1]

Although most of the principles guiding foreign investment policy in Papua New Guinea apply primarily to large-scale natural resource projects, the *Framework* also includes a few paragraphs on manufacturing and on tourism. The policy on manufacturing is mainly to encourage investment in small- and medium-scale enterprises, closely linked to agriculture, forestry, and fishing, which would serve internal markets. Tourism is to be encouraged under close controls intended to minimize adverse cultural effects and to maximize Papua New Guinean participation. Policies toward new investment in specific areas are determined by the appropriate ministers, and the terms and conditions for individual projects are negotiated individually between the potential investors and the government departments concerned. It is NIDA, however, that must ensure that the individual decisions are consistent with overall priorities.

MAJOR PROJECTS

Foreign investors who might hope for exceptional profits either from Papua New Guinea's relatively rich resources or from favorable price swings in world commodity markets are likely to be disappointed. They can expect sympathetic and fair, even generous, treatment in defining a reasonable return on investment: for large mining projects, a figure of 15 percent of total investment is used. A liberal exchange regime will permit foreign investors to recover debt and equity investments as rapidly as after-tax cash flows will permit. The government is opposed to granting tax holidays or accelerated depreciation allowances. The normal tax rate on company income is 33.3 percent, but those large natural resource projects whose products are subject to wide price swings must expect to pay higher marginal tax rates on above-normal earnings. In addition to the company income tax, there is a 15 percent withholding tax on dividends. The net result is tax rate flexibility, rates may vary from project to project, and abnormal profits will be divided on a basis

1. See, for example, the Papua New Guinea government statements, *Financial Policy Relating to Major Mining Projects* (Appendix F) and *Petroleum Policy and Legislation* (Appendix E).

tural processing, four agro- and marine-based industries, general construction on contracts over K50,000 and specialized construction below that figure, the provision of professional or technical services, and other activities specifically approved by the minister for labor, commerce and industry.

—*Restricted activities:* those in which new foreign investment will be restricted to enterprises in which a substantial part (normally, 25 percent or more) of the equity is owned by Papua New Guineans or to joint-venture partnerships. A list of twenty-two activities is specified, most of them in agriculture, agricultural processing, inland fishing, small-scale wholesale and retail trade, and construction involving nonspecialist contracts of less than K50,000.

—*Reserved activities:* those reserved for Papua New Guineans so far as new investment is concerned. Existing foreign investment in these fields is not affected, although it must be registered with NIDA. These activities include copra plantations, passenger transport on all roads and long-distance road hauling with trucks under eight tons, and a number of specific agricultural, handicraft, and trading activities.

Prospects for Additional Foreign Investment

In early 1976 some six or eight major projects were in various stages of discussion and negotiation with foreign firms. These included the following:

—The Ok Tedi copper deposit on the West Irian border, a project of approximately the same scale as Bougainville but located in more difficult terrain. Although one large U.S. firm had rejected (for internal company reasons) the terms offered by the government, the government subsequently negotiated and signed (in March 1976) a comprehensive agreement with a subsidiary of Australia's largest company, Broken Hill Proprietary Ltd. (BHP). In 1976, when the drilling program conducted by Papua New Guinea's Ok Tedi Development Company succeeded in proving up 250 million tons of copper ore averaging 0.85 percent Cu, BHP became committed to carrying out the full feasibility study needed to establish the project's bankability. Such a study will take a maximum of three years, with one additional year needed to arrange financing. Thus, it is likely to take about four years, starting from June 1976, to determine whether BHP will proceed with the project.

—Since about 1969, foreign oil companies have been spending about K10 million a year (about US$12.5 million a year at current exchange rates) on onshore and offshore oil and gas exploration. Recent analysis has centered future hopes on structures that are quite deep. Phillips Petroleum was scheduled to drill an initial deep well in 1976, but no results have yet been announced. Foreign investment in production facilities can be taken for granted if exploration results in commercial finds.

—In forestry, the government has recently been negotiating with five firms on five different projects. These include a K250 million U.S.–Australian consortium project at Vanimo; a K10 million Australian project at Kumusi; a K20 million project at Kapuluk with a South Korean group; and a K3 million project on New Ireland with a Japanese group. No one expects all these projects to materialize; the largest, Vanimo, is one of the more doubtful in terms of the potential investor's interest.

—The government is putting pressure on the four foreign offshore fishing companies to establish at least one major cannery in Papua New Guinea. CPO projections assume such a project by the late 1970s.

—The manufacturing sector does not yet offer as many opportunities to the foreign investor as the natural resource sectors. Nevertheless, an Australian milling firm has recently decided to build the country's first flour and feed mill at Lae. A feasibility study is currently being done for a cement mill. A similar study may be started on an electric furnace steel plant to produce reinforcing rods for the construction trade. It is considered doubtful that either a basic cement mill or the steel plant will be justified within the next several years. A cement grinding plant—a much more modest investment than a basic production unit—might possibly be justified.

It seems likely that the number of foreign investment projects will grow relatively slowly during the next few years and that no more than two or three large resource-based enclave projects—Ok Tedi copper, Vanimo forestry, and a possible oil or gas project—could materialize during the next decade. A much larger number of smaller foreign investments can be expected, although their combined volume is not likely to be large. For several years almost all factory-scale investment in manufacturing is likely to be foreign or joint venture. Much construction activity (including all large projects) also will be in foreign hands for the next several years, as will specialized technical and professional services. Because of language and historical association, Australia will probably continue to provide much the largest source of foreign interest in Papua New Guinea, at least outside the natural resource fields. Nevertheless, the Papua New Guinean government, without being in any way anti-Australian, would like to diversify the sources of its foreign investment, as it has begun to diversify the sources of expatriate employees in its public service.

The government has defined its policies and organized its promotional activities with considerably more energy and effectiveness than is characteristic of many newly independent countries. The generally excellent relations between expatriates and nationals in the country, the lack of any perceptible xenophobia, and a tradition of integrity in handling negotiations and administrative decisions all contribute to the generally favorable investment climate.

Section III

Prospects for Self-Reliance

6

Public Revenues and Expenditures

DURING THE YEARS WHEN PAPUA NEW GUINEA WAS A DEPENDENCY of Australia, much more than half the funds needed to finance the budget came as simple transfer payments from Australia.[1] Papua New Guinea's central long-term public finance problem is to increase the percentage of revenue from local sources and foreign loans; this percentage can be termed the "self-reliance index." In 1963, Papua New Guinea raised less than 30 percent of its budget requirements from domestic sources; during fiscal 1959–63, this figure averaged 31.7 percent. The World Bank survey mission of 1963 did not believe that the index could be raised above an average of 27.5 percent in the four-year plan period for which the mission was making recommendations, because the implementation of a development plan would add more to expenditures than to revenues. The self-reliance index has been rising since that time, however, and the index stood at 57 percent in the fiscal 1976 budget.

Transfers from the Australian budget (now called "foreign assistance") in 1976 still financed 35 to 40 percent of all government expenditures. This means that Papua New Guinea received (almost exclusively from Australia) foreign assistance of almost US$80 per capita—one of the highest assistance levels in the world.[2] The gov-

1. During its colonial period, Papua New Guinea had its own independent revenue system: that is, collections in Papua New Guinea did not flow into the Australian treasury.
2. Based on the exchange rate after the devaluation of the Australian dollar in late 1976.

Table 6.1. Central Government Finances, Fiscal Years 1968 and 1971–76
(Millions of current kina unless otherwise noted)

Item	Fiscal years							Percentage increase, fiscal 1968–76
	1968	1971	1972	1973	1974	1975	1976[a]	
Internal revenue	43.1	74.2	85.1	93.3	136.7	179.7	220.4	411
(tax revenue)	(30.6)	(61.8)	(71.6)	(74.5)	(95.1)	(134.8)	(186.3)	509
Current expenditures[b]	106.4	162.5	193.7	213.9	277.0	341.0	369.5	247
Current deficit	63.3	88.3	108.6	120.6	140.3	161.3	149.1	135
Capital expenditures[c]	22.5	42.2	40.1	36.5	30.5	33.1	43.0	91
Capital transfers[d]	0	n.a.	n.a.	4.7	34.8	0.3	n.a.	n.a.
Overall deficit	85.8	130.5	148.7	161.8	205.6	194.7	192.1	124
Total Australian grants	77.6	101.8	108.2	121.8	152.3	137.6	126.9	64
Australian budget grants	77.6	70.0	69.9	78.5	98.3	86.0	n.a.	n.a.
ASAG compensation[b]	n.a.	31.8	38.3	43.3	54.0	51.6	n.a.	n.a.
Miscellaneous borrowing, advances, and related income[e]	8.2	28.7	40.5	40.0	53.3	57.1	65.2	695
Self-reliance index[f] (percent)	33.4	36.2	36.4	37.2	44.4	48.0	53.4	

n.a.: Not available.

a. Fiscal 1976 does not include funds paid into the new Mineral Resources Stabilization Fund; only transfers from the Consolidated Revenue Account are included.

b. Includes salaries, allowances, and other expenses of members of the Australian Staffing Assistance Group (ASAG) paid out of the Australian budget until June 30, 1976. It also includes interest and repayments on public debt.

c. Fixed capital formation by central government only. Transfers and loans to local governments and public authorities, which are included in current expenditures, contain an element of capital outlays.

d. Transfer of assets in Papua New Guinea owned by the Australian government to the Papua New Guinean government.

e. Includes: (a) external financing, consisting of short-term advances and long-term borrowing from the Australian government, international organizations, and other sources (normally the largest source) plus changes in sinking fund balances; and (b) internal financing, consisting of changes in government cash balances, advances and borrowings from the Bank of Papua New Guinea, and domestic borrowing (mainly from commercial banks).

f. The ratio of internal revenue to current and capital expenditures.

Source: Adapted from material prepared by 1974 economic mission of World Bank; fiscal 1976, from Papua New Guinea Department of Finance, Estimates of Revenue and Expenditure.

92

ernment would like to reduce this figure very substantially in the next ten to fifteen years. To do so will require realization of the most favorable revenue and expenditure projections the CPO has made. This is perhaps unlikely, but the prospects for further improvement in the self-reliance index are good. Progress is not likely to be steady because the monetized economy provides only a limited revenue base. Any large revenue increases in the next decade must depend heavily on the development of two or three large enclave projects, with some important short-term help from higher indirect taxes. That Papua New Guinea's public finances will continue to be heavily dependent on Australian assistance for many years to come is recognized and fully accepted in both capitals.

Recent Growth of Revenues and Expenditures

An overall summary of Papua New Guinea's public finances and their recent evolution is presented in Table 6.1. The final column is of particular interest: it shows that during the fiscal 1968–76 period internal revenue increased 1.7 times faster than current expenditures, almost twice as fast as current plus capital expenditures, and more than six times faster than external grants from Australia. As a result, the self-reliance index rose from 33 percent in fiscal 1968 to 53 percent in fiscal 1976.[3] The use of domestic borrowing was low during this period, reflecting Papua New Guinea's conservative fiscal tradition.

Despite the relatively encouraging fiscal performance in preceding years, in 1976 Papua New Guinea experienced an extremely tight budget, and this situation is expected to persist at least for another two or three years, until world copper prices improve and bring in higher tax payments. This short-term pressure is reinforcing the long-term pressure on the government to find ways of reducing the heavy cost of government. In view of the narrow revenue base and the major role of new enclave projects in expanding revenues, maintaining fiscal viability for the next few years will depend more on measures to limit the growth of expenditures than on those to raise additional revenue. As long as Canberra believes that the government is exercising reasonable control over govern-

3. Revenues from BCL have moved the self-reliance index into a significantly higher range, but the sharp year-to-year fluctuations of company profitability will cause the index to show similar (but smaller) fluctuations. During fiscal 1977 and 1978, the index is likely to fall somewhat.

Table 6.2. Central Government Domestic Revenue, Fiscal Years 1971–76
(Millions of kina unless otherwise noted)

Item	Fiscal years						Percent distribution	
	1971	1972	1973	1974	1975	1976	Fiscal 1971	Fiscal 1976
Tax revenue	61.8	71.6	74.5	95.1	134.8	186.3	76.9	84.5
Taxes on income and profits	29.4	36.1	38.3	52.7	81.0	126.0	41.7	57.2
Companies	11.0	15.6	14.1	11.4	28.5	24.3	14.2	11.0
Individuals	18.4	20.5	22.2	30.1	42.4	55.0	23.5	25.0
Dividend withholding	...	...	2.0	11.2	10.1	1.7	4.1	0.8
Mineral Resources Stabilization Fund	...	...	...	...	...	45.0	...	20.4
Taxes on goods and services	9.0	10.5	12.9	18.7	22.0	27.6	12.8	12.5
Excise duties	8.0	9.0	11.4	17.1	20.3	25.6	11.6	11.6
Motor vehicle registration taxes[a]	0.8	1.2	1.2	1.3	1.4	1.7	1.0	0.8
Business and other licenses	0.2	0.3	0.3	0.3	0.3	0.3	0.2	0.1
Taxes on international trade and transactions	22.7	24.0	22.5	23.0	31.0	31.7	21.7	14.4
Import duties	22.7	24.0	22.5	22.9	29.7	29.6	21.4	13.4
Export taxes	...	...	...	...	1.1	2.0	0.2	0.9
Airport departure tax	...	...	...	0.1	0.2	0.1	0.0	0.0
Other taxes (stamp duties)	0.7	1.0	0.8	0.7	0.8	1.0	0.7	0.4
Nontax revenue	12.4	13.5	18.8	41.6	44.9	34.1	23.1	15.5
Sales of goods and services	3.3	3.6	3.7	3.9	4.4	5.2	3.3	2.3
Mining royalties	...	...	1.7	3.4	3.1	2.2	1.4	1.0
Income from investments	1.9	2.2	4.3	18.4	16.9	1.9	7.7	0.9
Rent	4.0	4.4	4.8	5.8	5.9	5.7	4.4	2.6
Fees and fines	0.7	0.7	0.9	1.0	1.5	1.6	0.8	0.7
Other	2.5	2.6	3.4	9.1	13.1	17.5	5.4	7.9
Total revenue	74.2	85.1	93.3	136.7	179.7	220.4	100.0	100.0

... Zero or negligible.
a. Includes drivers' license fees.
Sources: Papua New Guinea Department of Finance, *Estimates of Revenue and Expenditures* (various issues); and data provided by the Department of Finance.

ment expenditures, the Australian aid contribution is not in doubt, although both parties expect to negotiate over marginal amounts.

Sources of Domestic Revenue

Papua New Guinea's domestic revenues depend mainly on taxation, but a substantial proportion comes from other sources, such as sales of utility services, housing rentals, and—during the period of the first Bougainville contract—income from investments. The main sources of central government revenue during the past six years are shown in Table 6.2.

TAX REVENUES

Averaged over the five fiscal years 1971—75, the personal income tax was the single most important source of revenue, accounting for 24 percent of the total.[4] Import duties were in second place, with 21 percent; company income taxes provided 14 percent, and excise duties, 12 percent. The five-year average obscures the contribution of the Bougainville copper mine to domestic revenues. The probable growth of additional major foreign investments will strengthen the company income tax as a source of domestic revenue. In a small system, large enclave projects naturally have a very large effect on revenues, as they also do on foreign exchange earnings.

Because the profits of large mineral enterprises are highly erratic, the government in 1974 established the Mineral Resources Stabilization Fund (MRSF) to even out the budgetary effect of taxes on these profits. Payments into the MRSF originate only in large-scale mining enterprises (so far, only Bougainville). Payments into the fund include the revenues from company income and excess profits taxes, dividends on shares held by the government, and the proceeds of the withholding tax on dividends paid overseas (royalty payments do not enter the MRSF). MRSF funds are, in turn, transferred into the Consolidated Revenue Fund so as to produce a steady flow into each year's budget.

The strong growth of revenues since fiscal 1973 is not accounted for primarily by BCL. The first income tax payments by BCL that

4. These are collected from the employer on a PAYE (pay-as-you-earn) basis, so collections are very good.

carried through into the budget did not occur until fiscal 1976, and then they amounted only to K45 million. Thus, BCL revenues accounted for about one-third of the K127 million revenue growth between fiscal 1973 and 1976. The largest part of the increased revenues has come from a combination of successive increases in tax rates on individual incomes; a reduction in allowable deductions from individual incomes; sharp increases in excise and import taxes on luxury goods; and the introduction of a 15 percent dividend withholding tax, a 2 percent export tax on agricultural products, a 5 percent export tax on timber and fish exports, and an airport departure tax. Thus, the past three years have seen quite substantial increases in tax rates, and it has been these, rather than any substantial growth in the tax base or the advent of Bougainville copper, that have provided the largest part of the increase in revenues. The Ministry of Finance believes that for the next few years the main source of new revenues must come from an increase in the tax base, not from further increases in rates. Of course, this conviction does not rule out some increases in rates, particularly those which have not gone up in recent years.

STATUTORY BODIES

There are four important revenue-producing agencies whose finances are handled mostly—but not entirely—outside the budget. These bodies are the Electricity Commission (ELCOM), the Harbours Board, the Telecommunications Service of the Department of Posts and Telegraphs (P&T), and Air Niugini, the national airline (60 percent of which is owned by the government and 40 percent by the largest Australian domestic airline). In fiscal 1976, ELCOM, P&T, and Air Niugini each were expected to generate revenues on the order of K15 to 20 (US$19–25) million, and the Harbours Board about K3 million. Together, the four bodies account for revenues of K50 to 60 million, roughly equivalent to one-fourth of the government's total revenue from other sources.

ELCOM, P&T, and the Harbours Board are all profitable—or will be as a result of recent or pending rate increases. Indeed, the P&T Telecommunications Service has recently reached a point at which it is able to pay a modest dividend to the government (K3 million in 1975). Other revenue-earning statutory agencies may eventually be able to pay dividends, but no general policy on this point has yet been established. Air Niugini is currently earning far less than its management believes possible, despite the fact that customers now pay air fares that are among the highest in the world.

Before independence, the World Bank extended two loans each to ELCOM and P&T and one IDA credit to the Harbours Board. The Bank's assistance was conditioned on the willingness of these entities and of the government to set rate levels high enough to make a substantial contribution to future capital requirements. This policy does not mean that the government will never have to advance additional capital funds to these agencies. If the present financial objectives agreed upon between the World Bank and the Papua New Guinean government are met, however, the principal source of needed domestic capital will be the present and future users of the services, rather than the government. This will minimize the drain on government resources, preserving them for other investments that are less able to recover costs from users.

OUTLOOK FOR REVENUE GROWTH

It is not possible to estimate precisely the future growth of Papua New Guinea's domestic revenues. There is little doubt, however, that such growth will occur and that it will probably be faster than the growth of expenditures. The big uncertainties concern magnitudes and timing, mainly because of the system's new dependence on major foreign investments. Although the effect of such projects can be large, it is never certain until the projects are successfully in production. Nevertheless, such projects have a visibility roughly proportional to their size, and it is possible to take them into account in projecting the future behavior of revenues.

In 1976 the CPO made ten-year projections of the economy to anticipate how various components will evolve. The projections include one submodel designed to estimate the possible behavior of government revenues, assuming no changes in fiscal 1976 tax rates. Three assumed annual growth rates of public expenditures were tested—1 percent, 2.8 percent, and 5 percent. Only two major enclave projects (the Ok Tedi copper mine and the Vanimo pulp complex) could enter the system within this time horizon, and results are shown with and without both of these projects. The preliminary estimates indicate that with the two enclave projects total internal revenue would rise between 20 and 30 percent by fiscal 1985; without the two projects, the increases would be only 6 to 16 percent. The bottom line in this revenue projection is the size of the gap—the need for aid plus loans—in 1985. Only if the growth in government expenditures could be kept to 1 percent a year in real terms would the 1985 gap be less than it is today. It is highly unlikely that the real growth of government expenditures can be held to 1 percent a year, so these preliminary projections suggest that tax rates must eventually rise or new taxes must be added to prevent the absolute size of the gap from increasing.[5]

In February 1976 an International Monetary Fund (IMF) fiscal mission visited Papua New Guinea to assist the government in identifying possible new sources of revenue and means of economizing on expenditures. The mission identified a number of promising areas for raising additional revenue and estimated that these sources might add an average of nearly K20 (US$25) million a year to receipts over the next three fiscal years. The mission suggested that the government might take the following steps to increase revenues:

—Concentrate on raising indirect, rather than direct, taxes; an unusually high proportion of government taxes now is coming from direct taxes on individual and company incomes, and these are already at reasonably high rates.
—Raise import duties, which now amount to only 10 percent of the total value of imports, by an average of 40 percent within the next eighteen months.[6]
—Convert export duties from a flat to a progressive basis so as to capture for the government a larger share of the sales value when world prices are high.
—Increase highway-user charges, such as the import duty on petrol and fees on motor vehicle registration, and study a number of other government-service user charges that appear to be low.
—Put the company income tax on a pay-as-you-earn (PAYE) basis like that of the individual income tax; this one-time measure would move forward to the year of the change the tax income that otherwise would not be received until the following year.

5. Fiscal 1977 and perhaps 1978 may provide good tests of the government's ability to limit expenditure growth. 1977 is expected to be particularly tight, and the Ministry of Finance's initial budget guidelines to departments for their 1977 submissions stated the government's intention to hold the overall rise in expenditures to 1.5 percent. In fact, the 1977 budget provided for an expenditure increase of 5.5 percent at a time when inflation was running just over 8.5 percent—a successful containment of real expenditures.

6. The IMF did not suggest that all import duties be raised by 40 percent. This increased yield would be the net result of many differential increases, such as a suggested 50 percent increase in the duties on imports other than petroleum products and a 100 percent increase of the present 2.5 percent general levy.

It is too early to say what action the government will take on the IMF recommendations. Fiscal 1977 saw few changes in tax structure; although some of the IMF suggestions are viewed sympathetically, others are believed to raise problems that will make acceptance difficult. The thorniest issue is the effect of certain proposed tax increases on wage demands. The effect of wage increases on the expenditure side of the budget might almost completely offset the intended revenue effect of the higher taxes. There is also worry that higher import duties may bear too heavily on major investment projects. Once these problems have been sorted out, the government is likely to accept and act on at least some of the IMF suggestions; the net result will be a further growth of revenues of perhaps 8 to 10 percent from the present tax base.

Neither the IMF estimates nor the 1975 projections of the CPO take into account the fiscal consequence of a commercial oil or gas find. Estimates of the effect of an oil find are contained in the government's statement of March 1976, *Petroleum Policy and Legislation* (see Appendix E). These estimates show a range in the government's net cash flow between a high of US$117.6 million in the seventh year of production to a low of US$53.4 million seven years later, all in constant 1975 values. These values are substantially higher than the government's expected revenues from the Bougainville copper mine, despite the fact that the latter's sales values are considerably higher than those projected from a small offshore oil field. As a broad generalization, it appears that copper exports will do more for export earnings than for government revenues, and oil, if found, would do more for revenues than for exports. Both minerals are obviously of great importance in these critical financial areas.

Australian Assistance

The details of Australia's assistance to Papua New Guinea for the past six years are shown in Table 6.3. The main categories of assistance are (a) three types of outright grants that have always passed through the national budget; (b) payments to Australian government officers working in Papua New Guinea (since 1973, these payments have come directly from the Australian budget to the ASAG located in Brisbane); and (c) a miscellaneous collection of items that either are not considered aid by either government or are a disputable part of the aid package.

This assistance package was worked out in 1974, and it provided

Table 6.3. Australian Aid to Papua New Guinea, Fiscal Years 1971–76
(Millions of kina)

			Fiscal years			
Aid category	1971	1972	1973	1974	1975	1976 (budget)
Budgetary grants	70.0	69.9	78.5	98.3	86.0	122.9
Grants-in-aid	33.0	30.0	30.0	25.0	36.0	56.0
Development grants	37.0	39.9	48.2	52.1	40.0	41.3
Special grants	0	0	0.3	21.2	10.0	25.6[a]
Allowance and salaries of overseas officers[b]	31.8	38.3	43.3	54.0	51.6	37.0
Total	101.8	108.2	121.8	152.3	137.6	159.9
Other assistance						
Airport construction and other direct aid[c]	0	0	2.3	1.7	6.7	11.0
Direct expenditures by Australian government departments and instrumentalities in Papua New Guinea[c,d]	17.2	16.6	17.1	9.1	0.7	0.2
Transferred physical assets[e]	0	0	4.4	34.8	70.3	4.0
Termination and retirement benefits of overseas officers[c,f]	0	0	0.4	14.1	29.5	49.0

Note: In addition to Australian grants, Papua New Guinea receives small amounts of aid in the form of technical assistance provided by the United Kingdom, New Zealand, and the United Nations.

a. Includes K16 million of special grants to cover the salaries of Australian officers expected to transfer during the fiscal year to direct contract employment with the Papua New Guinean government.

b. Salaries and allowance paid directly out of Australian budget to its overseas officers in the Papua New Guinea public service until June 30, 1976.

c. Data provided by the Australian government.

d. Amounts paid directly out of the Australian budget to finance operations of various Australian government departments and instrumentalities in Papua New Guinea. Does not include defense expenditures.

e. Physical assets of the Australian government transferred to the Papua New Guinean government as grants.

f. Termination and retirement benefits paid out of the Australian budget to its former overseas officers who worked in the Papua New Guinean public service. Australian officers regarded this as part of their aid package, while Papua New Guinea did not. The March 1976 agreement ended this disagreement by excluding this item, now much reduced in amount.

Source: Papua New Guinea Department of Finance, *Estimates of Revenue and Expenditure* (various issues).

Papua New Guinea with assurance of a total of A$500 million (US$735 million at 1974 exchange rates) in Australian aid during the period fiscal 1975–77. This commitment was strengthened in March 1976, when the two governments agreed on a new five-year aid level with a minimum of A$180 million each year, starting on July 1, 1976. It was also agreed that annual supplements above this minimum would be considered, and that Australia would add supplements of A$10 million and A$20 million, respectively, during the first two years of the five-year period. In addition, a few minor special items were provided, so that in fiscal 1977 Australian aid to Papua New Guinea is estimated to exceed A$195 million, a figure that both governments agreed was "at least" A$33 million (or 20 percent) greater than in fiscal 1976. Because this increment over 1976 exceeds the current inflation in either country, it represents, for the first year at least, an increase in real aid.

This settlement was both larger and for a longer period than many observers had expected. Almost all of Australia's aid will continue to be on a general grant-in-aid basis, not in the form of program or project assistance. Putting aid on a program basis would draw Australian authorities into passing judgment on the details of the Papua New Guinean budget, something they wish to avoid unless they should become so disturbed by the trend of Papua New Guinea's fiscal performance that they feel they must raise questions. A shift to more project assistance would require a much greater investment of staff time on project work than Australian authorities believe to be justified to achieve their main aid objective.

Debt Financing

Papua New Guinea has an essentially conservative fiscal orientation. There is a statutory limitation on the amount of domestic borrowing the government is authorized to undertake. Borrowings are classified as long or short term depending on whether they are for more or less than one year. Long-term borrowings are defined as national debt and require amortization through annual contributions to a sinking fund; the size and investments of this trust account are published annually. Short-term borrowing consists of advances from the Bank of Papua New Guinea (BPNG) and the sale of 91- and 182-day treasury bills, a fairly recent introduction. The BPNG advances serve as the main residual source of short-term cash requirements, and treasury bills provide primarily a source of short-term investment for the surplus liquidity of commercial banks.

The volume of treasury bills increased sharply in fiscal 1975 and 1976 as a result of repatriation of commercial bank funds from Australia, where such funds had traditionally been placed; in the future, growth of the treasury bill market is expected to be much slower. As of June 30, 1975, the sum of BPNG advances and outstanding treasury bills totaled 4 percent of the 1976 budget. Both these forms of short-term borrowings are subject to statutory limitations, as are long-term borrowings.

Much the larger part of government domestic borrowing consists of long-term, rather than short-term, loans; on June 30, 1975, more than three-quarters of the total of K58.4 million (US$74.2 million) of domestic borrowing consisted of long-term loans covered by the sinking fund obligation. Much of the long-term borrowing consists of private treaty loans—individually negotiated private placements—many of them with the various provident funds that exist for government servants. The establishment of the National Provident Fund, covering both government and private employment, is expected within the next year or two; this should provide a major new pool of savings from which the government can borrow.

The government is currently carrying about four times as much foreign debt as internal debt (see Statistical Appendix Tabel SA20). Total debt service payments, internal and external, in fiscal 1976 were running at the relatively modest level of 11 percent of 1976 revenue.

The statutory limitations on domestic borrowing would not, of course, provide much protection against a government that is determined to make heavy use of deficit financing; such a government simply would repeal or ignore the law. The present government is strongly committed, however, to a regime of fiscal discipline. Even if it were not so committed to conservative fiscal policies and the maintenance of a hard currency, the government would quickly run up against foreign exchange limits should it repeal the debt restrictions and make heavy use of deficit financing. This is because of the economy's high import propensity; the government's awareness of this fact provides some additional protection against any temptation to pursue loose fiscal policies.

Expenditures

The fiscal year for Papua New Guinea begins on July 1.[7] The central budget is prepared on a cash basis and shows current and

---

7. As of January 1, 1978, the fiscal year will be changed to coincide with the calendar year.

capital expenditures separately.[8] The size and composition of actual expenditures for fiscal 1971−75 and the budgeted expenditures for fiscal 1976 are shown in Table 6.4. Expenditures increased at an average rate of 16 percent a year during these years. When allowance is made for inflation, real expenditures rose at a rate of about 6.5 to 7 percent a year, a greater rate than the maximum growth figure of 5 percent used in the CPO's ten-year projection to fiscal 1985.

Table 6.4. Economic Classification of Central Government Expenditures, Fiscal Years 1971−76
(Millions of kina)

Expenditure	1971	1972	1973	1974	1975	1976 (budget)
			Fiscal years			
Current expenditure	162.5	193.7	213.9	277.0	341.0	377.2
Salaries and wages	75.6	87.9	102.0	117.2	138.1	170.6
Paid by Papua New Guinea	43.8	49.6	58.7	63.2	86.5	133.6
Paid by Australian government[a]	31.8	38.3	43.3	54.0	51.6	37.0
Purchase of goods and services	68.2	76.8	76.0	99.7	134.8	139.4
Departmental operations	14.5	16.3	18.4	31.8	45.3	51.7
Maintenance	15.7	17.0	18.2	22.2	30.1	27.7
Other services	38.0	43.5	39.4	45.7	59.4	60.0
Public debt (interest)	3.7	6.1	8.6	10.4	14.2	18.5
Grants and loans[b]	15.0	22.9	27.3	49.7	53.9	48.7
Capital expenditure	42.2	40.1	36.5	30.5	33.1	45.5
Capital formation	29.7	40.0	33.4	27.9	32.0	42.2
Acquisition of existing assets	12.5	0.1	3.1	2.6	1.1	3.3
Total expenditure	204.7	233.8	250.4	307.5	374.1	422.7

Note: Excludes physical assets of Australian government transferred to Papua New Guinean government.
    a. Salaries and allowances paid directly out of Australian budget to its overseas officers in the Papua New Guinea public service.
    b. Contains an element of capital outlays.
    Sources: Papua New Guinea Department of Finance, *Estimates of Revenue and Expenditures* (various issues), and other data of the Department of Finance.

Government capital expenditures showed a declining trend until 1974, even in current terms. Their weight in total expenditures fell

8. It should be noted that "capital expenditures" refers to "capital works" as presented in the budget estimates; these do not include all investment expenditures in the budget.

from 21 percent in 1971 to about 11 percent in 1976. Capital expenditures budgeted for 1977 will be 19 percent greater than those for 1976, but this still represents only about 12 percent of all budgeted expenditures. Thus, the substantial growth in the budget in recent years has come entirely from current expenditures, which are dominated by wages and salaries (fairly constant at 40 to 50 percent of total current expenditures) and the purchase of goods and services (35 to 40 percent of the total).

During the period fiscal 1971–76, that part of the wage bill funded directly by the budget rose especially fast, and the part funded by the Australian government increased very slowly. Two factors caused this difference. One is the reduction in the number of Australians working in Papua New Guinea (from 4,500 in the early 1970s to 2,400 by the end of 1975) and the increase in the numbers of positions occupied by nationals; this shifted substantial numbers of employees from the Australian to the domestic payroll. The other is that total direct government employment rose rapidly—from 37,000 to 50,000 over the period June 1971 to June 1975—and there were substantial increases in government wage and salary levels. The government will have to cut the recent growth rate of its employment nearly in half if it is to limit the growth in real expenditures to the 5 percent figure used as a maximum in its ten-year projections. It should also pursue vigorously its review of the system of compulsory arbitration by which government salaries are now determined to see if a way can be found to reduce the extent to which the wages of most government employees are indexed to adjust for cost-of-living increases.[9]

The IMF fiscal mission to Papua New Guinea in 1976 expressed concern over the growth and cost of government employment. A slowdown in government hiring was among its principal recommendations for reducing government expenditures. A number of other areas where savings might be realized also received attention; the mission suggested that the following measures might be considered:

—Slow the recent growth in government staff (a freeze was suggested).
—Make the austerity program the responsibility of a ministerial committee, rather than leaving it to a committee of civil servants; this would make the government's seriousness in adopting such a program more credible.

9. An important 1976 arbitration award did, in fact, move from full to partial indexing.

—Issue immediate orders to reduce departmental expenditure on travel, new investment, consultants, overtime pay, printing, stationery, and telephones and other utility services.

—Review and reduce central government grants and subsidies.

—Require revenue-earning statutory bodies to raise funds on the regular capital markets rather than allowing them to use the government budget as a source of funds.

—Delay new public works projects for fiscal 1977 until new resources become available.

—Change financial management practices so as to recentralize spending controls, to link the creation and funding of new posts, and to clarify the budgetary implications of new spending proposals.

Projections of Future Fiscal Viability

Table 6.5 illustrates what may happen to the absolute size of the fiscal gap and the self-reliance index (SRI) over the next five, ten, and twenty years under different assumptions about the growth rates of revenue and expenditure. The five-year period coincides with the period of the five-year aid agreement concluded between the governments of Papua New Guinea and Australia in March 1976; the ten-year period coincides with the end of an assumed second five-year aid agreement; and the twenty-year period is an arbitrary two-decade time horizon. Five possible combinations are illustrated. Revenue is assumed to grow between a minimum average annual rate of 6 percent and a maximum of 8 percent; expenditure is assumed to grow between a minimum of 3 percent and a maximum of 5 percent.

The baseline figures are taken from World Bank estimates of the government's budget for fiscal 1977. These figures show a gap between expenditures and revenues—or a need for assistance plus domestic and foreign borrowings—of K175 (US$218) million and an SRI of 59 percent in fiscal 1977. The three projected outcomes may be summarized as follows:

—*Five years in the future:* If revenues grow only moderately faster than expenditures, the gap will either remain unchanged or may increase slightly. If revenues can be made to grow twice as fast as expenditures, however, the size of the gap can be reduced even in this relatively short period. A fair conclusion is that with a strongly disciplined fiscal effort, it should be possible for the next

Australian aid agreement to be set at a somewhat lower level than the one of fiscal 1977, but substantial aid will still be needed.

— *Ten years in the future:* Since revenue is assumed to grow faster than expenditures, the SRI rises under all combinations, and the longer the time horizon, the greater the rise. The overriding conclusion is that there will have to be a substantial difference in the growth rates of revenues and expenditures if the absolute amount of the gap is to fall below its level of fiscal 1982. It would not disappear within the decade under any of the growth assumptions used.

Table 6.5. Illustrative Projections of the Revenue-Expenditure Gap, Fiscal Years 1977–97
(Millions of kina unless otherwise noted)

	Fiscal years			
Projected growth rates	*1977*	*1982*	*1987*	*1997*
Case 1				
Revenue, 6 percent	250	335	448	803
Expenditure, 5 percent	425	554	693	1,126
Gap	−175	−219	−245	−323
Self-reliance index (percent)	59	60	65	71
Case 2				
Revenue, 7 percent	250	350	493	968
Expenditure, 4 percent	425	519	629	931
Gap	−175	−169	−136	+37
Self-reliance index (percent)	59	67	78	104
Case 3				
Revenue, 7 percent	250	350	493	968
Expenditure, 3 percent	425	493	570	769
Gap	−175	−143	−77	+199
Self-reliance index (percent)	59	71	86	126
Case 4				
Revenue, 6 percent	250	335	448	803
Expenditure, 3 percent	425	493	570	769
Gap	−175	−158	−122	+34
Self-reliance index (percent)	59	68	79	104
Case 5				
Revenue, 8 percent	250	368	540	1,165
Expenditure, 4 percent	425	519	629	931
Gap	−175	−151	−89	+234
Self-reliance index (percent)	59	71	86	125

Note: The self-reliance index measures the percentage of expenditures financed by domestic revenues plus foreign borrowing.
Source: Estimates developed by the 1976 World Bank mission to Papua New Guinea.

—*Twenty years in the future:* The effect of differential growth rates over time now show up clearly. In four of the five growth rate combinations, the gap has entirely disappeared, the country has become completely self-reliant in its public finances, and a budget surplus is realized. The fifth combination also carries a useful lesson: if revenues grow only marginally faster than expenditures, the SRI will increase slowly, but the absolute size of the gap will double (Case 1).

These estimates suggest that the government must make its revenue grow approximately twice as fast as expenditure if it is to achieve full self-reliance within the next two decades. Because of the difficulty the government will now have in mobilizing additional revenue from sources other than enclave projects and the probability that there will be no more than two or three major enclave projects other than oil during the next decade or two, the government should continue to do everything it can to intensify oil and gas exploration.

It should be noted that the gap measures the government's need for assistance plus loans. It is therefore misleading to think that the government must reduce the gap to zero in order to achieve full self-reliance; some reasonable fraction of capital expenditures can, of course, be financed from borrowings, thereby reducing the amount of expenditures that needs to be covered by domestic revenues. Long-term government borrowings (disbursements, not commitments) of K25 to 30 million (US$31–38 million) a year seem reasonable for the late 1970s, rising to perhaps K40 to 50 million (in real terms) by the early 1980s. Indeed, fiscal 1976 borrowings will total about K30 million in loans of more than a year's maturity; some 80 to 90 percent of this will be borrowed abroad. To the extent that an appropriate program of borrowing can fill the resource gap, the country can make somewhat faster progress toward fiscal self-reliance.

Critical Areas in Controlling the Growth of Expenditure

Rather than continuing to base them on Australian standards, Papua New Guinea needs to bring its expectations, living standards, and levels of public and private costs into a better relation to what it will be able to sustain from its own resources. Nowhere does this need show up more than in the public sector; nearly half of Papua

New Guinea's present government costs are supportable only because Australia is willing to pay for them. Papua New Guinea's fiscal self-reliance can grow only if there is unrelenting attention to the task of raising more domestic revenue and if there is a deliberate, continuing attack on the present high cost of government. It is unrealistic to expect that the absolute costs of government can be reduced, short of a crisis, which there is now no reason to expect. Future increases in the cost of government can be minimized, however, and the real cost of government reduced, if (a) inherited government functions are reviewed and decreased and new or expanded functions resisted unless there is strong justification for them; (b) the physical standards now applicable to most public investment are lowered wherever possible; (c) there is continuing localization of government posts; and (d) there is a determined effort to minimize future increases in wages, salaries, and other personnel costs.

REVIEW OF GOVERNMENT SERVICES

The government has already set in motion steps to restructure the public service. Although the main purpose is to change administrative structures to make them more appropriate for an independent nation, the proposed changes will have important financial, staffing, and legislative implications. The net financial result should be a reduction in administrative overhead. The present restructuring effort is not primarily concerned with reducing the costs of government, however. An effort toward this end needs to be mounted independently to see what specific functions and staff might be dropped. It should not be assumed, for example, that the departure of every expatriate should be followed by localization of the post; some posts might well be abolished: a strategy of slimming through attrition. The central question that needs to be asked of each existing or proposed function is: "Is this function or activity one that a newly independent government, striving to become financially independent, ought to have in its budget?"

REVIEW OF PHYSICAL STANDARDS

It should be possible to reduce the cost of capital works by deliberately looking for acceptable reductions in the physical or design standards applied to new projects. The current standards for government housing and for some government office buildings seem more appropriate to Australia than to Papua New Guinea, and these can probably be reduced without any sacrifice of safety standards. Roadbuilding standards will be especially important, because this will be a major category of capital works for many years to come; external donors must be as sensitive to this problem as the government. It is not clear that future expansion of the telecommunications network will need to have the exceptionally high technical standards that have given Papua New Guinea a system as convenient and reliable as the Australian service. Decisions regarding standards that directly affect human welfare, such as those for education, health, air safety, and law and order, will depend in part on studies of the relations between specific standards and costs and on the way administrators present these results to political leaders and to the public. The review of most physical standards should proceed on an opportunistic, piecemeal basis, as problems arise, rather than as an across-the-board, one-time effort. But the CPO and the Ministry of Finance should build a concern for physical standards into the review process by which departments are expected to justify their requests for funds.

CONTINUING LOCALIZATION

Although the pace of localization is not now governed—and should not be—by the need to reduce the cost of government, it does affect these costs. The cost of employing an expatriate for any given position is two to four times greater than that of employing a national, depending on the source from which expatriates are recruited. Serious localization began in the early 1970s, and it was given increasing priority as the Somare government prepared to assume responsibility for self-government in December 1973. The government hoped to halve the number of expatriates within three years. This has in fact happened, although too much of it occurred in the months immediately following self-government, when anxieties among many expatriates led to an unexpectedly rapid exodus. The government abandoned the targets it had originally set, gave reassurances to those who remained, and began to recruit a number of expatriates from countries other than Australia in order to diversify its sources of advice and expertise and to buy in cheaper markets.

Today, localization appears to be proceeding at a near optimal rate. The most difficult positions to localize will continue to be the professional and technical posts, in which extended education and experience are required, but CPO manpower forecasts suggest that by 1985 even these posts may be 80 to 90 percent localized. Tentative World Bank projections indicate that during the period 1971–85 the output of professional and semiprofessional manpower will fall short of requirements by only 4 percent (670 out of 17,180 persons). Requirements are based on a work force growth rate of 5 percent and assume 80 percent localization of professionals and 90 percent of semiprofessionals. If all skilled workers are localized, there will be a shortfall of 7,870 out of a needed 55,880 people, or 14 percent. Fortunately, it should be possible to make the most rapid progress in the occupations that now have the largest numbers of expatriates: secondary school teachers and the middle-to-higher clerical grades. Despite the limitations of manpower forecasts, it seems clear that the level of reliance on expatriates should be greatly reduced by 1985, or, if restructuring of the economy leads away from the Australian model to a lower demand for skilled manpower, dependence on expatriate manpower could be eliminated entirely.

WAGE RESTRAINT

As in every country, wages are the largest single item in the budget, accounting for nearly 50 percent of the total cost of government. Thus, wage policy has more influence than any other single factor on the rate of increase in total expenditure. Furthermore, changes in public sector wages, which are generally higher than those in the private sector, have set the standard for the entire monetized part of the economy. Because about 90 percent of all government employees are members of the Public Servants Association (PSA—a trade union), the government is not free to frame wage policy unilaterally. The country's negotiation, conciliation, and arbitration procedures for determining all wages have been patterned directly on Australian practice—so much so that the key individual in arbitration proceedings has served in both countries.

Recent inflation rates in Papua New Guinea have probably been slightly lower than those in Australia and some other Southeast Asian countries (see Statistical Appendix Table SA30). Nevertheless, price increases have been substantial, and the PSA and private sector trade unions naturally have pressed for compensating increases. Because cost-of-living increases apply only to a portion of each worker's salary, the people who have lost the most are those at the higher end of the wage scale. About a third of all government workers have experienced a fairly substantial erosion of real income, and the greatest losses are among senior officers, whose nominal salaries have increased only 5 percent in the past three years, when living costs rose 46 percent. Thus, despite the absence of any explicit policy to this effect, the government has been following a wage policy that will bring public sector wages into better line with what the country itself can support in the long run.

In early 1976 the government and the PSA went to arbitration over the question of how much of the wage scale should be indexed—that is, adjusted automatically to increases in the cost of living. The government's refusal to index voluntarily more than a modest fraction of its wage bill is further evidence that it means to continue with what is surely a correct, if politically difficult, policy. In effect, the current period of continuing world inflation is providing the government with an opportunity to reduce real wages somewhat by taking advantage of "the money illusion," which allows employers to reduce real wages at the same time they give employees more money.

The government has recently moved to review the present wage-setting machinery, which it feels deprives it of the degree of control it would like to have over incomes policy. It is too early to say what the result will be. Exerting more control will probably require a somewhat greater willingness to run the risk of strikes than that evidenced in the present system, in both the public and private sectors. The government's desire to review the principles governing salary adjustments reflects its fear that wages have been rising too fast and are unlikely to be slowed unless both government and private employers are given greater freedom to resist union demands.

7

The Balance of Payments

F OR COUNTRIES, AS FOR INDIVIDUALS, self-reliance implies the ability to "live within one's means." The two main tests of whether a country is doing this are its ability to finance its public budget and its ability to cover foreign expenditures without relying on grants from other countries. At present, Papua New Guinea is a long way from meeting either of these tests and still depends upon a large budget transfer from Australia each year to close both these gaps.

Independence and the Balance-of-Payments Problem

At the time of independence, the economy of Papua New Guinea was at such an early stage of development that it relied on imports for substantially all its capital goods, most of its fuel, almost all the raw materials used by its few industrial firms, a large part of its services (such as overseas transport, ship repairs, insurance, and professional and managerial services), and for a surprisingly high proportion of its consumer goods, including most of its nonsubsistence food requirements. With few exceptions, almost anything not produced by the subsistence sector has had to be imported. Papua New Guinea's exports have generally not been large enough to pay for all these imports. As long as the territory was a dependency of Australia, for all intents and purposes Papua New Guinea's foreign accounts were merged into those of Australia, and the problem of balance-of-payments viability existed only for Australia, not for Papua New Guinea. Australian authorities were, of course, interested in seeing how much of a drain on Australia's resources

Papua New Guinea was imposing, and they were naturally interested in promoting exports to minimize this drain, but there was no need for Papua New Guinea to achieve self-reliance in its external accounts. Indeed, Papua New Guinea had no such accounts in the usual sense.

Independence has created a balance-of-payments problem where there was none before, and it has forced the government to frame policies and to establish institutions to deal with the problem. Under the leadership of the minister of finance and his advisers, the following institutional changes were carried out:

—A central bank was organized to act as bookkeeper, trustee, and administrator for the country's foreign exchange earnings and reserves.
—A relatively simple set of foreign exchange controls was established.
—A division of exchange reserves was negotiated with Australia that provides Papua New Guinea with a clear measure of its initial stock of foreign exchange.
—A new currency, the kina, was successfully introduced; it was distinct from, but closely tied to, Papua New Guinea's former currency, the Australian dollar.
—The accounts of the private banking system were successfully disentangled from those of parent companies in Australia.
—The flexibility to relieve short-term pressures on exchange reserves by borrowing abroad was established by Papua New Guinea's new membership in the IMF and by the negotiation of a standby line of credit with the Reserve Bank of Australia; the Australian credit provides nearly four times as much potential accommodation as the IMF membership.
—With assistance from the IMF, an initial set of balance-of-payments accounts was worked out; with these accounts, changes in Papua New Guinea's external accounts can be measured without having to rely excessively on residual "balancing" entries, which mask important flows that were not adequately captured in the other accounts.

Papua New Guinea has one of the highest propensities to import of any country in the world.[1] The best estimate suggests that

---

1. The propensity to import is measured by the ratio of imports to the total value of goods and services bought; subsistence activities, which in Papua New Guinea account for 15 to 20 percent of GDP, are excluded.

roughly half of every kina spent in Papua New Guinea is spent on an imported good or service, and this proportion applies almost equally to kinas spent by nationals and to those spent by the expatriate population, which exercises such a large influence in monetized activity. Thus, increases in spending—consumer spending as well as capital spending and private spending as well as government spending—are reflected quickly and strongly in an increased demand for imports. There is some concern that the present high import propensity may even be rising as increasing numbers of Papua New Guineans enter the cash economy. This situation reflects the following factors:

—The almost complete absence of domestic manufacturing
—The dominance of export crops in monetized agriculture, resulting in inadequate domestic foodstuff production
—Very high internal transport costs, which partly explain the weak growth of home-market agriculture and manufacturing in the past
—The dominance of foreign goods in local markets, reflecting not only the lack of local production, but also the strong influence of expatriate incomes and tastes in the cash economy, a demand that expatriate-controlled trading firms naturally met through imports.

A major long-run problem for national economic policy is to sort out which imports serve the country's development interests and which do not, and to devise interventions that will discourage the latter without also discouraging the former. The government has not yet addressed itself vigorously to this problem, mainly because it has had to deal with too many more pressing problems.

Policy Orientation

In a series of carefully prepared speeches by the minister of finance, the government made clear that it intends to continue the hard-currency, open-economy policies that marked Papua New Guinea's economic relations with the rest of the world before independence.

THE HARD-CURRENCY POLICY

A hard-currency policy means that the government intends to maintain the external value of the kina in relation to major world

currencies; that is, it will do whatever it can to avoid using devaluation as a means of maintaining or restoring viability in its external
accounts. In a situation where national cost levels are very high and
there is a large adverse trade balance, devaluation could be super-
ficially attractive. By making all imports much more expensive,
devaluation would provide a means of "uncoupling" the Papua New
Guinean economy from its great dependence on Australian consumption standards and a means of increasing exports and decreasing imports. Under Papua New Guinea's institutional structure and
at the present stage of the economy's development, however,
devaluation would be unlikely to have any of the positive
equilibrating effects it sometimes has in economies with more
diversified and flexible production structures that are better able to
respond to changed price incentives. Devaluation of the kina would
undoubtedly be followed by irresistible union pressures to grant
compensating wage increases, thereby negating the attempt to
reduce imports. In addition, the cheapening of exports would not
lead to larger export earnings, because the economy does not have
any short-run excess capacity from which additional output might
come. In short, Papua New Guinea's problem of external viability is
a long-run problem of growth in productive capacity, involving
large investments in new export capacity and in import-substituting
domestic capacity. Devaluation could make no significant contribution to either of these objectives. The government's hard-currency
policy is therefore a wise one, because it puts the burden of self-
reliance on development policy, not on short-term shifts in financial
incentives.

In explaining the government's hard-currency policy, the minister of finance made clear that this policy need not mean that the
kina would always be pegged to the Australian dollar in the 1:1
relationship fixed when the kina was introduced. Initially, the kina
was pegged to the Australian dollar, because Australia was, and
continues to be, Papua New Guinea's major trading partner, and
there are many more Australians and Australian banking institutions
in Papua New Guinea than from any other currency area.[2] The
minister left open the possibility of changing the relationship of the
kina to the Australian dollar if changes in the dollar's relation to

2. "Pegging" simply means that a national currency is normally quoted in terms
of a particular foreign currency; the ratio between the two currencies is a separate
matter.

other major currencies should go against Papua New Guinea's own interests.

The second pillar of Papua New Guinea's external economic policy is to maintain an open economy. This is, of course, a matter of degree, and it is not negated by the establishment of a (liberal) set of exchange controls, of rules governing foreign investment, of controls on immigration and the employment of foreigners, or of taxes on imports or exports. An open economy is simply one in which individuals and firms are allowed to import and export with a minimum of controls, in which the controls that do exist rely primarily on market price incentives rather than on permissions secured from administrative authorities, and in which foreign capital and labor (particularly key managerial and technical labor) are made welcome on reasonable terms.

The underlying assumption of an open-economy strategy (as contrasted, say, with a policy of autarky, or administratively enforced self-sufficiency) is that the structure of the economy will evolve along lines of comparative advantage. Thus, Papua New Guinea would develop those activities it can do best and use this output to trade for other goods and services; this will bring the country the greatest return on the use of its national resources. The pursuit of such a policy does not mean a passive reliance on market forces alone. There is plenty of room and need for active interventions, such as identifying and promoting particular types of investment, laying down ground rules for foreign investment, influencing the location of industry, stimulating local entrepreneurship, preserving the still unspoiled natural environment, and protecting the weak from exploitation by the strong. The government is, in fact, active in all these endeavors.

Present Structure of the Balance of Payments

Until 1972 the balance of trade traditionally was heavily adverse. Exports were dominated by a few agricultural commodities, whose total value did not cover more than about half that of annual imports; the other half was covered by the Australian budget grant. The Bougainville copper mine at Panguna came into production in April 1972, and the fiscal 1971 level of agricultural exports of K74 million (US$83 million) was suddenly dwarfed by copper exports of

K126 million in 1973 and of K312 million in 1974.[3] Copper prices fell sharply in 1975, so that the Panguna mine contributed only about half the value of the country's exports instead of the nearly 70 percent recorded in the mine's first two years. BCL, almost alone, converted Papua New Guinea's traditional adverse trade balance to a favorable one beginning in 1973. In most years, however, BCL's impact was not large enough to create a favorable balance on the combined goods and services account. As Table 7.1 shows, Papua New Guinea still has to rely on the Australian grant to cover the combined costs of goods and services.

A number of interesting features become apparent relative to the capital account (Table 7.1). Papua New Guinea has experienced net receipts of capital in all of the years shown. In the first two years, fiscal 1971 and 1972, those receipts were very large; they reflected almost entirely the inflow of capital required during construction of the Panguna mine. A large enclave mining project actually generates a continuing stream of import requirements (trucks, equipment, fuels) amounting to perhaps 15 to 20 percent of its gross export earnings.[4] What is not clearly shown in the table, although it is reflected indirectly, is the large role played in the balance of payments by dividend and debt-service payments generated by major projects; BCL's factor-service payments (debt service and dividends) are much larger than those of the Papua New Guinea government. Although these transactions lead to large seasonal swings in the country's reserve position, they have become highly predictable and present no serious problem in reserve man-

3. The balance-of-payments treatment of the exports of large foreign enclave projects can be handled on either a gross or a net basis. The gross basis, upon which these statements are based, treats such exports as all other exports are treated, with the firm's factor-service payments (debt service and dividends) and its own import requirements entered in their appropriate accounts. The net basis deducts the use of foreign exchange by such projects each year and shows as "exports" only the net contribution of the project to the country's foreign exchange earnings. The logic for using the "net" treatment is that this type of large, foreign-owned, export project always has heavy foreign exchange requirements of its own, even though these are "self-financed" by its export activities. The World Bank's normal practice is to use the "net" approach, on the view that this provides a truer picture of the contribution such projects make to a country's balance of payments. Table 7.4 shows balance-of-payment projections in both gross and net terms.

4. It is worth noting that not all BCL's export proceeds accrue to Papua New Guinea as national foreign exchange earnings. BCL is permitted to hold back such amounts as are needed to service short-term debts expected to fall due within the next three months—in effect, normal trade bills.

agement; in fact, BCL furnishes the central bank with monthly statements of projected cash inflows and outflows.

Table 7.1. Balance of Payments, Fiscal Years 1971-76
(Millions of kina)

Item	Fiscal years					
	1971	1972	1973	1974	1975	1976[a]
Trade balance	−216.6	−190.9	21.3	235.3	15.0	8.2
Exports, f.o.b.	77.4	97.8	236.0	460.1	375.5	358.9
Imports, f.o.b.	294.0	288.7	214.7	224.8	360.5	350.7
Services	−75.0	−78.1	−124.7	−228.5	−156.1	−118.4
Receipts	41.0	47.7	60.0	71.4	65.8	80.0
Payments	116.0	125.8	184.7	299.9	221.9	198.4
Transfers (net)	124.3	128.8	145.9	151.4	115.5	96.6
Private	5.5	4.1	4.8	−11.6	−50.0	−59.7
Government	118.8	124.7	141.1	163.0	165.5	156.3
Current account balance	−167.3	−140.2	42.5	158.2	−25.6	−13.6
Capital account	222.0	210.4	60.1	109.3	76.1	45.2
Direct investment (net)	47.0	64.0	53.0	143.0	71.3	28.5
Private borrowing (net)	145.6	105.8	−23.9	−64.9	−25.1	−7.2
Public borrowing (net)	30.4	42.5	31.1	36.6	33.0	15.1
Capital n.e.i.	−1.0	−1.9	−0.1	−5.4	−3.1	−1.2
Errors and omissions	−63.3	−94.3	−73.4	−106.0	−101.7	−50.8
Changes in reserves[b]	8.6	24.1	−29.2	−161.5	51.2	19.2

a. Provisional. These data are more recent than, and therefore slightly different from, those upon which the projections in Table 7.4 are based.
b. A negative figure indicates an increase.
Source: Bank of Papua New Guinea, November 1976.

Net errors and omissions must also be accounted for in order to arrive at the overall balance-of-payments position, or change in reserves. In Papua New Guinea's accounts, this item has been exceptionally large, rising from about 20 percent of total imports in fiscal 1971 to more than 45 percent in 1974 before falling, in 1975, to about 30 percent. This item is believed to contain a large number of unrecorded private transfers, many of them transfers of Australians who departed during the early 1970s. Central bank authorities believe that the largest part of such unrecorded private transfers (which were extremely hard to detect before December 1975, when Papua New Guinea was part of the Australian currency system) has spent its force and will not be a source of large or volatile claims against reserves in the future. This is borne out by the provisional figures for 1976.

The final item in Table 7.1 shows the changes in holdings of foreign exchange by commercial banks and the central bank. In the last analysis, it is the changes in the reserves of the central bank, after its exchange transactions with the commercial banks, which bring the total system of accounts into balance. Since its establishment in November 1973, the Bank of Papua New Guinea has tended to gain, rather than lose, reserves.[5] In early May 1976 reserves stood at about K150 million (US$190 million) equivalent to approximately four months' imports—an adequate but not comfortable level.

The Composition of Imports

Table 7.2 shows the broad composition and trend of imports for fis-fiscal 1971 through 1975. In a normal year—one in which no major enclave investment is occurring—consumer goods account for the largest portion of total imports. Food and manufactured goods each account for almost half of all consumer goods; beverages and tobacco are minor items. Intermediate goods are much less important than consumer goods, and they are dominated by fuels, not raw materials (BCL quickly became much the largest importer of fuel in the country). Except during the height of construction of BCL, capital goods imports have not been nearly as large as consumer goods.

Another way of looking at imports is to say that capital goods are much more volatile than consumer goods and intermediates. Large foreign investments are normally self-financed, however, and do not exert much, if any, claim on export earnings or exchange reserves. This is not true of consumer goods and intermediate imports, which are sustained by export earnings. There are thus three important reasons for concentrating on consumer goods in any attempt to limit the growth of imports: (a) their heavy weight in total imports, (b) their sensitivity to increases in consumer incomes, and (c) their dependence on exports for financing. Given the policy emphasis on increasing self-reliance, a somewhat closer look at imports, particularly of consumer goods, is useful.

5. Papua New Guinea's reserves are published in the BPNG's quarterly *Bulletin*.

Table 7.2. Imports According to End Use, Fiscal Years 1971-75

	Fiscal years				
Import type	1971	1972	1973	1974	1975
Millions of kina					
Consumer goods	99.6	101.5	103.4	112.7	150.2
Food	41.5	45.4	47.7	57.4	71.4
Beverages and tobacco	6.3	6.0	5.0	4.3	5.6
Manufactured goods	51.8	50.1	50.7	51.0	73.2
Intermediate goods	16.0	21.1	19.1	28.5	54.9
Fuels	8.7	12.8	11.1	19.6	38.3
Other	7.3	8.3	8.0	8.9	16.6
Capital goods	175.8	162.8	89.3	80.4	138.9
Other imports	2.6	3.3	2.8	3.2	16.5
Total imports, f.o.b.	294.0	288.7	214.7	224.8	360.5
Percent of total					
Consumer goods	33.9	35.2	48.2	50.1	41.7
Intermediate goods	5.4	7.3	8.9	12.7	15.2
Capital goods	59.8	56.4	41.6	35.8	38.5
Other imports	0.9	1.1	1.3	1.4	4.6
Ratio (percentage)					
Consumer goods imports to private consumption[a]	40.0	39.3	38.9	39.2	42.1
Capital goods imports to fixed investment[a]	63.7	67.7	70.5	62.1	78.3

a. Private consumption and fixed investment refer to the market component only.

Sources: Papua New Guinea Bureau of Statistics, Ministry of Finance, and World Bank estimates.

Table 7.3 shows for the five-year period fiscal 1971–75 the composition of imports classified according to the Standard International Trade Classification (SITC) of the United Nations. Certain categories have not shown any strong growth over this period, notably manufactured goods (SITC 6 and 8, although paper and textile products have grown fast), miscellaneous items (SITC 9), and machinery and transport equipment (SITC 7, although this group has a volatility that reflects its dependence on major investment projects like the Panguna mine). The fastest growth has occurred in fuels; petroleum grew by about 350 percent, with an absolute growth of about K18 million in the last year shown (fiscal 1974 was the year of sudden worldwide increases in petroleum prices).[6] Chemical im-

6. The end use of petroleum imports is not clear. A breakdown of the figures for fiscal 1973 shows that automotive fuels accounted for more than 50 percent of the total, with aviation fuels and furnace oils accounting for about 20 percent each. By 1975, when the Panguna mine was in full operation, automotive and aviation fuels accounted for about a third of the total, with other uses not shown.

**Table 7.3. Value of Imports by Standard International Trade Classification
(SITC), Fiscal Years 1971–75**
(Millions of kina, f.o.b.)

SITC	Fiscal years				
	1971	*1972*	*1973*	*1974*	*1975*
0 Food and live animals	41.5	45.4	47.7	57.4	71.4
01 Meat and meat preparations	11.6	13.2	13.0	14.5	17.7
02 Dairy products and eggs	2.3	2.9	3.1	3.4	4.1
03 Fish and fish preparations	4.9	5.2	5.2	10.1	5.4
04 Cereal grains and cereal preparations	11.5	11.4	13.2	14.8	23.3
05 Fruits and vegetables	3.6	4.2	3.9	3.8	4.8
06 Sugar, sugar preparations and honey	3.2	3.8	4.4	5.7	8.4
Other	4.5	4.7	4.9	5.2	7.7
1 Beverages and tobacco	6.3	6.0	5.0	4.3	5.6
11 Beverages	3.7	3.7	3.0	2.1	2.8
12 Tobacco and tobacco manufactures	2.6	2.3	2.0	2.2	2.8
2 Crude materials, inedible (except fuels)	1.0	1.0	0.7	0.8	1.2
3 Mineral fuels, lubricants and related materials	8.7	12.8	11.1	19.6	38.3
33 Petroleum and petroleum products	8.6	12.7	10.0	19.5	38.0
Other	0.1	0.1	0.1	0.1	0.3
4 Animal and vegetable oils and fats	0.3	0.3	0.4	0.5	0.8
5 Chemicals	11.4	12.7	12.4	13.6	22.9
54 Medicinal and pharmaceutical products	2.3	2.6	2.4	2.3	3.3
55 Essential oils and perfume materials; toilet, polishing and cleansing preparations	3.1	3.1	3.1	3.7	5.1
Other	6.0	7.0	6.9	7.6	14.5
6 Manufactured goods	45.8	41.4	39.2	39.0	61.6
62 Rubber manufactures, n.e.s.	4.6	4.8	7.5	4.5	6.6
64 Paper, paperboard and manufactures thereof	4.7	4.5	5.0	5.3	8.9
65 Textile yarn, fabrics, made-up articles and related products	5.1	5.3	5.6	7.9	10.6
66 Non-metallic mineral manufactures n.e.s.	4.4	4.1	4.0	3.8	6.7
67 Iron and steel	8.8	7.8	6.2	7.0	10.9
69 Other metal manufactures	15.9	13.2	9.6	9.1	15.9
Other	2.2	1.9	1.3	1.2	2.0

(Table continues on following page.)

Table 7.3. (continued)

		Fiscal years			
SITC	1971	1972	1973	1974	1975
7 Machinery and transport equipment	101.4	93.1	73.5	61.7	112.2
71 Machinery (except electric)	51.2	46.7	37.3	33.9	65.1
72 Electric machinery, apparatus and appliances	21.0	22.8	15.5	12.3	18.4
73 Transport equipment	29.2	23.6	20.7	15.5	28.6
8 Miscellaneous manufactured articles	25.4	24.0	21.8	22.2	30.1
9 Miscellaneous transactions and commodities, n.e.s.	9.8	16.1	13.6	6.9	9.3
Total all sections	251.6	252.8	224.7	226.0	353.4
Outside packages	3.0	3.6	4.1	2.9	4.0
Total recorded imports	254.6	256.4	228.8	228.9	357.4
Unrecorded imports	49.7	48.8	–	2.6	–
Adjustment for balance-of-payments purposes	10.2	16.5	14.1	6.7	–
Total balance-of-payments imports	294.0	288.7	214.7	224.8	–

Source: Papua New Guinea Bureau of Statistics.

ports (SITC 5, most of them consumer-oriented chemicals) doubled during the period, although they became less important than petroleum. The largest category of consumer goods and the one with the most persistent import growth is food and live animals, which increased 72 percent between 1971 and 1975.[7] Four broad items dominate the food and animals imports: cereal grains (rice is three times as important as wheat flour), meat and meat products, fish (almost entirely tinned fish from Japan), and sugar.

The import data are also available broken down into six-digit SITC classifications. The broad categories suggest a number of agricultural, agro-industrial, and small manufacturing possibilities for import substitution, but the more detailed the categories become,

7. These values are all in current terms. If the food category values are deflated by the increase in the Australian consumer price index for this period, there would actually be a slight decline in real food imports. This probably reflects the substantial exodus of Australians from Bougainville in fiscal 1972 following completion of construction, as well as the additional exodus of Australian government workers in 1974 and 1975 in the eighteen months following self-government. Although an analysis of trends in real imports would be interesting, good figures are not readily available—and the payments problem occurs in terms of current, not constant, kina.

the more specialized the products, and the less likely it becomes that investments of a size large enough to be economic in operation can be justified. Thus, the import statistics, even at their most detailed level, provide only a starting point for the much more specific knowledge of products, markets, minimum economic size of investment, raw material requirements, and internal transport costs that would be needed to identify realistic possibilities for import substitution. NIDA has already identified some manufactured products that it believes can be justified for local production, but additional study would be worthwhile.

Import substitution is not the only way of limiting or reducing imports. As part of a drive toward self-reliance, customs duties could be used more energetically to discourage the import of nonessential and luxury items. This will not be popular with the expatriate community, but it can probably be made acceptable if well explained and not carried to extremes.

Balance-of-Payments Viability

Table 7.4 projects Papua New Guinea's balance of payments through fiscal 1985. For each balance-of-payments category affected by the copper sector, two alternate figures are shown: one including and one excluding transactions of the copper sector. The sum of the differences between the two sets of figures represents the overall net contribution of the copper sector to Papua New Guinea's balance of payments; these figures are shown at the bottom of the table.

The general outlook for Papua New Guinea's future balance of payments is reasonably good—given one key assumption: that the real growth of imports can be kept to a level below that of exports. The World Bank concluded that this is feasible if the government recognizes the critical importance of containing import growth and treats this objective as an independent policy variable to which other parts of the system, including the overall growth of GDP, should be expected to adjust. If imports grow at a faster rate than exports, reserves will be dragged down to hand-to-mouth levels, the government will be pushed into trying to borrow abroad at levels it cannot possibly expect to arrange, and the debt-service ratio will eventually deteriorate to dangerous levels.[8] These conclusions emerge when the growth rate of imports is assumed to be

---

8. The debt-service ratio is the ratio of debt-service payments to exports of goods and nonfactor services.

Table 7.4. Balance-of-Payments Projections, with and without Copper Contribution, Fiscal Years 1976–85
(Millions of U.S. dollars)

Item	Fiscal years									
	1976[a]	1977	1978	1979	1980	1981	1982	1983	1984	1985
Trade account	-44	-24	35	3	-104	-130	-52	251	261	279
	-225	*-245*	*-252*	*-271*	*-314*	*-357*	*-409*	*-468*	*-528*	*-588*
Exports	451	539	672	790	865	940	1,041	1,423	1,580	1,765
	220	*264*	*327*	*385*	*430*	*483*	*539*	*602*	*678*	*774*
Less imports	495	563	637	787	969	1,070	1,093	1,172	1,319	1,486
	445	*509*	*579*	*656*	*744*	*840*	*948*	*1,070*	*1,206*	*1,362*
Services, net	-152	-171	-199	-230	-250	-274	-298	-363	-407	-438
	-124	*-141*	*-156*	*-175*	*-194*	*-216*	*-241*	*-270*	*-301*	*-335*
Nonfactor services, net	-71	-81	-91	-103	-116	-131	-147	-166	-186	-209
Factor services, net	-81	-90	-108	-127	-134	-143	-151	-197	-221	-229
	-53	*-60*	*-65*	*-72*	*-78*	*-85*	*-94*	*-104*	*-115*	*-126*
Receipts	25	28	32	36	41	46	52	58	65	74
Less payments	106	118	140	163	175	189	203	255	286	303
	78	*88*	*97*	*108*	*119*	*131*	*146*	*162*	*180*	*200*
Transfers, net	203	200	210	220	220	220	170	170	170	170
Private	-13	-50	-40	-30	-30	-30	-30	-30	-30	-30
Public	216	250	250	250	250	250	200	200	200	200

124

Current account balance	7 *-146*	5 *-186*	46 *-198*	-7 *-226*	-134 *-288*	-184 *-353*	-180 *-480*	58 *-568*	24 *-659*	11 *-753*
Direct investment	18	21	24	54	95	100	69	48	55	63
Private borrowing, net	-17	27	24	76	146	126	53	-63	-61	-55
Public borrowing, net	0	2	3	4	5	6	7	8	9	10
Disbursements	23	5	0	1	3	4	6	6	7	3
Less repayments	29	14	11	14	18	20	22	24	26	23
Other capital[b]	6	9	11	13	15	16	17	18	19	26
	-93	0	0	0	0	0	0	0	0	0
Capital account	-69 *-52*	53 *28*	48 *27*	131 *32*	244 *39*	230 *46*	127 *54*	-9 *62*	1 *71*	11 *76*
Change in reserves[c]	62 *198*	-58 *158*	-94 *171*	-124 *194*	-110 *249*	-46 *307*	53 *426*	-49 *506*	-25 *588*	-22 *677*
Net contribution of copper to overall balance of payments	136	216	265	318	359	353	373	555	613	699
Bougainville	136	216	265	304	325	319	359	405	455	515
Ok Tedi	0	0	0	14	34	34	14	150	158	184

Note: Figures in roman type include contributions of the copper sector; figures in italics exclude the copper contribution. For categories unaffected by copper, only a single set of figures is shown. The two sets of figures differ by the amount of the copper contribution.

a. Preliminary.

b. Includes net capital from the International Monetary Fund, errors and omissions, and unidentified capital.

c. A negative figure indicates an increase.

Source: World Bank estimates.

slightly faster than the 5 percent annual rate upon which Table 7.4 is based.

IMPORTS

The value of imports is an independent variable in Table 7.4. Imports in fiscal 1976 are projected forward in time at a real growth rate of 5 percent a year plus a standard World Bank allowance for expected world inflation between 1976 and 1985. The justification for assuming a 5 percent real growth rate is that this appears to be a realistic maximum the economy can tolerate without finding itself in a crisis. This rate also appears to be consistent with the likely growth rates of other parts of the system, such as GNP, gross investment, monetized consumption, and exports.

The present income elasticity of demand for imports is believed to be close to 1.0, so a 5 percent growth in real imports assumes that monetized national income cannot grow faster than 5 percent unless the import propensity can be reduced. Thus, the key to limiting import growth without resorting to direct controls (which the government is determined to avoid) is to limit the growth of purchasing power, rather than to raise the price of imports. Limiting the growth of incomes will require careful control over government and private spending by continuing the present conservative fiscal and monetary policies; a key to the successful restraint of government spending will be the new incomes policy that the government is in the process of working out and implementing.

There appears to be relatively little hope that higher import duties on luxuries would discourage imports. About half of expatriates' nonfood consumption is composed of luxury imports. Duties on these have recently been raised to about 45 percent. It is also unrealistic to assume that many gains can be realized during the next decade from a program of import substitution, although a start should be made on the limited number of opportunities that may be identified.

EXPORTS

The export totals in Table 7.4 have been built up from separate estimates of the outlook for each major crop and for copper. Estimates were first made of expected volumes of exports, and then the World Bank's current estimate of future prices for each commodity was applied, year by year. The price estimates used were based on judgments about trends in relative prices for each commodity; the standard index of expected world inflation used was the same as for import values.[9]

A strong positive effect on exports is contributed by the improvement in relative commodity prices which the World Bank expects to occur around the end of this decade. Table 7.5 shows the projected export growth of major commodities in both constant and current values; both reflect the same growth in quantities (whose growth rates are shown in Table 7.6), but the current values are considerably higher than they would be if inflation were the only reason for the higher prices expected by the 1980s. The World Bank expects the prices of most of Papua New Guinea's major exports to rise faster than the average level of prices in the world, thus turning the terms of trade in its favor.

OTHER FACTORS

Australian aid. Table 7.4 assumes that the nominal amount of the Australian grant (a public transfer item) will be reduced by 20 percent after the current five-year agreement expires. In real terms, this would represent a near halving of Australian aid by fiscal 1985.[10]

Ok Tedi. The Ok Tedi project, if undertaken, would be of the same scale as the Panguna mine at Bougainville. Table 7.4 assumes that construction will start in fiscal 1979 and production in 1983. It now appears, however, that the mine will be delayed at least two years; in fact, it is by no means certain that the project will go forward at all, but there is considerable optimism that it will do so. As the last line of Table 7.4 indicates, the Ok Tedi mine could be an important factor in Papua New Guinea's balance-of-payments outlook; in full production, its net contribution could represent about 10 percent of Papua New Guinea's projected foreign exchange earnings.

9. The CPO has made independent preliminary projections of exports through 1985 (see Statistical Appendix Table SA17). The CPO projections for both series differ significantly from the Bank's, mainly because they are made in terms of constant 1976 prices. For purposes of balance-of-payments analysis, current prices are more appropriate than constant prices because they take account of relative prices—a key factor.

10. Changes in exchange rates which occurred after this table was constructed have reduced somewhat the value of Australian aid in U.S. dollar terms.

Table 7.5. Export Projections at Current and Constant Prices, Fiscal Years 1976–85
(Millions of U.S. dollars)

Item	Fiscal years									
	1976	1977	1978	1979	1980	1981	1982	1983	1984	1985
Exports at current prices										
Copra	22.6	25.4	28.6	30.1	31.6	35.9	40.8	46.3	52.6	59.7
Coconut oil	10.9	12.4	14.0	14.7	15.4	17.4	19.7	22.3	25.3	28.6
Coffee	57.8	75.0	97.4	108.6	121.0	132.6	145.4	159.3	174.7	191.5
Cocoa	41.4	44.5	47.9	49.4	50.9	53.6	56.5	59.5	62.6	66.0
Rubber	3.8	4.5	5.2	5.6	6.0	6.3	6.7	7.0	7.4	7.8
Tea	5.8	6.8	7.9	9.9	12.3	13.6	15.0	16.7	18.5	20.5
Palm oil	8.6	10.4	12.6	15.0	17.8	22.7	29.0	37.0	48.0	61.0
Fisheries	9.8	12.7	14.3	28.9	32.0	35.6	39.8	44.5	50.2	70.5
Forestry	21.1	29.3	49.8	67.4	81.2	94.8	107.0	121.7	139.3	156.7
Copper	231.0	275.0	345.0	405.0	435.0	457.0	502.0	821.0	902.0	991.0
Total	412.8	496.0	622.7	734.6	803.2	869.5	961.9	1,335.3	1,480.6	1,653.3
Price indexes										
Copra	100	121	129	127	146	158	177	197	219	244
Coconut oil	100	120	127	133	140	151	168	187	207	230
Coffee	100	129	150	162	165	170	178	186	194	203
Cocoa	100	103	109	111	110	111	115	118	122	126
Rubber	100	120	139	156	168	177	186	197	208	218

Tea	100	104	106	109	112	118	126	135	145	155
Palm oil	100	105	106	107	108	114	126	140	155	172
Fisheries	100	130	145	161	180	203	231	262	299	338
Forestry	100	111	128	142	155	169	184	200	218	237
Copper	100	120	150	176	189	204	224	247	272	298
Exports at constant 1976 prices										
Copra	22.6	20.9	22.2	23.7	21.6	22.7	23.1	23.5	24.0	24.5
Coconut oil	10.9	10.3	11.0	11.0	11.0	11.5	11.7	11.9	12.2	12.4
Coffee	57.8	58.1	64.9	67.0	73.3	78.0	81.7	85.6	90.1	94.3
Cocoa	41.4	43.2	43.9	44.5	46.3	48.3	49.1	50.4	51.3	52.4
Rubber	3.8	3.8	3.7	3.6	3.6	3.6	3.6	3.6	3.6	3.6
Tea	5.8	6.5	7.5	9.1	11.0	11.5	11.9	12.4	12.8	13.2
Palm oil	8.6	9.9	11.9	14.0	16.5	19.9	23.0	26.4	31.0	35.5
Fisheries	9.8	9.8	9.9	18.0	17.8	17.5	17.2	17.0	16.8	20.9
Forestry	21.1	26.4	38.9	47.5	52.4	56.1	58.2	60.9	63.9	66.1
Copper	231.0	230.0	230.0	230.1	230.0	224.0	224.1	332.4	331.6	332.5
Total	412.8	418.9	443.9	468.5	483.5	493.1	503.6	624.1	637.3	655.4
Implicit export price index	100	118	140	157	166	176	191	214	232	252
Import price index	100	108	117	125	135	144	154	165	176	189
Terms of trade index	100	109	120	126	124	123	124	130	132	134

Source: World Bank estimates.

Oil and gas. Table 7.4 does not take into account the possibility of a commercial find of oil or gas, although this possibility is considered reasonably good. If a commercial find is made, however, it will not necessarily provide any dramatic improvement in the balance of payments. The present expectation is that an oil field producing fewer than 35,000 to 40,000 barrels a day would not be economic. At this minimal scale of production, it is estimated that the country would net around US$60 to 80 million a year in 1975 prices. After allowance for inflation, this scale of oil exports would amount to around one-fifth the expected net exports from two major copper mines; it would, however, be equal to the country's total agricultural exports.

CURRENT ACCOUNT OUTLOOK

Given the assumptions in Table 7.4, including the World Bank's estimates of future commodity prices and of world inflation, Papua New Guinea's current account outlook for the next decade is for a few years of modest surplus followed by four years of moderate deficits. The deficits mean that net capital inflows will be needed—borrowings plus direct investments—in order to maintain exchange

Table 7.6. **Annual Real Growth Rates of Export Values, Fiscal Years 1976–80, 1981–85, and 1976–85**
(Percentage)

Export	Fiscal years		
	1976–80	1981–85	1976–85
Commodity			
Copra	−1.0	2.5	0.9
Coconut oil	. . .	2.4	1.4
Coffee	6.1	5.2	5.6
Cocoa	2.8	2.5	2.6
Rubber	−1.4	0	−0.5
Tea	17.5	3.7	9.6
Palm oil	17.7	16.5	17.0
Total agriculture	4.9	5.1	5.0
Fisheries	16.0	3.2	8.7
Forestry	25.0	4.8	13.5
Copper	. . .	7.6	4.2
Total exports	4.0	6.2	5.3

. . . Zero or negligible.
Source: Derived from Table 7.5 data on growth in constant prices.

reserves at a viable level. Without the Australian grant, the government would be forced to seek a level of foreign borrowing that it could not possibly expect lenders to supply. The continuation of Australian aid on a large scale is virtually certain; both of Australia's political parties are committed to heavy assistance to Papua New Guinea, and there would have to be a severe deterioration in relations between Port Moresby and Canberra or a major budget crisis in Australia for this aid not to materialize. After fiscal 1985, the current account is expected to strengthen as Ok Tedi pays off its debt and a larger share of its gross exchange earnings flows through to bolster the copper sector's net balance-of-payments contribution.

THE CAPITAL ACCOUNT

The capital account in Table 7.4 assumes a growing stream of direct (noncopper) investment and of public and private borrowings. These items are expected to consist of medium- and long-term capital inflows that will be project related. This reflects confidence that foreign investors will be attracted to Papua New Guinea in moderately increasing numbers and the government will increase the volume of its investment compared to the depressed level to which its capital expenditures have recently fallen. World Bank assistance will be needed to contribute to this healthy pattern of external borrowing. The financial result of such inflows will be to permit Papua New Guinea's central bank to maintain adequate foreign exchange reserves (between four and five months' worth of imports) throughout the decade.

The capital account and export projections in the preceding tables yield debt-service ratios that are comfortable throughout the period of fiscal 1976–85. These are shown in Table 7.7. The public debt-service ratio (government and government-guaranteed debt) reaches a maximum of 5.8 percent in 1976 and declines gradually thereafter. The broader ratio of gross factor-service payments (public and private debt service plus expected dividend payments) is dominated by the two copper projects whose factor-service payments account almost entirely for the high ratios at the end of the period. These ratios would fall substantially by the late 1980s as Ok Tedi's debt service declines. The "gross" ratios are misleading, however, because of the nature of enclave projects, whose factor service payments are self-financing. When the copper sector's transactions are treated on the net basis, the ratio falls to the levels shown in the second of the three ratios presented in Table 7.7.

Table 7.7. Debt-Service Projections, Fiscal Years 1976–85

Item	Fiscal years									
	1976	1977	1978	1979	1980	1981	1982	1983	1984	1985
Amount (millions of U.S. dollars)										
Debt-service payments										
Public	24	29	31	33	35	36	37	37	38	42
Public and private, net of copper	44	49	51	54	57	59	62	64	67	75
Gross factor service payments, including public and private debt service and dividends, with copper	72	79	98	117	125	133	136	236	251	251
Ratios (percent)										
Debt-service ratios[a]										
Public	5.8	5.3	4.7	4.2	4.0	3.8	3.6	2.9	2.6	2.6
Public and private, net of copper	10.7	9.0	7.7	6.9	6.5	6.3	6.0	5.0	4.7	4.6
Gross factor-service ratio[b]	14.2	13.1	13.2	13.4	13.1	12.8	11.8	15.2	14.5	13.0

a. Debt-service payments divided by exports of goods and nonfactor services and multiplied by 100. The denominator of both ratios shown here includes the net contribution of copper to the balance of payments.
b. Gross factor-service payments divided by exports of goods and nonfactor services, multiplied by 100. Both numerator and denominator include copper-sector transactions.

Source: World Bank estimates.

These levels are somewhat higher than the public debt-service ratio, but they decline throughout the period, because it is assumed that levels of private (noncopper) borrowing do not increase as fast as exports.

Conclusion

In summary it seems likely that Papua New Guinea's economy will be able to increase its external self-reliance quite significantly during the next decade. This conclusion depends crucially on the Ok Tedi project coming into production—by no means a certainty. Even if this should not occur or should be delayed, the underlying picture remains one of a natural resource base sufficiently rich and well proven so that eventually Papua New Guinea should become fully self-reliant in its external accounts. For the present, this conclusion is not unequivocally demonstrable, but enough evidence is at hand so that predicting self-reliance is a reasonable act of faith. This prediction can be realized, however, only by continued good central economic management that is able to restructure consumption and production so that the level of Australian aid can begin to fall. Unless the pressure of this requirement is constantly felt, self-reliance may never arrive.

The Bank's analysis of trends in Papua New Guinea's key debt-service ratios found these trends to be well within comfortable limits. This reassuring outlook is heavily influenced by the strong price trends expected for copper and for Papua New Guinea's other export commodities. Even if these price expectations were to be disappointed, however, or if noncopper factor payments were considerably higher than estimated, the ratios are not likely to rise to worrisome levels.

There are additional reasons for taking reassurance from these debt-service trends. First and foremost is the expected continuation of a substantial Australian budgetary grant, which provides a major source of foreign exchange not taken into account in the construction of the factor-service ratio. Adding foreign exchange provided by this grant to that stemming from exports would reduce the debt-service ratio by about 2 percentage points. In addition, Papua New Guinea will itself receive some factor income payments, perhaps K10 million a year by 1980; this will reduce the ratio by another percentage point or so.

It appears, then, that Papua New Guinea prudently could undertake a modest program of foreign borrowing. Because the country's external viability is so sensitive to trends in export prices and to the rate of import growth, the borrowing program should seek a mixture of hard and soft loans, arranged to avoid excessive bunching of debt service payments. For these same reasons, and because there is relatively little experience to guide Papua New Guinea's government or its foreign lenders, the country's continuing creditworthiness should be kept under close review.

The outlook for political viability is, of course, central to a country's ability to maintain orderly government and administration, a precondition for financial and economic viability. There are many question marks hanging over Papua New Guinea's political future. Against the obvious risks must be set the excellent start the Somare government has made in tackling the many difficult problems of independence and nation-building and the encouraging record of the government's performance since formation of the national coalition in 1972.

8

Postscript

IN EARLY 1976, when the report on which this book is based was being written, Papua New Guinea was in the middle of a recession. Preliminary estimates of real GDP, shown in Table 8.1, reflect the drop in the market component both in fiscal 1975 and fiscal 1976. This contrasts sharply with the 8.9 percent average annual rate of growth in real GDP during the five years preceding 1975.[1] In addition, the balance of payments (Table 8.2) showed an overall deficit of about K20 million (US$25 million) in 1976.

**Table 8.1. The Market Component of Gross Domestic Product,
Fiscal Years 1974–76**
(Millions of 1969 kina)

	Fiscal years		
Item	1974	1975	1976[a]
Consumption	373.0	396.7	383.9
Gross fixed capital formation	92.9	113.5	102.6
Exports of goods and services	312.1	299.1	301.3
Imports of goods and services	222.3	287.9	268.2
Gross domestic product, market component	555.7	521.4	519.6

a. Estimated.
Source: Papua New Guinea Central Planning Office, *Programmes and Performance,
1976–77* (August 1976), p. 2.

1. The data in Table 8.1 differ from those in the Statistical Appendix because they come from different sources.

Table 8.2. Balance of Payments, Fiscal Years 1975–77
(Millions of kina)

| | Fiscal years | | |
Item	1975	1976[a]	1977[b]
Trade balance	15.0	8.2	73.1
Exports, f.o.b.	375.5	358.9	495.1
Imports, f.o.b.	360.5	350.7	422.0
Services	−156.1	−118.4	−157.2
Transfers (net)	115.5	96.6	146.3
Private	−50.0	−59.7	−35.0
Government	165.5	156.3	181.3
Current account balance	−25.6	−13.6	62.2
Capital account	76.1	45.2	61.6
Errors and omissions	−101.7	−50.8	—
Changes in reserves[c]	51.2	19.2	−123.8

a. Provisional.
b. Projected.
c. A negative figure indicates an increase.
Source: Bank of Papua New Guinea, November 1976.

This situation has improved since 1976, and real GDP is expected to have grown by about 5 percent in 1977, ending the stagnation of the last two years. Several events have contributed to this improvement. Export prices rallied: cocoa and coffee prices rose rapidly, and copra and copper prices also increased, though more gradually. The inflation rate has slowed considerably, and the government has taken a strong anti-inflationary stand on wages. The political problems in Bougainville—now renamed North Solomons Province—were resolved in a calm and satisfactory manner, assuring the central government of continued revenue and foreign exchange earnings from the province's huge copper mine; in fact, 1977 saw the passage and initial implementation of self-government legislation affecting all the provinces. The longer-run outlook also brightened. Agreement was finally reached with a consortium to carry out feasibility studies of the Ok Tedi copper deposit, and exploration for oil and gas continued. The government set out its development priorities in two documents, *National Development Strategy* and *National Investment Strategy*, and it is preparing to undertake longer-term planning for economic development.

Net investment, especially private, fell in real terms in fiscal 1976. Expenditures on plant and equipment were mainly for replacement of depreciated assets. The registration of commercial vehicles also fell in fiscal 1976 but began to increase again in early fiscal 1977. Although the construction industry was depressed, it showed signs of picking up, with many more new building starts than in the previous year. The Housing Commission sharply increased its building rate of public housing compared to 1975.

The decline in the money supply that occurred during 1975 was reversed, and currency plus demand deposits increased by 27 percent in the first nine months of 1976. The supply of quasi-money— defined as term deposits and interest-bearing demand deposits— fell sharply in 1975, but it rose by 74 percent in the first three quarters of 1976. Domestic credit increased by 54 percent during the same period. (See Statistical Appendix Table SA21.) The latest statistics show that the money supply has continued to grow moderately.

Balance of Payments and Adjustments in the Exchange Rate

By July 1976 the outlook for trade and foreign reserves had so improved that the government decided to appreciate the kina by 5 percent in relation to other currencies in order to support internal anti-inflationary policies and to loosen the ties between the kina and the Australian dollar. Despite the balance-of-payments deficit in fiscal 1976, gross reserves (assets of the Bank of Papua New Guinea) stood at more than four months' worth of imports and net reserves at three months' worth in June 1976. The September quarter provided further gains, and the Bank of Papua New Guinea's balance-of-payments projections for 1977 predicted a K73 million (US$91 million) trade surplus, a K62 million current account surplus, and a K124 million overall surplus. The major factors generating this surplus were (a) a 38 percent increase in exports with only a 20 percent increase in imports and (b) a 16 percent increase in the size of the Australian transfer (see Table 8.2).[2]

On November 29, 1976, Australia devalued its dollar by 17.5 percent, and Papua New Guinea followed suit, though by a smaller amount. Depreciation of the kina to the full extent of the Australian devaluation would have had strong inflationary effects in Papua

2. The figures are based on data received from the government in November 1976 and do not reflect the numerous changes in exchange rates that occurred in late 1976. These adjustments have reduced the size of the Australian grant by about K16 million, but other compensating changes should reduce the effect on the balance of payments.

New Guinea through its imports from non-Australian sources, as well as through those Australian imports whose prices are determined in world markets. On the other hand, maintaining the value of the kina against other world currencies would have meant a substantial cut in the kina value of the Australian budgetary grant. The government settled on an appreciation of 12.5 percent against the Australian dollar and a depreciation of 7.2 percent against other world currencies. As a result of this and other small changes in 1976, the effective exchange rate appreciated by 2.4 percent on a trade-weighted basis. (See Statistical Appendix Table SA12 for a summary of exchange rate variations.)

Government Finances

Papua New Guinea follows a strategy that requires expenditures and receipts to be balanced over time. Deficits are kept to a modest level in difficult years and must be compensated by surpluses in better times. With independence and a desire for increasing self-reliance, there is greater pressure than ever on the government to keep a tight hold on expenditures and to try to increase revenues. Total budgeted government expenditures in 1977 are K435.3 million (US$544.1 million) adjusted for the budgetary effects of the July currency appreciation but not those of the devaluation in November. Total revenue is estimated at K426.5 million (US$533.1 million). Tables 8.3, 8.4, and 8.5 compare the budget for 1977 with that of 1976.[3] Total expenditures will rise by 5.5 percent in 1977. Because of the restraint on wage increases and limits on purchases of supplies and materials, current expenditures will rise by only 4 percent, but capital expenditures will rise by 19 percent. This will shift the composition of government expenditures toward development spending. Internal revenue will fall by nearly 2 percent, primarily because borrowing is lower and less excise tax revenue and dividend income is realized from the Bougainville copper mine. A substantial rise in the Australian grant will offset the decline, however, so that total revenues will rise by about 6 percent. The largest source of internal revenue continues to be direct taxation.

The 1977 Australian aid grant, which will supply more than 40

3. Data may differ slightly among these tables, because some are based on actual figures and some on estimates.

percent of total government revenues, was originally valued at K200 million, but was reduced to K181 million by the appreciation of the kina in July 1976 and even further, to about K175 million, by later currency readjustments. The drop in the value of Australian aid will not fall fully on the deficit side of the budget, however, because the appreciation of the kina against the Australian dollar will also reduce expenditures.

Table 8.3. Central Government Finances, Fiscal Years 1976–77
(Millions of kina)

| | Fiscal years | |
| | 1976 | 1977[a] |
Item	Actual	Budget
Internal revenue	220.4	216.6
(Tax revenue)	(186.3)	(187.7)
Current expenditures	369.5	384.2
Current deficit	149.1	167.6
Capital expenditures	43.0	51.1
Overall deficit	192.1	218.7
Australian grant	126.9	181.3
Loans and advances	65.2	37.4
(International agencies)	(13.1)	(15.6)

a. Takes into account only the July 1976 appreciation of the kina.
Source: Papua New Guinea Department of Finance, *Estimates of Revenues and Expenditures for the Year Ending 30th June 1977.*

This is the first budget prepared since the five-year Australian $1 billion aid agreement was concluded in March 1976. For the first time, the Papua New Guinean government was able to make projections of the resources that will be available to it during the next few years and to plan its expenditures accordingly. An additional source of budget stability is the Mineral Resources Stabilization Fund, established in late 1974 to smooth the peaks and troughs of revenue from mineral exports. Instead of the more than K40 million drop in revenues that would have resulted from the lower copper prices of 1976, budget income will decline only K10 million because the stabilization fund will absorb part of the loss; the fund will still

Table 8.4. Central Government Revenue, Fiscal Years 1976–77
(Millions of kina)

	Fiscal years	
Source	1976[a]	1977[a]
Internal revenue		
Direct taxation		
Companies	19.5	20.5
Individuals	58.5	59.2
Dividend withholding tax	1.9	1.6
Indirect taxation		
Import duties	30.0	35.5
Excise	29.0	26.6
Export tax and other charges	2.1	4.3
Drawings from Mineral Resources		
Stabilization Fund	45.0	35.0
Other internal sources	37.6	33.9
Australian aid	126.9	181.3[b]
Loans		
General	27.0	13.0
International agencies	13.1	15.6
Other[c]	11.2	—
Total revenue	401.8	426.5

a. Estimate.
b. Takes into account only the appreciation of the kina in July 1976.
c. Consolidated revenue, Budget Equalization Reserve Fund, and an advance from the Bank of Papua New Guinea.
Source: Papua New Guinea Department of Finance, *Estimates of Revenues and Expenditures for the Year Ending 30th June, 1977.*

retain some surplus from previous years.[4] New coffee and cocoa stabilization funds set up to protect producers from sudden price declines may also lend stability to the budget.

The major thrust of the 1977 budget, according to the minister of finance, is twofold: to provide increased economic opportunities in rural areas and to encourage and direct the development of the modern sector, especially in resource-based industries. The first of these goals is reflected in the more than proportionate increases in the allocation of funds to economic and planning services and research and development in the Department of Primary Industry

4. Flows into the fund in fiscal 1976, the first year of its operation, reached K65.9 million, of which K45 million went into government revenues. In 1977 inflows are expected to be K22.3 million, compared with drawings by the government of K35 million.

Table 8.5. Central Government Expenditures, Fiscal Years 1976–77
(Millions of kina)

Item	Fiscal years	
	1976[a]	1977[b,c]
Department expenditures	224.4	258.2
National Parliament; Prime Minister	8.8	10.3
Defense; Police; Justice	42.4	46.6
Education; Administrative College	47.2	59.4
Finance	4.2	5.0
Foreign Affairs and Trade	4.2	5.1
Health	28.7	32.2
Labor, Commerce, and Industry[c]	3.3	4.8
Primary Industry; Natural Resources	33.7	36.4
Provincial Affairs[c]	7.6	14.6
Public Services Commission	4.5	6.8
Transport, Works, and Supply; Public Utilities	39.8	37.0
Works and services	70.8	83.1
Capital works	43.0	51.1
Grants and financial transactions	59.1	54.2
Expenditure on transferred functions[d]	20.0	0
Advances to the Secretary for Finance[e]	0	8.0
Special appropriations	31.4	30.5
Other	6.6	5.7
Total expenditures	412.3	439.7

a. Estimate.

b. Budget allocation; does not take into account any currency adjustments; the July 1976 appreciation reduces the total to K435.3 million.

c. Departmental allocations in 1977 include for the first time Australian salaries previously paid by Australia. This fact accounts in large part for the increases in Provincial Affairs and Labor, Commerce, and Industry.

d. Purchase of assets from the Australian government (offset to zero in the revenue estimates by a grant from the Australian government).

e. These advances will be used in part to pay the provinces their 1.25 percent share of export earnings.

Source: Papua New Guinea Department of Finance, *Estimates of Revenues and Expenditures for the Year Ending 30th June, 1977.*

(formerly the DASF) and to capital works for rural infrastructure construction.[5] The second goal is aimed at increasing government revenues generated by the growth of the modern sector. The budget allocation to the Department of Labor, Commerce, and Industry is more than 40 percent greater than the prior year's expenditures, partly because of the cost of staff transferred from the

5. The allocation of the Rural Improvement Program, K6.2 million, is about the same as that in 1976. However, a new program, Special Rural Projects, has been allocated K2 million to carry out larger-scale projects than those funded by the Rural Improvement Program.

Australian budget, but increases also go to the promotion of industry and to the Office of Business Development.

The establishment of provincial governments puts some apparent strain on the budget. The large increase in the 1977 allocation for the Department of Provincial Affairs is, however, largely for salaries of Australians previously paid by the Australian government. In addition, the budget provides an unconditional grant of K2.3 million to the Bougainville provincial government, representing royalties plus 1.25 percent of its export earnings less royalties paid; grants of unspecified amounts will be made to other provincial governments. The right of provinces to retain 1.25 percent of their export earnings will cost the central government K1.25 million in revenues, and the estimated K2 million loss of royalties will add an additional cost. The losses in central government revenues are expected to be offset by a shift in responsibilities from the central government to the provincial governments.

Inflation and Incomes Policy

There has been a low rate of inflation in Papua New Guinea in recent months. The consumer price index (CPI) grew by 5 percent in 1976 and 2.3 percent in the first half of 1977, compared with 11 percent in 1975 and 20 percent in 1974 (see Statistical Appendix Table SA30). Although this reduction in the inflation rate is partly the result of external influences, it also reflects strong efforts on the part of the government to restrain wage and price increases.

A number of decisions concerning wages and salaries have contributed to the low rate of inflation in 1977. The Minimum Wages Board met during the first half of 1976 to rule on minimum urban and rural wages.[6] It declared a freeze on wage increases through March 1977, after which all urban salaries would be allowed to rise at a rate equal to two-thirds the rate of increase in the CPI, and rural wages at three-fourths of the price increase, to a maximum of 12.5 percent. A new formula announced in April 1977 allows public service salaries to rise at the full inflation rate for the next three years, with the understanding that public employees will not pursue new claims on economic grounds during that time.

---

6. Minimum wages since 1960 are shown in Statistical Appendix Table SA4. In recent years, wages have risen far more rapidly than the rate of inflation.

Another step taken by the government to hold down both wages and its own budget was the recent rejection of the proposed salary increases for employees from Great Britain and New Zealand. This is the first time the cabinet has used its power to reject the recommendation of an arbitration tribunal. Subsequently, a board of inquiry into salaries of all overseas public servants was opened, and the government declared to the board its opposition to the introduction of common conditions of employment for all overseas employees, a step that could increase government expenditures on salaries by raising all expatriate incomes to the level of Australian employees.

Public Service Employment

Replacement of expatriates by Papua New Guineans in the public service is proceeding at a slow but steady rate, which is to be expected since the level of localization is already quite high. Greater emphasis is being placed on training Papua New Guineans for all government positions, and at the end of fiscal 1977 the public service was 89 percent localized, compared with 87 percent the year before. Thirty percent of the expatriate public employees are teachers. The composition of the expatriate group has changed considerably, however. The Australian Staffing Assistance Group came to an end formally on June 30, 1976, when those Australians wishing to remain signed contracts directly with the Papua New Guinean government; approximately 1,800 Australians still work in Papua New Guinea's government. To some extent the departing Australians have been replaced by other expatriates, mainly from the United Kingdom and the Philippines. Replacing Australians represents a saving for the government, because they cost somewhat more than other expatriates. Only 40 percent of the new recruitment of paid expatriates in 1976 was Australian.

Salaries and wages make up 63 percent of all government departmental spending, and the size of the public service and of the salaries paid to public employees has a large impact on the government budget. In the 1971–75 period public employment grew at an average annual rate of 5.7 percent. The minister of finance announced in 1977 that as part of the effort to hold down government spending future growth of the public service will be held to 1.4 percent a year.

Development Policies

A recently published government white paper, *National Development Strategy*,[7] sets out the priorities and key policies to be implemented through government expenditures over the next few years. The paper explicitly states that the strategy is not one of maximum growth and recognizes that tradeoffs may exist between the goals of growth and of equitable distribution of income. The primary policy is to devote a higher proportion of the nation's resources to rural areas by generating income-earning opportunities. In order to reduce income inequalities, special efforts would be made in regions with the lowest income levels.

EMPLOYMENT

The decision to concentrate on self-employment in rural areas grew out of an analysis indicating that opportunities for both wage employment and self-employment in urban areas will be limited to a small proportion of the growing work force. The growth rate of the population is close to 3 percent a year, and almost 40,000 people enter the labor force yearly. Severe pressure on land has begun to be felt in some areas, making the cash economy an increasingly important source of income. Participation in the cash economy can occur either through production of cash crops and local trading or through migration to plantations or urban areas in search of jobs. Although rural-urban migration is high, 80 percent of both the population and the labor force remains in rural areas. Most members of the urban and of the rural labor forces are engaged in some kind of money-raising activity, but only 150,000 to 170,000 people — 12 to 14 percent of the total labor force of 1.25 million — are engaged in wage employment of any kind. Few jobs have been created in the last few years, and although wage employment is expected to increase, its growth is not expected to exceed 3 percent a year over the next decade.

A recent survey of 114 major enterprises in the private sector found that 44 percent of them had Papua New Guineans in senior executive positions, compared with only 26 percent in 1975. Almost half of the companies planned to appoint additional Papua New Guineans to executive posts this year. The average proportion of Papua New Guinean employees in the companies was 88 percent.

7. Central Planning Office, October 27, 1976.

This type of employment involves only a small segment of the labor force, however. Further, even if the government were to subsidize modern sector activities to raise the growth rate of wage employment to 5 percent, this type of employment would still involve only 15 percent of the labor force by 1986. The urban informal sector is small at present, limited by inappropriate, restrictive regulations. Even when these restrictions are removed, however, the urban informal sector will be able to absorb only a limited proportion of the work force, because at least two-thirds of the labor force will remain in rural areas.

RURAL DEVELOPMENT

The key policies in the area of rural development deal with coordination of extension services, which are now provided by specialists from a number of departments; diversification and improvement of agricultural production, with high priority given to food for domestic markets and improved nutrition; introduction of appropriate, usually labor-intensive, technology; promotion of small-scale industries that are located in rural areas or that support rural industry; development of means to mobilize local savings for local investment; redirection of the educational system away from formal schooling toward informal and vocational training; redistribution of health services toward rural areas; introduction and improvement of marketing and storage facilities; and extension of rural electrification. In addition, recognizing that the high cost and slow speed of transport are major obstacles to rural improvement in many areas, the government will give high priority to developing feeder road systems and improving coastal shipping in order to increase accessibility to markets.

In keeping with the emphasis on rural development, policies for urban development will concentrate on redirecting the pattern of development away from Port Moresby and Lae toward smaller centers. These smaller towns will become growth centers, providing marketing and other services for the surrounding rural areas.

INVESTMENT POLICY

Investment policy, set out more fully in the *National Investment Strategy*,[8] will promote small-scale investments by ensuring that

8. Ministry of Labor, Commerce, and Industry, November 1976.

adequate credit is available. A few large-scale projects based on natural resources will be encouraged and are expected to become the main source of revenue to reduce reliance on foreign aid. The renegotiation of the agreement with BCL set the standard for future agreements, guaranteeing the government a reasonable share of the proceeds from Papua New Guinea's natural resources. In order to allow for steady growth, rather than disruptive swings, of government expenditure, revenues from all major projects will be paid into stabilization funds and released gradually into annual budgets. Medium- and large-scale manufacturing and service activities will be financed in large part by foreign investors. The government will particularly encourage such investment in sectors that will provide employment, increase government revenue, and improve the balance of payments—and that will not lead to inefficient import substitution. Subsidies or import tariffs and quotas will be considered only for short-term protection of industries that eventually can produce at competitive prices in Papua New Guinea.

LONG-RANGE PLANNING

Except in a few instances, these policies have yet to be translated into specific programs or projects. Details will be worked out in a four-year national public expenditure plan scheduled to start in 1978. This plan will involve the selection of a small number of key targets, expressed in physical terms and backed by the commitment of funds. The selection of targets and design of the projects will be done by central government departments in consultation with provincial governments. Working groups have been established to assist in and coordinate the development of projects in five policy fields; food, subsistence, and nutrition; less developed areas; education for rural development; technology policy; and transport and marketing. These projects will then be submitted to the Budget Priorities Committee, which will assess their relative priorities and make appropriate recommendations to the National Executive Council. The *National Investment Strategy* calls for the annual preparation of estimates of the proposed investment expenditures of major private companies, both foreign and national, by industry for each province. These estimates, along with the national expenditure plan, will enable the government to plan for the rational and effective allocation of the total resources, both public and private, that are available to the country.

The government recognizes that its expenditure goals will require several years to implement fully. For several reasons, total government expenditures cannot grow by more than about 3 percent a year in real terms over the next five years: the Australian aid agreement will probably fall in real terms, overseas borrowing is limited by the debt-service burden it imposes, and internal revenue is expected to increase only gradually. The *National Development Strategy* calls for all real growth in expenditures to be allocated only to activities linked to clearly identified objectives. Expenditures in high-priority areas can be substantially increased only if cutbacks are made in other areas. Such cutbacks are possible, but it will require several years to reduce standards and fulfill technical and political commitments. Decisions must be made now in order that the allocation of government and national resources in the next five years will reflect the policies of the *National Development Strategy*. This attitude on the part of the government is a realistic appraisal of the difficulties of rural development, which will help prevent unrealistic expectations and subsequent disappointment for rural groups.

1977 Elections

In July 1977 the first national election since independence resulted in a vote of confidence for Somare and the two parties that have formed the core of the national coalition government. Somare has been reappointed prime minister for another five years. His Pangu party, which increased its seats in the national parliament from 23 to 38, now has the largest representation in the 109-seat parliament. The opposition United party, formerly the largest bloc, lost nearly one-third of its seats, falling from 44 seats in 1972 to 32. The People's Progress party, a coalition member headed by Minister of Agriculture and Deputy Prime Minister Chan, increased its strength to 19 seats. The Papua Besena movement has 7 seats, while independent members hold 13 seats, with their support divided between the coalition and the opposition.

Appendix A

National Income Statistics

GROSS DOMESTIC PRODUCT (GDP) measures the value of goods and services produced within a country's borders during any given year, but it does not provide an accurate measure of the incomes of the country's residents. Not all the income generated by GDP is distributed to residents; some is sent abroad. Furthermore, residents do not get all their incomes from values produced within the country; some is received from other countries. GDP must be adjusted for these factors in order to arrive at the value of incomes received by Papua New Guinean residents—that is, national income (NI).

Table A1 shows GDP adjusted for production-generated incomes sent out of the country and for income received from other countries for the fiscal years 1971–75. Domestic factor incomes— domestic incomes generated by domestic production—average about 11 percent less than GDP during the period covered in the table. National income at market prices is derived by adjusting domestic factor incomes for (a) net property and entrepreneurial income exchanges with other countries, and (b) the net effect of indirect taxes paid and subsidies received. NI, then, represents income received by Papua New Guinean residents in return for their productive contributions of labor and property, whether production takes place inside or outside Papua New Guinea. Until 1972, NI in Papua New Guinea was traditionally slightly larger than domestic factor incomes. As soon as the Bougainville project entered the picture, its heavy debt service and dividend payments abroad reduced NI below domestic factor incomes, which were already lower than GDP.

NI does not represent the total income at the disposal of Papua New Guinean residents, because it does not include unearned income received from abroad, nor does it exclude transfers to residents of other countries. Disposable income is arrived at by adding net transfers (payments unrelated to the recipients' contributions to production) to the NI figure. In Papua New Guinea's case, this is a major adjustment, because the large annual grants to Papua New Guinea from Australia fall into the category of transfers. Except in 1974 the Australian grant has been sufficient to push Papua New Guinea's national disposable income slightly above the value of its GDP—that is, residents have had more to spend than they have

Table A1. Gross Domestic Product, National Income, and National Disposable Income at Current Market Prices, Fiscal Years 1971–75
(Millions of kina)

Item	Fiscal years				
	1971	1972	1973	1974	1975
Compensation of employees	296.9	311.5	317.4	406.2	453.2
Operating surplus	265.8	266.6	380.9	527.9	430.4
Market component	127.2	116.1	215.8	368.4	267.8
Nonmarket component	138.6	150.5	165.2	159.5	162.6
Equals domestic factor incomes	562.7	578.1	698.3	934.1	883.6
Plus property and entrepreneurial income receivable from the rest of the world (net)	−26.6	−35.4	−37.4	−79.1	−68.7
Plus indirect taxes	32.0	34.7	36.2	42.4	53.6
Less subsidies	1.8	3.2	2.7	2.8	1.8
Equals national income at market prices	566.4	574.1	694.5	895.3	868.1
Plus other net current transfers from the rest of the world	103.5	118.2	121.3	129.3	147.3
Equals national disposable income	669.9	692.3	815.8	1,024.6	1,015.3
Plus consumption of fixed capital	28.7	35.9	57.0	66.8	73.6
Less property and entrepreneurial income receivable from the rest of the world (net)	−26.6	−35.4	−37.4	−79.1	−68.7
Less other net current transfers from the rest of the world	103.5	118.2	121.3	129.3	147.3
Equals gross domestic product	621.7	645.4	788.8	1,040.6	1,009.1

Source: Papua New Guinea Bureau of Statistics, National Accounts Statistics, various issues.

produced within the country. Even in 1974 it was record copper prices realized by the Bougainville mine that temporarily—and somewhat artificially—inflated GDP more than they inflated disposable income.

This pattern of relationships among GDP, NI, and disposable income is not unusual for small economies that have large foreign-owned enclave sectors and that rely on substantial foreign aid to meet essential budget needs. As Papua New Guinea moves towards greater self-reliance and as Australian aid diminishes, it will have to depend increasingly on its own domestic production as the source of its disposable income. As long as a large share of GDP originates in the enclave sector, there will be large net factor payments leaving the country, and disposable income will fall short of GDP unless the gap is filled by foreign aid or other incoming transfer payments.

Appendix B

Agricultural Prospects

THE DEPARTMENT OF PRIMARY INDUSTRY (DPI, formerly the Department of Agriculture, Stock, and Fisheries) has prepared some tentative forecasts of the production volume of major agricultural exports for fiscal years 1976 through 1980, and the World Bank has made similar projections for fiscal 1985. These projections and the actual data for three previous years are shown in Table B1.

Table B1. Actual and Projected Volumes of Major Agricultural Export Commodities, Fiscal Years 1969–85
(Thousands of metric tons)

Commodity	Actual			Projected					
	1969	1972	1975	1976	1977	1978	1979	1980	1985[a]
Copra	95.2	87.5	99.7	91.0	90.0	89.0	88.0	87.0	96.0
Coconut oil	20.9	26.5	25.2	27.0	27.0	27.0	27.0	27.0	30.0
Coffee	20.2	28.2	36.8	41.0	43.0	46.0	49.0	52.0	68.0
Cocoa	27.7	30.0	35.3	34.0	35.0	36.0	37.0	38.0	44.0
Rubber	5.8	5.9	5.5	5.9	5.7	5.6	5.5	5.4	5.4
Tea	0.3	1.8	4.5	5.4	6.3	6.8	8.3	10.4	13.0
Palm oil	. . .	3.5	18.4	25.0	29.0	34.5	39.5	48.0	100.0

. . . Zero or negligible.

a. Projections for 1985 made by the World Bank assumed the following expansion of volumes between 1980 and 1985: copra, 10 percent; coconut oil, 10 percent; coffee, 30 percent; cocoa, 15 percent; rubber, nil; tea, 25 percent; and palm oil, 108 percent.

Sources: Actual data through 1975 from Papua New Guinea Bureau of Statistics, *Statistical Bulletin;*1975 data are preliminary. Data for 1976 through 1980 are tentative and unpublished projections made by the DPI. Data for 1985 are World Bank projections.

Principal Crops

In the decade extending from the last year for which actual data are available, 1975, to the end of the projection period in 1985, copra production (including the portion that is crushed and exported as coconut oil) is expected to remain virtually unchanged. Cocoa production will rise by 25 percent, coffee by 85 percent, and tea (a minor export) by 189 percent. The 1985 production of palm oil, an almost unknown crop in 1970, is expected to more than quadruple its 1975 level. Rubber production is not expected to increase at all, and rubber will replace tea as the smallest of the "big seven" agricultural exports.

Most of the country's principal export crops require a lead time of three to six years before production begins, so output of export crops through 1980 depends on plantings made in or before 1976. As Table B2 indicates, planting trends among smallholders have been somewhat different from those on plantations. Although the table does not show replacement requirements, available data indicate that between 1969 and 1972 smallholder new plantings for the three most important export crops—coconut, coffee, and cocoa—were considerably in excess of replacement needs. In the same period, new plantings in the plantation sector for coconut and cocoa were considerably lower, and coffee plantings were higher, than in the previous decade. Although accurate statistics are not available for the latest three years, the DPI believes that there have been significant cocoa, coffee, and coconut plantings in the smallholder sector during this period. In the largely expatriate plantation sector, political uncertainties during the past three years have discouraged investment. Expansion in coffee and cocoa was only marginal, and coconut declined. In view of these considerations, the DPI projections from 1976 through 1980 appear realistic.

For a steady expansion of the major crop exports beyond 1980, it is essential that large-scale replanting and acreage expansion start immediately. Such replanting is especially important for copra, because nearly 50 percent of Papua New Guinea's coconut palms are more than fifty years old and hence senile and low yielding. The government is aware of the need for incentives to encourage replanting and for active expansion programs. It intends to implement a program of hybrid coconut planting for output expansion; the likely magnitude of the program is not yet known.

A coffee acreage expansion program is being undertaken for arabica coffee in the highlands and for the less important robusta

Table B2. Annual New Plantings, 1955–63 and 1969–72
(Thousands of hectares)

Producer	Coconut	Coffee	Cocoa	Rubber	Tea	Oil palm
			1969–72			
Plantation	1.4	0.33	1.69	0.15	0.15	0.42
Smallholder	5.0	1.10	1.18	0.35	0.07	0.45
			1955–63			
Plantation	2	} 0.30	{ 4.25			
Smallholder	6		{ 0.57			

Source: Papua New Guinea Department of Primary Industry.

coffee in the lowlands; both plantation and smallholder plantings will be promoted. Coffee production became well established in the 1950s, preceding the signing of the International Coffee Agreement. That agreement slowed the expansion of Papua New Guinea's coffee industry until the suspension of quotas in 1973. Although Papua New Guinea is only a small supplier to the world market, it could expand coffee output considerably faster if the agreement did not exist.[1] So far in the 1970s, coffee production has increased by about 10 percent a year. Now that Papua New Guinea is not constrained by the International Coffee Agreement to restrict acreage expansion, a considerable increase in production could occur in the 1980s.

Papua New Guinea is also a small factor in the world cocoa trade, but some European buyers are anxious to see its output expand substantially to reduce European dependence on West Africa. There is no international agreement in cocoa to limit Papua New Guinea's expansion in this field, and a considerable amount of new planting is now going on: the experimental station at Keravat in East New Britain has a twelve-month waiting list for growers who want to buy

1. Coffee industry affairs in Papua New Guinea are monitored by a governmental Coffee Marketing Board, whose headquarters are in Goroka. The board does not in fact do any marketing, preferring to leave the trade entirely in private hands. The board does operate a stabilization fund, financed by a tax on exports, which currently stands at K3.5 million and is growing by about K2 million a year (1972 was the only year in which payments have had to be made). Similar marketing boards exist for copra and cocoa. The Copra Marketing Board handles export marketing in addition to operating a stabilization fund. The Cocoa Marketing Board, established in 1975, operates much like the coffee board, preferring not to exercise its control and marketing powers as long as private operations appear to be yielding satisfactory results to all interests.

new cuttings. Except in disease-free Bougainville, cocoa output has been held down somewhat in recent years by a die-back disease, but research on the disease has begun to yield encouraging results.

As Table B3 indicates, the smallholder share in coffee production is already large. The smallholder share in coconut and cocoa is likely to grow over time. The continued expansion of smallholder production of these three export crops is both feasible and vitally important for raising rural incomes. The outlook is promising, because smallholders are already acquainted with the growing of these crops, which do not require any difficult adjustment to unaccustomed work discipline. Although smallholder cocoa and coconut production is increasing, the role of the plantation sector is expected to remain important. This will require that Papua New Guinean managerial capability (or hired managers) be developed in pace with measures for localization (nationalization) of plantations. Recent success in oil palm development on nucleus estates, which are combined with smallholdings, indicates good production prospects for this export crop.[2] Prospects for expansion of tea exports after 1980 are not very clear; agronomically, the crop can be grown well in the highlands, but the world market outlook is somewhat discouraging.

Although price prospects for Papua New Guinea's export crops, except for coffee, are not encouraging for the late 1970s, they should improve in the early 1980s. Rural wages are fixed by the minimum wage laws and are another important determinant of the profitability and attractiveness of export crop production and of its expansion. Although Papua New Guinea's growing conditions are favorable and yields are high, continuously increasing wages are unmatched by increasing labor productivity. This may hamper the country's agricultural export growth by reducing its competitive strength relative to other exporters of tropical agricultural products. The government is, however, becoming increasingly aware of this problem. The DPI intends to continue to advocate wage restraint in the interest of satisfactory growth of Papua New Guinea's agricultural exports.

The country's earnings from agricultural exports over the next decade will depend on changes in the volume of production of in-

2. The pioneer project has been the World Bank–assisted operation at Hoskins in West New Britain. A Japanese project at Bialla on the same island is in an earlier stage of development but is already producing. A second Bank-assisted project, relying entirely on smallholder production, is being prepared at Popondetta in Northern Province on the mainland.

Table B3. Production of Major Export Crops by Papua New Guineans and by Expatriates, Fiscal Year 1973

Crop and producer	Crop area (thousands of hectares)	Percentage composition	Production (thousands of metric tons)	Percentage composition	Average size of holdings, 1972 (hectares)
Coconuts					
Papua New Guineans	139.9	56.4	51.9	40.1	1.28
Expatriates	108.3	43.6	77.4	59.9	163.30
Total	248.2	100.0	129.3	100.0	
Cocoa					
Papua New Guineans	22.9	28.8	6.8	30.5	0.63
Expatriates	56.7	71.2	15.5	69.5	129.50
Total	79.6	100.0	22.3	100.0	
Coffee					
Papua New Guineans	22.9	76.6	25.0	71.8	0.13
Expatriates	7.0	23.4	9.8	28.2	28.00
Total	29.9	100.0	34.8	100.0	
Rubber					
Papua New Guineans	3.6	21.8	0.2	3.4	1.43
Expatriates	12.9	78.2	5.6	96.6	185.61
Total	16.5	100.0	5.8	100.0	
Tea					
Papua New Guineans	0.4	10.8	0.7	19.4	0.52
Expatriates	3.3	89.2	2.9	80.6	135.72
Total	3.7	100.0	3.6	100.0	
Oil palm					
Papua New Guineans	4.9	64.5	22.0[b]	59.8	3.19
Expatriates[a]	2.7	35.5	14.8[b]	40.2	132.84
Total	7.6	100.0	36.8	100.0	

a. Expatriate companies are involved in equal partnership with Papua New Guineans in nucleus estate-factory operations.

b. Estimated.

Sources: Acreage and production in 1973 DPI unpublished data; average size of holdings in 1972, Papua New Guinea Bureau of Statistics and *Rural Industries, 1971–72.*

dividual crops and changes in the prices received. Table B4 shows actual and projected export earnings in current prices, which reflect a continuation of recent world and Papua New Guinean inflation, as well as projected earnings in real prices of individual crops. The table suggests that real agricultural exports will increase by 52 percent during the next decade. Virtually all of this increase will come from three crops, coffee, copra, and palm oil. More than half the growth will come from coffee alone, and this will strengthen the position of coffee as Papua New Guinea's leading agricultural export. Palm oil exports will earn about three times as much in 1985 as in 1976, but they will still earn less than a third as much as coffee. Earnings from other crops—except for tea, a minor source of export earnings—are expected to be essentially stagnant.

With the exception of cocoa, changes in the volume of production are expected to have a much greater influence on real export earnings than are changes in real prices. The percentage increases in quantities and in export earnings expected during the next decade for the four high-growth crops are as follows:

	Percentage growth	
Export	*In output*	*In real earnings*
Coffee	66	75
Cocoa	29	−16
Tea	131	82
Palm oil	300	273

These figures mean that coffee price trends are expected to boost coffee earnings above the level to which output expansion alone would take them; tea, cocoa, and palm oil prices will tend to decline in relation to other prices and will therefore offset the expected growth in output of these three crops.

No current developments give much promise that any major new crops will be produced for export. A limited amount of work on spices has been done at the Lowlands Experiment Station at Keravat, New Britain, but nothing of much promise has so far materialized. Growing conditions for spices appear to be generally uncompetitive. An Australian firm has expressed some interest in developing lime production, but demand would be exceedingly small. There is talk of introducing Japanese mint at Popondetta, but none is growing as yet. The Keravat station has done some work on vanilla, but New Britain does not have the right insects for natural pollination, and pollination by hand is uneconomic.

Table B4. Actual and Projected Export Earnings from Agriculture and Fishery, Fiscal Years 1974–85

| | Actual earnings (millions of current kina) | | Projected earnings | | | | | | | |
| | | | (Millions of current kina) | | | | (Millions of 1973 kina) | | | |
Export	1974	1975	1976	1978	1980	1985	1976	1978	1980	1985
Copra	23.7	29.4	17.8	22.5	24.9	47.0	12.6	13.7	13.2	17.6
Coconut oil	13.8	13.8	8.6	11.0	12.1	22.5	6.1	6.7	6.4	8.5
Coffee	28.8	33.5	45.5	76.7	95.3	150.8	32.3	46.8	50.5	56.6
Cocoa	23.5	39.1	32.6	37.7	40.1	52.0	23.2	23.0	21.2	19.4
Rubber	3.6	2.6	3.0	4.1	4.7	6.1	2.2	2.4	2.4	2.3
Tea	2.6	3.8	4.6	6.2	9.7	16.1	3.3	3.8	5.1	6.0
Palm oil	2.7	5.4[a]	6.8	9.9	14.0	48.0	4.8	6.1	7.5	17.9
Total	98.7	127.6	118.9	168.1	200.8	342.5	84.5	102.5	106.3	128.3
Total agriculture[b]	101.4	130.0	121.4	171.0	204.0	347.0	86.0	104.5	108.5	131.0
Fishery[c]	14.2	18.5	n.e.	n.e.	40.0	80.0	n.e.	n.e.	22.0	30.0

n.e. Not estimated.

Note: Values shown here for fiscal 1976 and 1985 differ from those shown in Table B1 because of (a) the application of different sets of prices and (b) minor differences in the projected quantities.

a. Estimated from data for five months.

b. In addition to listed items, includes mainly copra pellets, dessicated coconut, oil palm nuts and kernels, pyrethrum, fruits, and fruit juice.

c. Fish and prawn.

Sources: Actual 1974 and 1975 data, from the Papua New Guinea Bureau of Statistics. Projections, based on quantities in Table B1 and World Bank price forecasts.

Papua New Guinea's cost competitiveness relative to other producers of its major agricultural exports varies from crop to crop. Broadly speaking, Papua New Guinea's natural growing conditions are good to excellent for all the crops it now grows for export. This is a major advantage for physical productivity of plantation and smallholder export-cropping, although for all crops except oil palm yields on smallholdings are often only about half those on plantations. Smallholders now use little or no fertilizer on their crops, and they do a minimum of scientific cultivation, so there would appear to be considerable room for increasing output by intensifying smallholder output as well as by extending acreage. Yields may increase as the extension service is able to reach the smallholder and as the latter's interest in higher cash income rises.

Expansion of plantation acreage will continue to depend heavily, but not exclusively, on expatriate activity for the next decade or so. In turn, expatriate activity will depend on confidence in the investment climate in agriculture and on profit expectations as determined by (a) expected price trends in world markets and (b) expected trends in wage costs and labor productivity. Papua New Guinea's nationwide system of uniform minimum wages for hired rural labor has imposed high money costs on plantation operators. Owners of copra plantations (and perhaps some others) have tried to counter this by devising incentive systems that require minimum output in order to establish eligibility for the minimum wage, but this device has been contested. The result is that plantation output has considerably higher labor cost than its main competition in Southeast Asia, a burden that is only partly offset by high-yield growing conditions. Although the DPI and the fifty-year-old Planters' Association of New Guinea are becoming increasingly aware of Papua New Guinea's high labor costs, this problem deserves considerably more attention than it has so far received if Papua New Guinea is to avoid a profit squeeze that could make it a marginal producer in certain crops.

Import-Substitution in Food

In the past there were no internal markets of any significance, and until the 1970s efforts at agricultural development were concentrated almost entirely on export crops. But with the growth of urban centers and the monetization of parts of the rural economy, internal markets for agricultural products have grown and are no longer so heavily dependent on expatriate demand. In fiscal 1974 the country imported for domestic consumption more than K57 million worth of food, mainly cereals, livestock and poultry products, fruits and vegetables, fish, and sugar. Thus, lack of demand is not the main constraint on food production for internal markets. Because the country is rugged and geographically fragmented, and cross-country transportation is costly, a single national market for most of these products is not practical. Small regional markets, meeting demands of towns and population centers with food supplies from nearby rural areas, could be developed through existing and anticipated transport links.

Many products now imported could be produced locally. This would provide an important opportunity to increase rural incomes and at the same time contribute to the improvement of the balance of payments. The government is giving priority to replacing imported foodstuffs by domestic production. Some progress has been achieved in recent years in livestock, poultry, and fruits and vegetables. In fiscal 1974, K4 million (less than a third the imported value) in livestock and an estimated K7 million (twice the imported value) in fruits and vegetables were supplied to the domestic markets from local production. The size and the impact of a systematic import replacement program over the next five or ten years have not yet been outlined. Except for meat and vegetables, expanding marketed production and replacing imports will be a very slow process until fiscal 1980.

To achieve self-sufficiency in meat supplies, the government is expending considerable effort (an estimated 31 percent of extension staff time in fiscal 1976) toward increasing production of livestock (cattle and pigs) and poultry. The cattle population is rapidly increasing, both on large ranches and on smallholdings. The country has extensive grassland for sustaining large cattle populations in many areas, but especially in Morobe, the Eastern Highlands, Madang, and the Northern and Central provinces. The Papua New Guinea Development Bank is providing the credit necessary to build up herds. Commercial pig production, mainly by smallholders in rural and semiurban areas, is making some progress. Poultry production is increasing rapidly despite difficulties in many areas in obtaining inexpensive poultry feed. Under an IDA credit, poultry production is increasing dramatically in areas around Lae. Papua New Guinea has applied for a World Bank loan for a food and feed grain project based on imported wheat and possibly some locally produced corn and sorghum. This project is likely to increase the availability, and reduce the costs, of feed for pig and poultry production. The country can be expected to be self-sufficient in meat within a few years.

The government is increasing DPI extension service efforts (about 16 percent of extension staff time in 1976) to encourage production of fresh fruit and vegetables. Producer response has reportedly been so good that village communities and area authorities are increasing their requests for extension services. On Bougainville, BCL has reportedly achieved considerable success in its private efforts to introduce new types of vegetable production to villagers for their own consumption as well as for the market. In several areas religious missions have done the same. Difficulty in transportation and the consequent high waste are the main problems. The IDA-financed report on fruits and vegetables[3] provides guidelines for marketing development. With greater extension efforts and improvement in transport, cold storage, and marketing arrangements, there are good prospects for the virtual elimination of fresh fruit and vegetable imports, perhaps by the early 1980s.

Despite some government efforts, the domestic production of rice has stagnated at about 1,000 tons a year, although imports have been growing at about 10 percent a year and are now at 50,000 tons a year. The popularity of rice as an item of daily food is spreading. Unless domestic production is increased or importation restricted, rice imports are likely to increase from the current level to well over 100,000 tons a year in the early 1980s. The government, through a trade agreement, has virtually fixed annual rice imports at about 50,000 tons. It intends that more rice be grown locally and that people be encouraged to consume more of the traditional foods instead of rice.

There are differences of technical opinion in regard to the economic feasibility of rice production and the appropriate organization of production in suitable areas. According to a recent study by an FAO expert, (a) villagers' response to rice cultivation is poor because the return to their time and effort from rice cultivation is much less than from other village agriculture in that calorie yield per hectare is higher from sweet potato than from rice; (b) there is no tradition of paddy cultivation, and costs of extension efforts for

---

3. ULG Consultants (Warwick) Ltd., "Internal Marketing of Fruit, Vegetables, Meat, and Fish in Papua New Guinea," Report of the Reconaissance and Identification Mission for the United Nations Development Programme and the World Bank (Burgess Hill, Sussex, England: ULG Consultants, 1975).

village rice cultivation are high; (c) only large-scale mechanized cultivation has good prospects and only in one large area (Markham Valley); and (d) village dry-land rice cultivation under the bush-fallow system can be expanded only in the Sepik and the Mekeo Valley areas.

The government considers that the best prospects for increased rice production from smallholders lie in the bush-fallow system. The major aims of the government are to improve rice varieties and cultivation techniques and to provide more processing facilities. A few Filipino rice farmers have recently been brought into the country to train local farmers. A few rice mills will be established in promising areas. For large-scale rice production and milling, the government faces both financial and manpower constraints, and it intends to ask for World Bank assistance to overcome these. The outlook for any major progress in import-replacement of rice is still unclear, but it deserves further investigation.

Sugar cane is indigenous to Papua New Guinea,[4] and it can be grown for commercial production in several areas, particularly the Markham Valley. Imports of refined sugar are around 20,000 tons at present and the demand is increasing. The country has the potential to meet domestic demand and eventually to become a sugar exporter. The government intends to start cane production in the villages, and it is seeking World Bank assistance for the purpose.

Fish is another increasingly popular food item. Imports (mainly of lower-priced tinned mackerel) are large and growing. At the same time, Papua New Guinean fish exports are becoming an important source of foreign exchange to the nation. While tuna and prawn exports are carried out by large-scale operations involving foreign companies, barramundi and crayfish exports provide direct income and employment to many local fishermen who handle their own catching and processing. The country's rich potential for fish production can meet the domestic demand and make an increased contribution to export earnings. Reduction or replacement of imported tinned fish would require the establishment of one or more canneries, supplemented by improved storage, transportation, and marketing of fresh and dried fish. The government intends to tackle these problems by developing cold storage, ice production, and fish drying. With Asian Development Bank assistance, Papua New Guinea is also considering a major fish-processing and canning project that would serve both export and domestic markets.

4. A substantial amount of raw cane is consumed annually by the local population. There is no production of unrefined sugar as a village industry.

Improving Traditional Agriculture

The government's eight-point plan implicitly puts great emphasis on improving traditional agriculture in order to raise rural living standards. These improvements would include:

—Continuing to change agriculture from purely subsistence production of root crops to an increasing participation in producing new cash crops, either for export or for domestic markets—two quite different sets of crop possibilities.
—Trying to increase yields and nutritional values of the traditional subsistence crops, something that is particularly important in some of the highland districts where there is population pressure on the land.
—Trying to diversify traditional subsistence crops and to include new subsistence production mainly of nonroot crops, poultry, and livestock, which would improve nutrition and help to restore soil fertility.
—Introducing some combination of these measures.

There is as yet no clear strategy for improving traditional agriculture, although the spread of cash-cropping has clearly been given the most attention in recent years. The diversification of subsistence production for nutritional reasons is likely to be more important—and more feasible—than further improving yields of traditional crops. Present yields of traditional crops (sweet potatoes, taro, yam, cassava) are quite high, and there are serious limitations to further increasing yields of these traditional crops without the intensive application of nonfarm inputs such as fertilizers and pesticides and a strain on extension services. Moreover, market demand outside the subsistence sector itself has been growing mostly for nontraditional products. If rice imports continue to be fixed at the current level, a strong possibility, then with improved storage and transport some of the traditional root crops would find a fairly large and growing internal market outlet.

Appendix C

Framework for Industrial Development

A S APPROVED BY THE CABINET, *A Framework for Industrial Development in Papua New Guinea* does not represent any great changes in government policy. Rather, it endeavors to suggest specific objectives that should be concentrated upon in each sector. The following paragraphs are excerpts from this document and present its major elements.

Our present industrial sector is very small by international standards and thus limits the immediate opportunities to increase the value of domestic primary production through further processing. It also limits our ability to develop a more self-reliant economy and increase the productivity of our work force. Further, we must develop our industrial sector so that we are not governed by severe fluctuations in primary produce prices. This in turn will help us to achieve an internationally competitive economy and a strong stable currency. A development strategy is therefore necessary which leads to an expansion of industrial activities in line with the overall development objectives of the government.

Industrial development must specifically:

1. Promote self-reliance by generating government revenue, increasing exports and replacing selected imports with locally produced products;

2. Promote rural development by increasing income earning opportunities in rural areas and providing inputs to agriculture and the rural sector in general;
3. Create productive employment opportunities and in particular create job opportunities to deal with problems of urban drift and the increasing number of unemployed school leavers;
4. Provide opportunities for manpower development through the acquisition of entrepreneurial, management and technical skills; and
5. Contribute to regional equality by dispersing industrial activities.

Respect for the worker and the environment will be key considerations in defining both the direction and form of this development. While the fact that increasing numbers of Papua New Guineans are becoming involved in the money economy makes employment creation a major goal of government policy, industrial development must take place in a manner which maintains the worker's dignity. The involvement of employees in decisionmaking and profit sharing will be actively encouraged.

Every effort will be made to guarantee the stability of the environment and to ensure that the growth of the total economy does not result in polarization into urban industrialized and rural nonindustrialized economies.

Public and Private Sector Investment

Rather than concentrating our limited financial and human resources on government ownership of industrial undertakings, the government will concentrate its efforts in the industrial sector on the promotion and encouragement of private sector activity in a form and manner consistent with our industrial development policies. The overall policy of increasing participation of Papua New Guineans in the economy will be a major aim in extension programs relating to the promotion of industrial activities. The focus will be on the development of appropriate technologies for village and small-scale industries and the promotion of these industries in both rural and urban sectors to serve local demand.

We recognize that foreign investment can contribute to our overall development aims by promoting the diversification of the economy and by providing government revenue, foreign exchange, capital, employment, and technical know-how and management skills. It can also contribute to the development of infrastructure, the training of our people, and the development of small-scale enterprises.

Therefore, foreign investment will continue to be encouraged in selected sectors and activities, provided that the investor is willing to operate within the government determined policy guidelines—in particular, the National Investment Guidelines—and the terms and conditions established by the government at the time of registration with the National Investment and Development Authority.

The government will concentrate most on the provision of finance and support of local business undertakings through the Development Bank and other government programs aimed at promoting Papua New Guinean businesses. To ensure that the limited international capital and finance available flows primarily to our own local businesses, as a general rule foreign enterprises will be expected to raise their capital from external sources. Government equity participation may be sought in selected foreign undertakings, particularly in the natural resources sectors. Government corporations will be established only in those priority areas in which private investment is unavailable or which are considered to be in the national interest. Where possible, such government involvement will be with a foreign partner who will provide the necessary skills.

Sectoral Development

In the sections below are listed the sectors of industry where we feel a particular contribution can be made. Each sector is discussed in terms of local and foreign enterprise and their roles. An indication is also given as to what emphasis should be made in each sector in the next two years. Sector programs and industry plans will be laid down to a greater or lesser degree to ensure that regional and sectoral balance is maintained along with increases in overall development.

NATURAL RESOURCES

Recognizing that our country is richly endowed with natural resources, the most important development of industrial activity must be based on these resources. Their utilization must be controlled in a manner which will ensure that the maximum benefits accrue to the people and the country with minimum social and environmental costs. Extraction of our natural resources should take place only at a rate necessary to augment the government's revenue base and foreign exchange requirements, and to promote its regional development plans. Environmental impact studies will be required to ensure that the detrimental effects of natural resource extraction are minimized.

Mining, gas, and oil. This government will actively encourage further exploration [by foreign enterprises] for oil and gas and minerals.

Forests. The utilization of our forest resources must be carefully planned. We will not allow systematic logging or clear felling of our forest areas purely for the export of the unprocessed wood. The export of logs as a revenue earner is no longer appropriate and will be eliminated. Existing operations will be encouraged to increase the degree of processing and vertical integration within Papua New Guinea. New activity by foreigners must be in the form of integrated forest industries or in enterprises which further process timber now being logged. In any forestry development, reforestation must be undertaken as a means of renewing the resource and sustaining the industry.

The main objectives in the development of timber-based industries will be their contribution to the regional dispersal of economic activities and regional welfare, and this to greater regional equality. This will happen particularly through royalty revenue to the people of an area and through employment creation. Forest based industries will also be expected to contribute to government revenue, foreign exchange earnings, training, the development of infrastructure and the promotion of small-scale Papua New Guinean enterprises.

Fishing. Like forest industries, the main objective in the development of our fishing industry will be its contribution to regional dispersal and thus greater regional equality. The development of the industry requires an integrated approach between local and foreign fishermen. Foreign enterprises involved in fishing will also be a source of government revenue and foreign exchange and will, in particular, be expected to train Papua New Guineans and to encourage the further development of Papua New Guinean fishing ventures. The government will continue to encourage the development of cooperative Papua New Guinean fishing ventures on a commercial scale and the processing of fish caught both by commercial and traditional methods for internal consumption. The eventual aim will be the establishment of Papua New Guinean fishing fleets to replace foreign fishing fleets. Fishing by foreign fleets in the waters of Papua New Guinea will continue to be encouraged, provided that enterprises agree to land their catch in Papua New Guinea and process to the maximum extent feasible on Papua New Guinea soil.

As with the forestry sector, our aims in this sector are better served in the immediate future by finding ways to process fish presently being caught. Of equal priority with further processing is the integration of foreign capital with local fishing skills. Both these forms of industry development rank much higher than the need to increase our total catch at this time.

MANUFACTURING

The key focus in the manufacturing sector will be on the encouragement of industries which are complementary to and integrated with the rural sector, with the main emphasis on agro-based industries, which will provide inputs required by agriculture and which will process agricultural commodities and industries which are supportive of activities in forests, mining and fishing. However, the expansion of urban industry, including manufacturing, will continue to be important and investment proposals in these activities are welcome, if they confer net benefits on the Papua New Guinea economy, and will be considered on their merits.

While the employment creation effect, direct or indirect, will be a major concern in manufacturing, the activities will also play important roles in the development of a more self-reliant and balanced economy. Special attention will be given to the opportunity for maximum local participation in the further processing of agricultural commodities. A key to this development will be further researched on, and application of technologies appropriate to Papua New Guinea. Priorities for the development of small-scale industries are now being established by the Small Industries Committee.

The government will actively encourage and provide special assistance to foreign investment in labor-intensive agro-industries which either provide inputs which are utilized in agricultural activities or which process agricultural products as well as to investment in other manufacturing activities either for the home market or for export, to meet the industrialization objectives of the country.

TOURISM

If planned appropriately, this sector will foster and preserve the traditional customs and culture of our Papua New Guinean society. Large scale "enclave" type tourism development will not be encouraged in nonurban areas with the exception perhaps of special areas where other economic opportunities are scarce.

It is expected that a large part of the tourism development outside of the urban areas will be carried out by local enterprises or joint ventures. The ability of tourism to create work opportunities outside of the urban areas will receive special attention.

Foreign investment in larger scale tourist ventures in urban areas will be encouraged. Special attention will be given to those forms of development which involve overseas linkages in areas of tourism marketing and promotion.

INFRASTRUCTURE

The development of a national road system and the improvement of coastal shipping services are both related to our industrial policy. They can be the basis for encouraging a variety of local enterprises and they will also require selected foreign investment.

Appendix D

Second National Investment Priorities Schedule

THE FOLLOWING LIST SHOWS the areas of activity in which foreign investment will be promoted, permitted, restricted, or prohibited:

1. *Priority activities,* in which the government is actively seeking new foreign investment:
   —Exploration for minerals and ancillary activities.
   —Exploration for natural hydrocarbons and ancillary activities.
   —Major timber projects and ancillary activities.
   —Offshore fishing and further processing of fish.
   —Agriculture, including cultivation and processing of tea, oil palm, and sugar cane; and cultivation of legume, grain, and root crops for processing.
   —Manufacture, including:
   Further processing of agriculture and livestock products, including coconut and other vegetable oils; coir products, except brooms and brushes; canning and preserving of fruits and vegetables; manufacture and processing of palm oil; processing and manufacturing of rubber and rubber products; and manufacture of cocoa butter and tanned hide.
   Further processing of fish and fish products.
   Further processing of timber.

Manufacture of cement, asbestos cement, lime, sacks, tools, and nuts and bolts; steel rolling; blending of fertilizers; assembly or manufacture of agricultural machinery and low cost radio receivers; and ship breaking, repairing, and building.

—Construction of dwellings.

—Coastal freezer and coastal cargo shipping services.

—Professional-technical services: industrial electrical contracting; light engineering, fitting and turning establishments; general engineering; motor vehicle and electrical repair; aircraft maintenance.

2. *Permitted activities,* in which new foreign investment will be permitted, but not actively promoted:

—Extraction of timber for utilization in a priority timber-based industry.

—Nucleus estate or agricultural activities integrated with further processing activities.

—Manufacture of instant coffee; collection and marketing of prawns and lobsters; pearl culturing; and tobacco growing.

—Construction activities, involving contracts in excess of K50,000 and those less than K50,000 which require specialist expertise; and hotel/motel/building construction.

—An activity involving the provision of a professional or technical service.

—Minor activities involving an estimated capital investment not exceeding K75,000.

—Activities resulting from acquisition of certain assets from another foreign company which carried out the same activity with those assets before December 6, 1974.

—Activities approved by the Minister for Labor, Commerce and Industry after consultation with the appropriate minister(s).

3. *Restricted activities,* in which new foreign investment will be restricted to enterprises with substantial (25 percent or more) Papua New Guinean equity or to joint-venture partnerships between foreigners and Papua New Guineans:

—Agriculture and related activities: coffee and rubber plantations; sago cultivation and processing; inshore and inland fishing and fish farming; spice growing; crocodile farming; silk worm cultivation; processing of cocoa (collection through to dry bean), copra (collection through to dry copra), and coffee (collection through to green bean); tea packaging for the home market; coffee roasting, grinding, and packaging.

—Trade and services: taverns; urban trade stores; retailing and wholesaling businesses involving investment of less than K25,000; hire, repair, and maintenance of vending and amusement machines; boot and shoe repairing; amusement parlors; restaurants and take-away food bars involving investment of less than K25,000.

—General construction work, excluding civil engineering projects, involving contracts not exceeding K50,000 and not requiring specialist expertise unavailable to Papua New Guinean contractors.

—Plant and equipment hire.

4. *Reserved activities,* in which foreign investors will not be allowed to undertake new ventures:

—Agriculture: copra plantations; growing of root crops for sale as a fresh product; pig raising for slaughter; raising of broilers; cultivation, collection, wholesaling, and exporting of orchids; gathering, wholesaling, retailing, and exporting of uncultivated natural products; hunting, farming, and trading in nonprotected insects and other nonprotected fauna.

—Crafts: handloom weaving; silkscreen printing of piece goods; manufacture of handicrafts.

—Trade and services: purchase of coffee, copra, or cocoa (grower to factory or exporter); rural trade stores; retailing of petrol (not including integrated service stations); mobile food canteens and trading establishments; refreshment stands, sandwich, and coffee shops; second-hand clothing stores.

—Transport: all road passenger transport; long-distance trucking businesses operating trucks under 8 tons (unladen).

Appendix E

Petroleum Policy and Legislation

THE FOLLOWING IS A SUMMARY of the thirty-page government statement *Petroleum Policy and Legislation* (March 1976):

1. *Ownership and Participation*
   (a) The state will take a minority participation interest in all
       petroleum developments. The exact percentage will be
       negotiated in each case between the company and the state.
   (b) The state's share of exploration and development costs will
       be provided by the company, which will, in effect, lend the
       money to the state. Repayment will be made to the com-
       pany from the income from the state's share of production.
   (c) The state will meet its share of operating costs from year to
       year.
   (d) A specialized government agency, the National Petroleum
       Authority, will be established after the first commercial
       petroleum discovery to administer the state's participation
       interests.
2. *Taxation*
   (a) All petroleum production will pay a royalty of 1.25 percent
       of the wellhead value of production.
   (b) Companies will pay a petroleum income tax of 50 percent of
       taxable income. This tax will take the place, for companies
       producing oil and gas, of the current company income tax
       and the dividend withholding tax.
   (c) Once a reasonable rate of return on investment has been
       achieved, companies will pay an additional profits tax of 50

percent of net cash receipts (that is, net profit plus depreciation less capital expenditure).

(d) The reasonable return is defined as a 25 percent money return on total funds invested in the project. When a realistic assessment of inflation is taken into account, this amounts to a real return in excess of 15 percent. The reasonable return on shareholders' funds will be substantially in excess of this.

(e) The overall impact of the financial provisions with a 30 percent state participation is more generous than a 70:30 production-sharing contract.

(f) Both petroleum income tax and additional profits tax will be assessed on a license-by-license basis. Companies will be allowed deductions for exploration expenditure within a license that includes a producing field at the time the expenditure is made. Exploration expenditure outside the license will be deductible beginning at the time when the area in which such exploration was incurred is fully surrendered.

(g) Exploration expenditure will be deductible at a rate up to 20 percent a year. Capital expenditure will be deductible at a rate up to 10 percent a year or over the actual life of the asset as determined by the chief collector of taxes, whichever is the faster rate.

(h) Only exploration expenditure incurred less than eleven years before issue of a development license will be allowable as deductions.

(i) Operating expenses will be deductible in the year they are incurred. Operating losses may be carried forward for up to eleven years, but not carried back.

(j) No deductions will be allowed for payments to the parent company or affiliated companies for technology fees, licenses, royalties, and so on. Reasonable management fees will, however, be deductible.

(k) Deductions for interest on loans will be limited to a reasonable margin above the then current prime international lending rates of interest.

(l) There will be provisions for accelerated depreciation deductions in the early years of a project, if cash flow falls below 25 percent of initial capital and exploration expenditure.

(m) Additional profits tax will not apply to natural gas operations. Instead, the government will receive a free participation interest—for which it will not have to repay the company—equivalent to an 8 to 16 percent royalty, depending on the size of the field and the rate of production.

3. *Pricing and Marketing*
   (a) The government expects companies to sell petroleum products at a world market price, and mechanisms will be established to ensure that such a price is the one used in calculating tax liability and in calculating the value of the state's share of production which it receives through its participation interest.
   (b) The price for natural gas will normally be the actual contract price realized by the producer. All long-term sales contracts will, however, be subject to prior government approval.
   (c) In setting a reasonable norm price for oil, the government expects to use the actual price realized by the producer, but in the case of intracompany sales it may use other recent sales, or the price of Arabian light or Sumatran light crude oils, with appropriate quality and transportation cost adjustments, as reference points.
   (d) The pricing mechanism will be flexible, and capable of achieving periodic adjustment in price to reflect changing world conditions.

4. *The Structure of Licenses*
   (a) There will be two basic types of licenses, both on- and offshore: prospecting licenses for exploration; and development licenses for production.
   (b) Prospecting licenses will be issued for an initial term of six years, and will provide exclusive prospecting rights over the license area.
   (c) Prospecting licenses will normally be issued over areas of up to 60 blocks of five minutes of longitude by five minutes of latitude. (One block is approximately 86 square kilometers.) In certain cases, licenses may be issued over areas of up to 200 blocks. Companies will be able to hold more than one license.
   (d) Companies will be required to relinquish 25 percent of the original license area after three years, and if the license is renewed, a total of 50 percent of the original area after six years and 75 percent of the original area after nine years.
   (e) All new prospecting licenses will be awarded through a

Table E1. Hypothetical Cash Flow from a Small Offshore Oil Field in Papua New Guinea
(Millions of kina)

Item	Year 1	2	3	4	5	6	7	8	9	10
Project										
Exploration	50	1.5	12.7	13.5						
Capital expenditure					46.2	146.3	76.4			
Output							8.2	16.4	16.4	16.4
Value of output							98.4	196.8	196.8	196.8
Operating costs							11.8	11.8	11.8	11.8
Company										
Sales receipts							68.9	137.8	137.8	137.8
Costs							8.3	8.3	8.3	8.3
Normal depreciation							29.7	29.7	29.7	29.7
Accelerated depreciation							30.0			
Royalty							0.9	1.7	1.7	1.7
Trading profit							0	98.1	98.1	98.1
Petroleum income tax							0	49.1	49.1	49.1
Additional profits tax								—	—	—
Government loan repayment							26.0	55.5	22.5	
Cash flow					−123.9	−146.3	9.3	134.2	101.3	78.8
Net cash receipts					−123.9	−146.3	+9.3	134.2	101.3	78.8
Accumulated value at 15 percent					−123.9	−288.8	−322.8	−237.0	−171.2	−118.1
Government										
Loan account borrowing					37.2	43.9	22.9	59.0	59.0	59.0
Value of government share of oil							29.5	3.5	3.5	3.5
Costs							3.5	55.5	22.5	
Loan repayment							26.0	55.5		
Loan account balance							78.0	22.5		
Cash from government share							0	0	33.0	55.5
Petroleum income tax							0	49.1	49.1	49.1
Additional profits tax								—	—	—
Royalty							0.9	1.7	1.7	1.7
Government cash flow							0.9	50.8	83.8	106.3

Table E1. (continued)

Item	Year									
	11	12	13	14	15	16	17	18	19	20
Project										
Exploration										
Capital expenditure										
Output	16.4	14.8	13.3	12.0	10.8	9.7	8.7	7.9	7.1	6.4
Value of output	196.8	177.6	159.6	143.6	129.2	116.3	104.7	94.2	84.8	76.3
Operating costs	11.8	11.8	11.8	11.8	11.8	11.8	11.8	11.8	11.8	11.8
Company										
Sales receipts	137.8	124.3	111.7	100.5	90.4	81.4	73.3	65.9	59.4	53.4
Costs	8.3	8.3	8.3	8.3	8.3	8.3	8.3	8.3	8.3	8.3
Normal depreciation	29.7	18.8	18.8	18.8	18.8	18.8	–	–	–	–
Accelerated depreciation										
Royalty	1.7	1.6	1.4	1.2	1.1	1.0	0.9	0.8	0.7	0.7
Trading profit	98.1	95.6	83.2	72.2	62.2	53.3	64.1	56.8	50.4	44.4
Petroleum income tax	49.1	47.8	41.6	36.1	31.1	26.7	32.1	28.4	25.2	22.2
Additional profits tax	–	0.5	30.2	27.5	24.9	22.7	16.0	14.2	12.6	11.1
Government loan repayment										
Cash flow	78.8	66.1	30.2	27.5	24.9	22.7	16.0	14.2	12.6	11.1
Net cash receipts	78.8	66.6	60.4	54.9	49.9	45.5	32.1	28.4	25.2	22.2
Accumulated value at 15 percent	–56.9	+1.0								
Government										
Loan account borrowing										
Value of government share of oil	59.0	53.3	47.9	43.1	38.8	34.9	31.4	28.3	25.4	22.9
Costs	3.5	3.5	3.5	3.5	3.5	3.5	3.5	3.5	3.5	3.5
Loan repayment										
Loan account balance										
Cash from government share	55.5	49.8	44.4	39.6	35.3	31.4	27.9	24.8	21.9	19.4
Petroleum income tax	49.1	47.8	41.6	36.1	31.1	26.7	32.1	28.4	25.2	22.2
Additional profits tax		0.5	30.2	27.5	24.9	22.7	16.0	14.2	12.6	11.1
Royalty	1.7	1.6	1.4	1.2	1.1	1.0	0.9	0.8	0.7	0.7
Government cash flow	106.3	99.7	117.6	104.4	92.4	81.8	76.9	68.2	59.4	53.4

Note: Field is assumed to produce 45,000 barrels a day; DCF internal rate of return to the company is assumed to be 18.5 percent.

Correction: Due to computation error, the total depreciation and amortization deductions exceed the total capital expenditure by US$30 million. This affects cash flow in years 15 and 16 when deductions should be 7.6 and 0, respectively. This does not significantly alter the DCF rate of return.

Source: Government statement on *Petroleum Policy and Legislation* (March 1976).

competitive bidding procedure, in which the minister for natural resources advertises areas available for license. Bids will be evaluated on the basis of the extent of the work program proposed and the terms of the petroleum agreement.

(f) Development licenses will be issued with respect to a single block within a prospecting license in which there has been a commercial discovery. The development license will be for a term of twenty-five years and will be granted automatically.

(g) The minister may also issue nonexclusive reconnaissance permits for seismic or other survey work over areas not currently held under license. These permits will carry no automatic rights to licenses.

(h) Transitional provisions will ensure that the position of current license holders is safeguarded.

(i) All new prospecting licenses will be issued only after the negotiation of a petroleum agreement between the state and the company setting out all details of how the project would proceed in the event of a commercial discovery—in particular, the arrangements governing the state's participation share. Current offshore license holders will be required to negotiate such an agreement before the current term of their permit or license expires (and in no event later than the end of 1977).

5. *Other Issues*

(a) Environment: Oil companies will be subject to strict pollution controls, including requirements that the companies demonstrate their ability to prevent environmental damage in the event of oil spills or leaks. Companies will be financially responsible for any damage or rehabilitation expenses resulting from their operations.

(b) Training and localization: Companies will be subject to normal immigration and labor controls during exploration. In the event of a commercial discovery, they will be required to prepare complete localization and training programs covering the life of the project.

(c) Local purchasing and business development: Companies will be expected, wherever possible, to use Papua New Guinean supplies and equipment. Holders of development licenses will also be expected to prepare plans for assisting Papua New Guinea citizens to set up service businesses associated with the industry.

(d) Legal controls: Companies will be subject to the normal laws of Papua New Guinea, including the specific laws on petroleum taxation and licensing. In addition, relations between the state and each company will be governed by a petroleum agreement between the two. Disputes will normally be settled in accordance with Papua New Guinea law and under Papua New Guinea arbitration procedure, but the agreement may provide a procedure for selecting an arbitrator from outside the country.

Appendix F

Financial Policy Relating to Major Mining Projects

THE PAPUA NEW GUINEA GOVERNMENT released the following statement in 1975:

1. Major mining projects should be undertaken within the private sector, and it is understood that for the foreseeable future this will mean foreign investment.

2. The government welcomes offers of minority shareholdings in major projects. The holding should be sufficiently small to make it clear that the government has no major management responsibilities (perhaps 20 to 25 percent). The government expects to pay the full value of its shares. It also expects to be rewarded with equity for the full value of any infrastructure provided for a project.

3. After long deliberation, the Papua New Guinea government decided during 1974 that charges for the use of highly valuable mineral resources should take the form of an additional profits tax, rather than a royalty or high equity. A new investor can thus expect to work within the following tax regime:

   (a) There will be only one charge on sales, a 1.25 percent royalty on proceeds of sales, net of transport and smelting charges. This royalty will be paid to the central government, which will in turn make the proceeds available in some combination to the local landowners and the district in which the mine is established. This payment can be seen as meeting any obligations to reward local groups for the use of the resource.

(b) Companies will work within the Papua New Guinea Income Tax Act, which is based on the Australian Act. The Income Tax Act provides for a tax on company income (presently 33.3 percent) and on dividends paid overseas (a dividend withholding tax of 15 percent). There is no withholding tax on interest.

4. At present, the act provides for the amortization of nondepreciable assets over the life of the mine. Under the new Bougainville agreement, nondepreciable assets are written off over twenty years. The government recognizes that this is severe in times of high inflation and uncertainty, and amendments to the Income Tax Act are possible.

5. There are no plans to change the rate of either the income tax or the dividend withholding tax. However, the government will consider reasonable limits to these taxes: 15 percent for dividend withholding tax throughout the life of the project and probably 40 percent for income tax during the investment recovery period. The investment recovery period is defined as the period required for the accumulated value (at corporate borrowing rates ruling at the time the project is established) of profits before tax less income tax plus depreciation plus interest paid less interest earned less capital expenditure, all calculated annually, to exceed zero.

6. The government will agree not to impose any export taxes and will place reasonable limits on all other significant taxes, including import duties.

7. The government will seek to negotiate an additional profits tax on income above a "reasonable return" on investment. The "reasonable return" will reflect market factors, such as interest rates ruling at the time of investment. The "reasonable return" will be well in excess of international average returns in the relevant industry. For example, the government would not have expected any additional profits tax to be paid on income from a project, established in time of low inflation and interest rates during the 1960s if the internal rate of return (DCF) on total expenditure at the project did not exceed 15 percent. The internal rate of return that would justify additional profits tax would be correspondingly higher in the current circumstances of high interest rates and inflation.

8. The renegotiated Bougainville agreement provides one exam-

ple of the application of the government's policy, that investors are entitled to a "reasonable return" on investment but that a high proportion of income in excess of that "reasonable return" should accrue to the government. It is a complicated agreement, but, roughly, it provides that the company should pay only normal corporate income tax up to an after-tax income representing 15 percent on total funds employed (adjusted automatically for currency variations and capital additions less retirements and by agreement for abnormal inflation), and income tax at the rate of 70 percent on income in excess of the 15 percent after tax return, following about twenty-one months of high, tax-free profits.

9.   The government appreciates that the Bougainville formula will not be applicable precisely to a new project. For example, if the general form of the Bougainville tax were adopted for a new project with high risk, the government would not expect additional profits tax to be paid during the investment recovery period.

10.   The government wants new private investment in major mining projects and will not let unreasonable taxation demands get in the way of new projects. It is prepared to be flexible about the form of the additional profits tax, with the principle that investors are entitled to a reasonable return that is well in excess of industry averages and is related to market conditions, but that a high proportion of income in excess of that return should accrue to the government as payment for the use of highly valuable national resources.

Statistical Appendix

Table SA1. Population Size, Growth Rate, and Density, by District, Actual 1971 and Estimated 1986

District	Population (thousands) 1971	Population (thousands) 1986	Population as percentage of total 1971 population	Compound annual growth rate 1966–71	Compound annual growth rate 1971–86	Approximate area in square miles	Population density per square mile 1971	Population density per square mile 1986	Rank in 1971 Size	Rank in 1971 Density
Indigenous population	2,435.4	3,566	97.8	2.5	2.6	183,500	13.3	19.4		
Papua	670.5	1,020	26.9	2.5	2.8	90,000	7.5	11.3		
Western	70.3	104	2.8	2.7	2.6	40,000	1.8	2.6	13	18
Gulf	58.2	86	2.3	1.1	2.6	15,000	3.9	5.7	17	17
Central	175.5	336	7.0	5.4	4.4	12,000	14.6	28.0	6	12
Milne Bay	108.5	161	4.4	1.8	2.7	7,800	13.9	20.6	9	13
Northern	65.9	96	2.6	2.6	2.5	9,000	7.3	10.7	14	15
Southern Highlands	192.0	237	7.7	0.9	1.4	6,200	31.0	38.2	4	4
New Guinea	1,764.9	2,546	70.9	2.5	2.5	93,500	18.9	27.2		
Eastern Highlands	236.8	339	9.5	3.2	2.4	5,000	47.4	67.8	3	2
Chimbu	159.7	161	6.4	−0.9	0.1	2,800	57.0	57.5	8	1
Western Highlands[a]	343.3	489	13.8	3.5	2.4	9,200	37.3	53.2	1	3
West Sepik[b]	93.5	129	3.8	−1.2	2.2	19,700	4.7	6.5	11	16
East Sepik[b]	180.1	211	7.2	2.9	1.1	10,500	17.2	20.1	5	8
Madang	168.2	232	6.8	2.3	2.2	10,800	15.6	21.5	7	9
Morobe	240.9	389	9.7	3.3	3.2	12,700	19.0	30.6	2	7
West New Britain[b]	60.8	132	2.4	6.7	5.3	7,100	8.6	18.6	15	14
East New Britain[b]	108.2	157	4.4	0.6	2.5	7,000	15.5	22.4	10	10
New Ireland	58.5	93	2.4	3.5	3.1	3,800	15.4	24.5	16	11
Bougainville	90.4	168	3.6	4.7	4.2	4,100	22.0	41.0	12	6
Manus	24.4	46	0.9	3.2	4.3	800	30.5	57.5	18	5
Nonindigenous population	54.5[c]		2.2	9.4[c]						
Total population	2,489.9		100.0	2.7		183,500	13.6	19.4[d]		

Note: 1971 is the latest census year.

a. As of 1974 comprises Western Highlands and newly formed Enga district.

b. In December 1968, Ambunti subdistrict was transferred from West Sepik to East Sepik and Gasmata Census Division from East New Britain to West New Britain.

c. By 1976 the nonindigenous population had declined to about 37,000.

d. Indigenous population only; if 30,000 foreigners are assumed, the figure rises to 19.6.

Source: Adapted from Papua New Guinea Bureau of Statistics.

Table SA2. Activity and Work Force Status of Local Population Ten Years of Age and Over, July 1971

Activity status	Males		Females		Persons	
	Thousands	Percentage of all males	Thousands	Percentage of all females	Thousands	Percentage of all persons
Primary activity						
Money raising	261.5	31.88	83.0	10.79	344.5	21.67
Subsistence	355.1	43.29	297.4	38.66	652.5	41.05
Unpaid home duties	52.8	6.44	306.7	39.87	359.6	22.62
Students attending school or college	117.4	14.31	60.0	7.80	177.5	11.17
Other activities	33.5	4.08	22.1	2.87	55.6	3.50
Total	820.3	100.00	769.3	100.00	1,589.6	100.00
Work force status[a]						
Worked 15 hours or more[b]	260.9	31.81	93.4	12.14	354.3	22.29
Worked 1–14 hours[b]	36.0	4.39	37.0	4.81	72.9	4.59
Temporarily absent[c]	33.1	4.04	19.7	2.56	52.8	3.32
Looked for work[d]	6.8	0.83	1.5	0.19	8.3	0.52
Money raising work force	336.8	41.06	151.5	19.69	488.3	30.72
Did not work[e]	483.5	58.94	617.8	80.31	1,101.3	69.28
Total	820.3	100.00	769.3	100.00	1,589.6	100.00

a. During week preceding census.
b. To earn money.
c. Temporarily absent from work during reference week due to illness, holiday, or strike or temporarily laid off without pay.
d. Looked for a paid job, including first paid job, during reference week.
e. Did no work to earn money in the last 12 months and did not look for paid job during reference week.
Source: Papua New Guinea Bureau of Statistics, 1971 Census.

Table SA3. Employment of Nationals in the Public Service, 1971–75

Occupational category	1971		1972		1973		1974		1975	
	Total	Percentage nationals	Total	Percentage nationals	Total	Percentage nationals	Total	Percentage nationals	Total	Percentage nationals
Professional	1,169	6.7	1,403	6.7	1,487	7.6	1,530	10.7	1,553	12.6
Subprofessional	5,354	34.1	5,427	35.7	5,704	44.7	5,798	52.2	6,563	50.8
Skilled workers	10,147	77.6	11,145	76.4	12,763	81.1	13,916	86.5	14,429	87.8
Semiskilled workmen	9,894	84.3	9,575	84.5	9,534	88.5	9,914	93.4	8,397	92.6
Unskilled workmen	15,190	99.5	16,570	99.6	17,668	99.8	18,968	100.0	21,142	100.0
Total	41,754	79.6	44,120	79.2	46,975[a]	83.2	50,126	86.6	52,084	86.6
Local	33,236		34,943		39,083		43,409		45,105	
Expatriate	8,518		9,177		7,892		6,717		6,979	

a. Data as given do not add to totals.
Source: Papua New Guinea Central Planning Office, Programmes and Performance, 1975–76, p. 333. Figures presumably refer to the end of the fiscal year, June 30.

Table SA4. Minimum Wages, 1960−75

	Rural		Major towns	
Year	Kina per week	Annual increase (percent)	Kina per week	Annual increase (percent)
1960	0.62[a]			
1961	0.75−0.88[b]	21−42	6.00	
1964	n.c.		n.c.	
1965	n.c.		6.50	8
1966	n.c.		n.c.	
1967	1.00−1.25[a,b]	33−42	n.c.	
1968	n.c.		n.c.	
1969	n.c.		n.c.	
1970	n.c.		7.00	8
1971	1.50−1.75[a,b]	33−42	8.00	14
1972	5.90[c]	237−293	11.50	44
1973	n.c.		13.80	20
1974	6.40[d]	8	20.00	45
1975	10.75[e]	68	25.80	29

n.c. No change.

a. In addition, the employer was obliged to provide food, clothing, and housing.

b. The wage depends on length of employment.

c. In 1972, the minimum all-cash wage was introduced, with deductions for housing (K0.87), food (K2.50), and clothing (K0.36).

d. Along with the increase, housing deductions were abolished and food and clothing deductions were raised to K3.00 and K0.43, respectively.

e. In 1974, a two-tiered rural minimum wage was introduced. The minimum wage for those employed in primary industries was raised to K8.90, while that for other rural employees was K10.75.

Source: Unpublished data from Papua New Guinea Department of Labor, Commerce and Industry.

Table SA5. Overseas Migration, Fiscal Years 1970−75
(Number of persons)

	Fiscal years					
Migration status	1970	1971	1972	1973	1974	1975
Arrivals	73,960	85,726	89,185	87,795	81,859	80,605
Long-term and permanent	38,622	41,184	44,558	43,698	40,104	41,507
Short-term	35,338	44,542	44,627	44,097	41,755	39,098
Holiday	14,366	16,651	19,940	21,660	20,797	18,390
Business	12,092	10,720	10,016	10,722	11,390	10,956
Other	8,880	17,171	14,671	11,715	9,568	9,752
Departures	69,482	82,702	94,471	93,010	91,021	82,495
Permanent	35,816	45,844	52,257	50,048	50,629	42,468
Short-term	33,666	36,858	42,213	42,962	40,392	40,027

Sources: Papua New Guinea National Investment and Development Authority, *Papua New Guinea: A Handbook for Industrialists* (December 1975), p. A210; Papua New Guinea Bureau of Statistics, *Abstract of Statistics* (September 1975) and other unpublished data.

Table SA6. Schools and Enrollments, by Type and Level of School, 1960, 1967, 1972, 1975

Level	Total				Government				Nongovernment			
	1960	1967	1972	1975	1960	1967	1972	1975	1960	1967	1972	1975
Number of schools[a]	1,263	1,849	1,703	1,952	305	526	648	881	958	1,323	1,055	1,017
Primary[b]	1,187	1,712	1,547	1,762	267	449	554	757	920	1,263	993	1,005
Secondary[c]	39	60	67	78	26	24	36	48	13	36	31	30
Technical/vocational	11	60	79	102	7	50	55	73	4	10	24	29
Teacher training	26	17	10	10	5	3	3	3	21	14	7	7
Students enrolled[d]	95,366	220,796	251,557	278,611	22,164	82,649	110,534	n.a.	73,202	138,147	141,023	n.a.
Primary[b]	92,029	204,509	220,193	238,318	20,428	72,289	90,755	n.a.	71,601	132,220	129,438	n.a.
Secondary[c]	1,947	11,864	23,523	29,762	1,076	7,092	13,808	18,972	871	4,772	9,715	10,790
Technical/vocational	576	3,208	5,998	8,131	407	2,831	5,071	n.a.	169	377	927	n.a.
Teacher training[e]	814	1,215	1,843	2,400	253	437	900	1,052	561	778	943	1,348

n.a. Not available.

a. From July 1, 1970, includes only schools within national education system.

b. Excludes fifty-three multiracial primary schools.

c. Includes data for intermediate schools before 1960–61, postprimary schools before 1963–64, and junior high schools before 1964–65; excludes four multiracial schools in 1975.

d. These statistics refer to the number of students enrolled on the school census date. They exclude correspondence and special class students and, from July 1, 1970, students enrolled at schools outside the national education system.

e. Includes enrollments for further training.

Source: Papua New Guinea Department of Education.

Table SA7. Teachers and Student-Teacher Ratios, by Level of School, 1960, 1967, 1972, 1975

| | Number of teachers[a] | | | | | | | | | | | | Average student-teacher ratios, all schools | | | |
| | All teachers | | | | Local | | | | Foreign | | | | | | | |
Level	1960	1967	1972	1975	1960	1967	1972	1975	1960	1967	1972	1975	1960	1967	1972	1975
Primary[b]	1,918	6,388	7,381	7,824	1,449	5,207	6,383	7,518	469	1,181	998	306	48.0	32.0	29.8	30.5
Secondary[c]	102	533	1,079	1,282	20	49	179	430	82	484	900	852	19.1	22.3	21.8	23.2
Technical/vocational	39	221	389	569	3	51	93	170	36	170	296	399	14.8	14.5	15.4	14.3
Teacher training	39	116	213	166	3	10	29	27	36	106	184	139	20.9	10.5	8.7	14.5
Total	2,098	7,258	9,062	9,841	1,495	5,317	6,684	8,145	623	1,941	2,378	1,696	45.5	30.4	27.8	28.3

a. From July 1, 1970, includes only teachers employed by the Papua New Guinea Teaching Service Commission; includes teachers in both multiracial and Papua New Guinea schools in 1975.

b. Excludes fifty-three multiracial primary schools.

c. Includes data for intermediate schools before 1960–61, postprimary schools before 1963–64, and junior high schools before 1964–65; excludes four multiracial schools in 1975.

Source: Papua New Guinea Department of Education.

Table SA8. Gross Domestic Expenditure and Gross National Product, Fiscal Years 1961–76
(Millions of kina)

Item	Fiscal years									
	1961	1968	1969	1970	1971	1972	1973	1974	1975	1976[a]
Consumption	205.9	410.2	453.9	510.2	570.2	614.5	655.9	716.1	849.0	864.6
Government	58.7	139.8	150.7	163.7	183.1	207.1	228.0	270.1	331.0	319.1
Private	147.2	270.4	303.2	346.5	387.1	407.4	427.9	446.0	518.0	545.5
Market	76.6	157.6	176.1	215.2	248.7	258.3	265.9	287.6	356.7	380.1
Nonmarket	70.6	112.8	127.1	131.3	138.4	149.1	161.9	158.4	161.3	165.4
Gross fixed capital formation	26.6	83.1	91.4	182.4	276.1	241.7	129.8	130.5	178.8	174.1
Market	25.4	81.9	91.3	180.1	276.0	240.3	126.6	129.4	177.4	172.6
Nonmarket	1.2	1.2	0.1	2.3	0.1	1.4	3.2	1.2	1.4	1.5
Increase in stocks	3.4	7.0	6.7	5.5	15.5	8.5	19.0	3.7	28.8	25.8
Exports (goods and services)	34.9	76.5	86.8	99.4	113.6	157.2	290.4	530.5	434.3	418.0
Less imports (goods and services)	61.0	163.0	184.2	267.5	354.2	383.8	308.2	328.7	486.2	481.9
Statistical discrepancy	0.7	−0.9	−1.2	1.2	0.5	7.3	1.8	−11.4	4.6	12.5
Gross domestic product	210.5	413.0	453.3	531.0	621.7	645.4	788.8	1,040.6	1,009.1	1,013.2
Market	138.7	298.9	326.1	397.4	483.1	494.9	623.6	881.1	846.5	846.2
Nonmarket	71.8	114.0	127.3	133.6	138.6	150.5	165.2	159.5	162.6	167.0
Less net factor payments	2.4	2.6	4.0	8.6	26.6	35.4	37.2	78.5	67.5	38.2
Gross national product	208.1	410.4	449.3	522.4	595.1	610.0	751.6	962.1	941.6	975.0

a. Preliminary.
Sources: Papua New Guinea Bureau of Statistics, *National Accounts Statistics, 1960/61–1973/74*; and Papua New Guinea Statistical Bulletin, *National Accounts Statistics, Bulletin no. 2, 1971/72–1975/76*, April 1977.

191

Table SA9. **Distribution of Gross Domestic Product at Current Market Prices, Fiscal Years 1961–76**
(Millions of kina)

Item	Fiscal years									
	1961	1968	1969	1970	1971	1972	1973	1974	1975	1976[a]
Wages and salaries	98.5	187.8	198.9	240.7	296.9	311.5	317.4	406.2	453.2	476.1
Profits	102.4	195.5	221.0	245.3	265.8	266.6	380.9	527.9	430.4	403.9
Market	30.6	81.5	93.7	111.6	127.2	116.1	215.8	368.4	267.8	237.0
Nonmarket	71.8	114.0	127.3	133.6	138.6	150.5	165.2	159.5	162.6	167.0
Depreciation	5.0	14.2	16.8	22.7	28.7	35.9	57.0	66.8	73.6	74.6
Indirect taxes	5.2	16.9	18.6	24.9	32.0	34.7	36.2	42.4	53.6	60.4
Less subsidies	0.6	1.5	1.9	2.6	1.8	3.2	2.7	2.8	1.8	1.9
Gross domestic product	210.5	413.0	453.3	531.0	621.7	645.4	788.8	1,040.6	1,009.1	1,013.2

a. Preliminary.
Sources: Papua New Guinea Bureau of Statistics, *National Accounts Statistics, 1960/61–1973/74;* and Papua New Guinea Statistical Bulletin, *National Accounts Statistics, Bulletin no. 2, 1971/72–1975/76,* April 1977.

Table SA10. National Income at Current Market Prices, Fiscal Years 1961–76
(Millions of kina)

Item	1961	1968	1969	1970	1971	1972	1973	1974	1975	1976[a]
					Fiscal years					
Wages and salaries	98.5	187.8	198.9	240.7	296.9	311.5	317.4	406.2	453.2	476.1
Profits	102.4	195.5	221.0	245.3	265.8	266.6	380.9	527.9	430.4	403.9
Market	30.6	81.5	93.7	111.6	127.2	116.1	215.8	368.4	267.8	237.0
Nonmarket	71.8	114.0	127.3	133.6	138.6	150.5	165.2	159.5	162.6	167.0
Domestic factor income	200.9	383.3	419.9	486.0	562.7	578.1	698.3	934.1	883.6	880.1
Net factor income from abroad	-2.4	-2.6	-4.0	-8.6	-26.6	-35.4	-37.2	-78.5	-67.5	-38.2
Indirect taxes	5.2	16.9	18.6	24.9	32.0	34.7	36.2	42.4	53.6	60.4
Less subsidies	0.6	1.5	1.9	2.6	1.8	3.2	2.7	2.8	1.8	1.9
National income at market prices	203.1	396.1	432.7	499.7	566.4	574.1	694.5	895.3	868.1	900.4
Other net current transfers from abroad	26.7	80.0	88.3	94.6	103.5	118.2	121.3	129.3	147.3	161.4
National disposable income	229.8	476.1	521.0	594.3	669.9	692.3	815.8	1,024.6	1,015.3	1,061.7

a. Preliminary.
Sources: Papua New Guinea Bureau of Statistics, *National Accounts Statistics, 1960/61–1973/74*; and Papua New Guinea Statistical Bulletin, *National Accounts Statistics, Bulletin no. 2, 1971/72–1975/76*, April 1977.

Table SA11. Capital Formation and Financing, Fiscal Years 1961–76
(Millions of kina)

Item	Fiscal years									
	1961	1968	1969	1970	1971	1972	1973	1974	1975	1976[a]
Gross fixed capital formation	26.6	83.1	91.4	182.4	276.1	241.7	129.8	130.5	178.8	174.1
Market	25.4	81.9	91.3	180.1	276.0	240.3	126.6	129.4	177.4	172.6
Nonmarket	1.2	1.2	0.1	2.3	0.1	1.4	3.2	1.2	1.4	1.5
Increase in stocks	3.4	7.0	6.7	5.5	15.5	8.5	19.0	3.7	28.8	25.8
Net lending abroad	11.2	25.5	23.3	−41.1	−127.2	−105.7	109.5	300.5	61.7	86.6
Gross accumulation	41.2	115.7	121.4	146.7	164.4	144.5	258.4	434.8	269.2	286.5
Domestic savings	23.9	65.9	67.0	84.1	99.7	77.8	160.0	308.6	166.4	197.1
Depreciation	5.0	14.2	16.8	22.7	28.7	35.9	57.0	66.8	73.6	74.6
Net capital transfers from abroad	13.0	34.7	36.3	41.1	36.5	38.1	43.2	47.9	33.8	27.3
Statistical discrepancy	−0.7	0.9	1.2	−1.2	−0.5	−7.3	−1.8	11.4	−4.6	−12.5
Finance of gross accumulation	41.2	115.7	121.4	146.7	164.4	144.5	258.4	434.8	269.2	286.5

a. Preliminary.
Sources: Papua New Guinea Bureau of Statistics, National Accounts Statistics, 1960/61–1973/74; and Papua New Guinea Statistical Bulletin, National Accounts Statistics, Bulletin no. 2, 1971/72–1975/76, April 1977.

Table SA12. Exchange Rates, Fiscal Years 1971–76

Date	Value of K1	
	U.S. dollar	Australian dollar
1971 (average)	1.12	1.00
1972 (average)	1.18	1.00
1973 (average)	1.29	1.00
1974 (average)	1.47	1.00
1975 (average)	1.37	1.00
1976 (average)	1.27	1.00
July 25, 1976	1.29	1.05
November 27, 1976	1.20	1.18
June 1977	1.25	1.13

Sources: International Monetary Fund, *International Financial Statistics;* and various issues of the Port Moresby *Post-Courier.*

Table SA13. Exports of Major Commodities, by Quantity and Value, Fiscal Years 1966 and 1970–75

Commodity	Unit[a]	Fiscal years						
		1966	1970	1971	1972	1973	1974	1975[b]
Tuna	K1,000	n.a.	n.a.	1,317	2,806	3,025	10,189	
	1,000 pounds	n.a.	n.a.	19,802	31,835	26,554	81,388	
Crayfish and prawn	K1,000	17	659	875	2,051	1,354	3,432	
	1,000 pounds	30	590	812	1,731	1,048	2,740	
Dessicated coconut	K1,000	...	1,211	1,203	1,065	1,198		
	1,000 cwt.	...	72	72	64	72		
Coffee beans	K1,000	8,787	20,182	20,572	20,454	23,395	28,847	33,513
	1,000 cwt.	216	508	471	555	613	654	735
Cocoa beans	K1,000	4,435	15,549	13,643	11,021	11,175	23,338	40,377
	1,000 cwt.	336	467	548	576	434	575	710
Tea	K1,000	11	645	1,094	1,500	2,048	2,602	3,828
	1,000 cwt.	219	13,570	23,020	35	54,958	79,300	88,680
Crocodile skins	K1,000	1,001	452	264	198	650		
Peanuts (green)	K1,000	527	550	518	616	305		
	Cwt.	30,659	32,969	33,793	34	16,819		
Copra	K1,000	14,298	13,340	14,207	9,392	8,083	23,672	29,287
	1,000 cwt.	1,757	1,685	1,811	1,723	1,571	1,471	1,922
Copra oil	K1,000	5,864	5,801	7,805	5,880	4,982	13,761	14,286
	Metric tons	21,900	21,327	26,896	26,081	27,277	26,807	26,565
Copra oil pellets	K1,000	725	607	893	588	950		
	1,000 cwt.	238	220	315	296	334		
Rubber	K1,000	2,576	2,798	2,297	1,995	1,998	3,563	2,575
	1,000 cwt.	107	125	125	117	111	123	109

Item	Unit							
Timber (logs)	K1,000	884	2,570	5,300	4,997	5,646	11,588	7,480
	1,000 sup. feet	26,545	65,619	140,726	144,594	139,679		
Timber (sawn)	K1,000	813	1,210	1,070	1,991	2,688	5,163	3,248
	1,000 sup. feet	5,153	7,173	6,173	1,211	15,629		
Plywood	K1,000	1,903	2,529	2,504	1,996	2,368	3,571	2,663
	1,000 square feet by 3/16 inch	17,784	26,719	26,400	21,981	26,243		
Copper ore and concentrates	K1,000	...	5	...	22,284	125,625	311,909	236,657
	Dry tons	...	...	...	96,612	495,088	717,140	627,580
Gold	K1,000	947	798	696	792	953		
	Fine ounces	n.a.	25,523	22,276	25,353	23,029		
Pyrethrum	K1,000	89	332	286	227	192		
	Cwt.	15	424	365	280	232		
Palm oil	K1,000	...	...	...	515	1,148	2,685	6,785
	Tons	...	...	...	3,409	7,939	8,734	18,441
Other	K1,000	n.a.	n.a.	2,903	2,672	2,765		
Total	K1,000	43,544	71,443	77,447	93,039	200,542		
Reexports	K1,000	6,286	22,117c	24,485	34,142	29,072		
Total, including reexports	K1,000	49,830	93,560	101,932	127,182	229,614		

n.a. Not available.

... Negligible.

a. K1,000 units are f.o.b.; cwt. = hundredweight; sup. feet = superficial feet (1 superficial foot true volume = 0.00236 cubic meters).

b. Preliminary; incomplete.

c. Includes floating oil rig valued at K8 million.

Sources: Papua New Guinea Bureau of Statistics, *Summary of Statistics, 1972/73;* and "Abstract of Statistics," March 1976.

Table SA14. Value of Imports by SITC Section, Fiscal Years 1973 and 1975, and by Country of Origin, Fiscal Year 1973
(Thousands of kina)

Commodity	Federal Republic of Germany	Nether-lands	Other E.E.C.[a]	United Kingdom	Rest of Europe and U.S.S.R.	Australia
Food and live animals	284	123	150	275	94	40,129
Beverages and tobacco	97	59	119	268	88	3,154
Crude materials, inedible	33	13	...	7	2	483
Minerals fuels, lubricants, and related materials	1	2	...	7	...	1,620
Animal and vegetable oils and fats	...	...	1	10	4	314
Chemicals	748	309	118	610	112	8,558
Manufactured goods	525	86	381	1,059	388	23,352
Machinery and transport equipment	1,141	808	778	4,900	1,095	27,503
Miscellaneous manufactured articles	475	167	100	790	419	11,643
Miscellaneous transactions and commodities	68	3,043	5	1,258	53	4,584
Total all sections	3,372	4,608	1,652	9,185	2,254	121,340
Outside packages	86	36	19	57	27	2,168
Total imports	3,459	4,644	1,672	9,242	2,281	123,507

Commodity	New Zealand	Other Oceanian	Hong Kong	Japan	Singapore	Other Asian
Food and live animals	850	3	315	4,306	16	917
Beverages and tobacco	1	11	1	5	1	71
Crude materials, inedible	14	...	10	31	18	42
Minerals fuels, lubricants, and related materials	4	...	...	3	7,406	2,012
Animal and vegetable oils and fats	1	...	11	5	7	3
Chemicals	118	...	182	921	50	158
Manufactured goods	420	8	1,102	7,385	269	2,215
Machinery and transport equipment	217	10	378	20,433	158	262
Miscellaneous manufactured articles	150	7	3,262	1,859	1,291	610
Miscellaneous transactions and commodities	54	12	25	88	24	10
Total all sections	1,829	50	5,285	35,037	9,241	6,301
Outside packages	15		104	610	56	55
Total imports	1,844	50	5,389	35,647	9,297	6,355

... Negligible.
a. Includes Belgium, Luxembourg, and Italy.

Table SA14. (continued)

(Thousands of kina)

Commodity	U.S.A.	Canada	All other[b]	1973 Total	1975 Total[c]
Food and live animals	191	22	59	47,734	71,448
Beverages and tobacco	266	3	882	5,025	5,672
Crude materials, inedible	55	1	39	749	1,247
Minerals fuels, lubricants, and related materials	48	...	...	11,102	38,306
Animal and vegetable oils and fats	...	...	...	357	805
Chemicals	546	2	2	12,435	22,951
Manufactured goods	1,947	17	32	39,214	61,663
Machinery and transport equipment	15,210	570	71	73,533	112,577
Miscellaneous manufactured articles	899	97	21	21,791	29,892
Miscellaneous transactions and commodities	1,744	20	2,567	13,556	9,279
Total all sections	20,933	732	3,674	225,495	353,839
Outside packages	40	2	45	3,320	3,975
Total imports	20,973	734	3,719	228,815	357,814

... Negligible.

b. Includes Antarctica, Africa, other America, and unknown.

c. Preliminary data; detail by country not available.

Sources: 1973, Papua New Guinea National Investment and Development Authority; 1975, Papua New Guinea Statistical Bulletin, *International Trade,* August 1976.

Table SA15. Value of Major Domestic Export Commodities, by Major Countries of Destination, Fiscal Year 1973
(Thousands of kina)

Commodity	Belgium and Luxembourg	France	Federal Republic of Germany	Netherlands	Italy	United Kingdom	Rest of Europe and U.S.S.R.	Australia
Tuna	...	...	...	...	...	...	...	...
Prawns	...	...	...	...	...	...	...	790
Desiccated coconut	...	...	...	...	...	44	...	1,142
Coffee beans	846	110	2,542	156	5	1,392	1,757	5,323
Cocoa beans	553	1,370	1,520	333	...	890	9	2,119
Tea	...	...	61	209	...	823	...	732
Peanuts (green)	...	...	...	...	...	...	...	305
Copra	...	...	...	...	...	3,447	...	1,578
Copra oil	...	...	...	...	...	3,569	...	1,261
Copra oil pellets	...	...	700	250	...	...	...	...
Rubber	...	...	...	...	...	...	...	1,998
Timber, logs	...	...	...	4	...	...	...	69
Timber, sawn conifer	2	...	...	...	...	...	...	974
Timber, sawn nonconifer	9	1	7	25	...	3	...	1,384
Plywood	...	...	...	...	...	...	...	2,335
Copper concentrate	...	...	48,405	...	...	...	11,660	...
Pyrethrum extract	...	...	...	77	...	192	...	...
Palm oil	...	...	...	...	...	683	...	...
Gold	...	...	...	...	...	...	...	953
Crocodile skins	...	...	...	...	...	...	...	31
Other	2	4	76	47	46	101	23	1,485
Total domestic exports	1,411	1,485	53,312	1,103	51	11,145	13,449	22,480
Reexports	2	110	123	108	7	220	72	23,579
Total exports	1,413	1,595	53,435	1,211	58	11,365	13,521	46,059

... Negligible.
Source: Papua New Guinea National Investment and Development Authority, *PNG: A Handbook for Industrialists*, p. A2.7.

Table SA15. (continued)

Commodity	New Zealand	Other Oceanian	Japan	Other Asian	U.S.A.	Canada	All other[a]	Total
Tuna	...	313	2,570	...	142	...	...	3,025
Prawns	...	...	517	...	...	...	...	1,307
Desiccated coconut	...	...	...	...	...	6	...	1,192
Coffee beans	503	...	1,689	1,984	7,046	4	38	23,395
Cocoa beans	29	...	9	66	3,665	387	225	11,175
Tea	39	...	18	...	104	61	...	2,048
Peanuts (green)	...	...	...	...	...	...	...	305
Copra	...	...	3,058	...	...	...	...	8,023
Copra oil	...	...	152	...	...	...	...	4,982
Copra oil pellets	...	...	...	...	...	...	...	950
Rubber	1	...	...	...	...	...	...	1,998
Timber, logs	2	10	5,573	...	...	...	...	5,646
Timber, sawn conifer	1	93	26	...	...	...	...	1,013
Timber, sawn nonconifer	...	...	144	...	6	...	...	1,675
Plywood	10	22	...	...	...	...	...	2,368
Copper concentrate	...	...	64,516	...	...	...	1,043	125,625
Pyrethrum extract	...	...	...	...	...	...	...	192
Palm oil	...	...	112	...	...	...	274	1,148
Gold	...	...	...	...	...	...	...	953
Crocodile skins	...	...	47	572	...	...	...	660
Other	6	214	527	75	175	19	12	2,813
Total domestic exports	591	652	78,958	2,697	11,138	478	1,592	200,542
Reexports	340	1,273	2,482	408	317	9	22	29,072
Total exports	931	1,925	81,440	3,105	11,455	487	1,614	229,614

... Negligible.
a. Includes Antarctica, Africa, other America, and unknown.
Source: Papua New Guinea National Investment and Development Authority, PNG: A Handbook for Industrialists, p. A2.7.

Table SA16. Inflow of Private Overseas Investment, by Sector, Fiscal Years 1969–75
(Millions of Australian dollars)

Industry	Fiscal years						
	1969	1970	1971	1972	1973	1974	1975
Agriculture, hunting, forestry, and fishing	4,607	4,507	5,286	2,892	3,708	221	3,472
Agriculture and hunting	2,911	3,354	1,393	2,302	2,543	−1,885	1,816
Forestry and logging	38	774	2,756	−1,282	1,078	975	615
Fishing	1,658	379	1,137	1,872	87	1,131	1,041
Mining and quarrying	22,061	73,895	161,356	150,005	30,018	75,920	−47,491
Crude petroleum and natural gas production	11,174	5,728	2,954	7,902	5,146	8,977	736
Other mining and quarrying	10,887	68,167	158,402	143,003	24,872	66,943	−48,227
Manufacturing	2,722	6,427	3,102	4,180	10,090	5,320	4,055
Construction	960	1,978	2,593	4,148	−68	264	−901
Wholesale and retail trade restaurants, and hotels	3,843	7,554	12,059	9,304	3,541	−3,843	13,780
Wholesale trade	2,077	4,032	9,814	10,342	4,821	−1,020	6,983
Retail trade	1,451	3,379	1,904	−2,322	−2,700	−2,768	3,195
Restaurants and hotels[a]	315	143	341	1,284	1,420	−55	3,602
Transport, storage, and communication	−177	2,589	3,989	1,114	−3,416	−7,024	3,725
Financing, insurance, real estate, and business services	3,381	1,301	4,254	−2,714	−14,619	25,460	2,778
Total	37,397	98,251	192,639	169,829	29,254	96,318	−20,582

a. Includes some personal services from SIC major division 9 which could not be published separately.
Source: Papua New Guinea Bureau of Statistics, Papua New Guinea Statistical Bulletin, *Private Overseas Investment 1968/69 to 1974/75,* April 1977.

Table SA17. **Central Planning Office Preliminary Projections of Export Growth, with and without Ok Tedi and Vanimo Projects, Fiscal Years 1976–85**
(Millions of 1976 kina)

Exports	Fiscal years									
	1976	1977	1978	1979	1980	1981	1982	1983	1984	1985
Projection A										
Bougainville, Ok Tedi, and Vanimo	254.4	254.4	254.8	256.6	287.7	289.7	290.0	456.3	457.5	430.4
Other exports	220.9	241.8	256.4	288.1	302.5	327.6	342.4	370.8	381.7	390.3
Endogenous[a]	15.8	12.6	9.6	9.2	8.4	7.9	7.2	6.7	6.4	6.4
Total	491.1	508.8	520.8	553.9	598.6	625.2	639.6	833.8	845.6	827.1
Projection B										
Bougainville only	254.4	254.4	254.8	256.6	257.3	250.9	245.1	242.6	242.6	242.6
Other exports	220.9	241.8	256.4	288.6	302.5	327.6	342.4	370.8	381.7	390.3
Endogenous[a]	15.8	12.6	9.3	8.4	7.1	6.6	6.4	6.3	6.1	6.1
Total	491.1	508.8	520.5	553.6	566.9	585.1	593.9	619.7	630.4	639.0

Note: Projections made February 1976. Because the projections are in constant prices, they differ markedly from those made by the World Bank; there are also some different assumptions on quantitative growth, but these are relatively minor.

a. Endogenous exports are generated by the model used to make the projections.

Source: Papua New Guinea Central Planning Office.

**Table SA18. Financial Operations of the Central Government,
Fiscal Years 1971–76**
(Millions of kina)

	Fiscal years					
Item	*1971*	*1972*	*1973*	*1974*	*1975*	*1976 budget*
Domestic revenue	74.2	85.1	93.3	136.7	179.7	243.5
Tax	61.8	71.6	74.5	95.1	134.8	202.8
Nontax	12.4	13.5	18.8	41.6	44.9	40.7
Current expenditure[a]	162.5	193.7	213.9	277.0	341.0	377.2
Current deficit	88.3	108.6	120.6	140.3	161.3	133.7
Foreign grants	101.8	108.2	121.8	152.3	137.6	159.9
Capital expenditure	42.2	40.1	36.5	30.5	33.1	45.5
Overall deficit	28.7	40.5	35.3	18.5	56.8	19.3
Financing (net)	28.7	40.5	35.3	18.5	56.8	19.3
External sources (net)	28.2	41.2	35.0	32.1	30.9	18.4
Advances (Australian government)	−3.0	...	1.4	−1.4	...	...
Borrowing	32.3	43.1	33.7	42.5	34.0	18.8
Australian government	18.8	11.7	3.0	2.2	−2.5	−2.2
International organizations	2.6	8.1	7.9	9.1	14.4	13.3
Other	10.9	23.3	22.8	31.2	22.1	7.7
Sinking fund balances[b]	−1.1	−1.9	−0.1	−9.0	−3.1	−0.4
Domestic sources (net)	0.5	−0.7	0.3	−13.6	25.9	0.9
Cash	0.5	−0.8	0.4	−14.4	8.6	6.2
Bank of Papua New Guinea	...	...	...	...	7.0	1.3
Advances	...	...	...	...	7.0	1.0
Special borrowing[c]	...	...	...	...	...	5.0
Claims[d]	...	...	...	...	...	−4.7
Mineral Resources Stabilization Fund	...	...	...	...	...	−20.5
Domestic borrowing[e]	...	...	...	...	10.3	13.9
Other	...	0.1	−0.1	0.8	...	...

... Zero.
a. Includes loan repayments, salaries, and allowances paid by Australian government.
b. Include some portion of Papua New Guinea securities.
c. To finance contributions to international agencies.
d. Counterpart of International Monetary Fund contribution.
e. Until 1974, included in external borrowing.
Sources: Papua New Guinea Department of Finance, *Estimates of Revenue and Expenditure* (various issues); and data provided by the Department of Finance.

Table SA19. Domestic Revenue of the Central Government, by Source,
Fiscal Years 1971–76
(Millions of kina)

Source	1971	1972	1973	1974	1975	1976 budget
			Fiscal years			
Tax revenue	61.8	71.6	74.5	95.1	134.8	202.8
Taxes on income and profits	29.4	36.1	38.3	52.7	81.0	135.0
Companies	11.0	15.6	14.1	11.4	28.5	75.5
Individuals	18.4	20.5	22.2	30.1	42.4	55.0
Dividend withholding	...	...	2.0	11.2	10.1	4.5
Taxes on goods and services	9.0	10.5	12.9	18.7	22.0	29.5
Excise duties	8.0	9.0	11.4	17.1	20.3	27.5
Motor vehicle registration taxes[a]	0.8	1.2	1.2	1.3	1.4	1.7
Business and other licenses	0.2	0.3	0.3	0.3	0.3	0.3
Taxes on international trade and transactions	22.7	24.0	22.5	23.0	31.0	37.2
Import duties	22.7	24.0	22.5	22.9	29.7	36.0
Export taxes	...	...	...	...	1.1	1.0
Airport departure tax	...	...	...	0.1	0.2	0.2
Stamp duties	0.7	1.0	0.8	0.7	0.8	1.1
Nontax revenue	12.4	13.5	18.8	41.6	44.9	40.7
Sales of goods and services	3.3	3.6	3.7	3.9	4.4	5.1
Mining royalties	...	...	1.7	3.4	3.1	2.0
Income from investments	1.9	2.2	4.3	18.4	16.9	10.6
Rent	4.0	4.4	4.8	5.8	5.9	5.5
Fees and fines	0.7	0.7	0.9	1.0	1.5	1.5
Other	2.5	2.6	3.4	9.1	13.1	16.0
Total revenue	74.2	85.1	93.3	136.7	179.7	243.5

... Zero.
a. Includes drivers' license fees.
Sources: Papua New Guinea Department of Finance, *Estimates of Revenue and Expenditure*
(various issues); and data provided by the Department of Finance.

Table SA20. Outstanding Public Debt, by Creditor, Fiscal Years 1971—75
(Millions of kina)

Creditor	Fiscal years				
	1971	1972	1973	1974	1975
External debt	56.3	96.7	127.7	165.6	211.4
Australia	52.3	84.6	94.1	102.3	103.7
Government[a]	17.7	29.4	32.4	38.6	36.1
Private institutions	34.6	55.2	61.7	63.7	67.6
International agencies	4.0	12.1	19.8	26.7	44.8
World Bank	1.4	5.5	12.2	16.7	29.0
International Development Association	2.6	6.6	7.6	9.0	14.5
Asian Development Bank	...	...	...	1.0	1.3
Germany	...	...	13.8	13.3	16.2
Switzerland	...	...	...	11.3	15.0
Japan	...	...	...	12.0	12.8
Eurobond market	...	...	...	...	18.9
Internal debt	36.6	39.4	42.0	48.0	58.4
Marketing boards	9.3	8.3	4.1	5.0	6.2
Superannuation funds	3.0	3.1	3.0	3.2	3.6
Banks[b]	18.8	21.5	25.6	30.1	37.9
Statutory authorities	5.4	6.2	8.9	9.3	10.3
Other	0.1	0.3	0.4	0.4	0.4
Total debt	92.9	136.1	169.7	213.6	269.8

... Zero.
a. Excludes advances of K1.4 million in fiscal 1973 repaid in fiscal 1974.
b. Excludes advances of K7.0 million from Bank of Papua New Guinea in fiscal 1975.
Source: Papua New Guinea Department of Finance.

Table SA21. Monetary Survey, 1971–76
(Millions of kina)

Item	1971 June	1971 December	1972 June	1972 December	1973 June	1973 December	1974 June	1974 December	1975 June	1975 December	1976 June	1976 September
Net foreign assets	-40.3	-44.4	-65.6	-40.7	-40.2	20.7	113.5	99.0	80.6	70.2	50.7	106.8
Bank of Papua New Guinea	—	—	—	—	—	17.5	22.2	23.2	36.0	139.7	119.2[a]	173.1[a]
Commercial banks	-40.3	-44.4	-65.6	-40.7	-40.2	3.2	91.4	75.8	44.6	-69.6	-68.5	-66.3
Net domestic credit	129.0	138.4	154.4	133.2	137.5	133.1	125.5	161.2	174.5	134.1	195.3	206.0
To government	16.8	17.9	19.1	19.6	19.3	-4.0	-12.4	11.1	8.8	-31.9	18.5	23.8
To private sector[b]	112.2	120.6	135.3	113.6	118.3	137.1	137.9	150.1	165.6	166.0	181.8	182.1
Excluding Eurodollar loans[c]	52.1	60.4	78.9	60.8	65.5	91.9	92.6	98.9	115.9	112.5	127.4	130.4
Papua New Guinea currency	...	...	...	...	...	...	...	...	21.6[d]	40.6[d]	45.7	51.0
Demand deposits	33.7	36.7	33.6	36.8	37.3	42.6	59.0	61.9	59.5	62.6	68.7	79.8
Quasi-money[e]	56.0	58.0	56.2	56.5	60.5	109.6	158.6	179.2	159.1	96.1	109.8	166.9
Other items (net)	-1.0	-0.7	-1.0	-0.7	-0.5	1.6	21.4	19.1	14.9	5.0	21.8	15.1
Memorandum item												
Australian currency in circulation	39.5	40.6	44.3	43.3	51.5	57.8	66.4	76.7	62.1[d]	51.9[d]	...	...

... Zero; that is, the dual currency period ended December 31, 1975.

Notes: Data exclude the operations of the Reserve Bank of Australia, which had an office in Port Moresby until November 1, 1973, handling the issue of Australian currency.

a. Excludes from the Bank of Papua New Guinea's foreign liabilities the reserve position in the International Monetary Fund, which is treated in this table as a liability of the Bank of Papua New Guinea to the government.

b. Includes claims of public enterprises and small amounts of commercial bank advances to central and local governments.

c. The amount excluded is the domestic counterpart of a US$67.4 million Eurodollar obligation raised for financing Bougainville Copper Ltd., which has been valued at the prevailing market rates between the kina and the U.S. dollar at the dates indicated.

d. This represents currency on issue during the dual currency period, when currency held by the commercial banks and the Bank of Papua New Guinea was not separated between Australian and Papua New Guinea currency.

e. Demand deposits bearing interest and term deposits.

Sources: Bank of Papua New Guinea and Papua New Guinea authorities.

207

Table SA22. Movement of Selected Monetary Aggregates, Fiscal Years 1972–76
(Millions of kina)

	Fiscal years				
Item	1972	1973	1974	1975	1976
Net foreign assets of banking system	−25.3	25.4	153.7	−32.9	−29.9
Net domestic credit[a]	29.1	−13.2	−4.6	44.5	21.2
To government	2.3	0.2	−31.7	21.2	9.7
To private sector excluding Eurodollar loan	26.8	−13.4	27.1	23.3	11.5
Demand deposits plus quasi-money	0.1	8.0	119.8	1.0	−40.1
Demand deposits	−0.1	3.7	21.7	0.5	9.2
Quasi-money	0.2	4.3	98.1	0.5	−49.3
Memorandum item					
Australian currency in circulation	4.8	7.2	14.9	−4.3	−10.2[b]

a. Excluding valuation changes associated with the Eurodollar loan.

b. This represents the fall in Australian currency in circulation as of December 31, 1975, when the dual currency period ended. The amount of A$51.9 million of Australian currency not presented for exchange into kina probably reflects some overestimation of currency in circulation, some hoarding, and some capital flight.

Sources: Data provided by the Bank of Papua New Guinea and Papua New Guinea authorities.

Table SA23. Loan Approvals by the Papua New Guinea Development Bank, by Type of Borrower, Fiscal Years 1970–76 and Nine-Year Total

| | Fiscal years | | | | | | | |
| | 1970 | | 1971 | | 1972 | | 1973 | |
Borrower	Amount	Percent	Amount	Percent	Amount	Percent	Amount	Percent
Number of loans								
Papua New Guineans	1,176.0	83.2	1,889.0	94.5	2,203.0	92.0	1,392.0	92.8
General	823.0	58.2	1,684.0	84.2	1,866.0	77.9	n.a.	n.a.
Land settlement schemes	353.0	25.0	205.0	10.3	337.0	14.1	n.a.	n.a.
Expatriates	201.0	14.2	100.0	5.0	181.0	7.5	92.0	6.1
Joint enterprises	37.0	2.6	10.0	0.5	11.0	0.5	15.0	1.0
Total approved	1,414.0	100.0	1,999.0	100.0	2,395.0	100.0	1,499.0	100.0
Value of loans (thousands of kina)								
Papua New Guineans	1,673.8	34.2	2,290.0	55.2	3,884.2	48.4	2,920.6	50.0
General	1,013.7	20.7	1,906.5	45.9	3,254.0	40.5	n.a.	n.a.
Land settlement schemes	660.1	13.5	383.5	9.2	630.2	7.8	n.a.	n.a.
Expatriates	2,581.5	52.7	1,723.3	41.5	3,664.4	45.6	1,431.1	24.7
Joint enterprises	643.0	13.1	138.2	3.3	480.5	6.0	1,429.5	24.7
Total approved	4,898.3	100.0	4,151.5	100.0	8,029.1	100.0	5,781.2	100.0
Average loan value (kina)								
Papua New Guineans	1,423.0		1,212.0		1,763.0		2,098.0	
General	1,232.0		1,132.0		1,744.0		n.a.	
Land settlement schemes	1,870.0		1,871.0		1,870.0		n.a.	
Expatriates	12,843.0		17,233.0		20,245.0		15,555.0	
Joint enterprises	17,378.0		13,820.0		43,682.0		95,300.0	

n.a. Not available.
Source: Papua New Guinea Development Bank, Annual Report and Financial Statements, 1975–76.

(Table continues on following page.)

Table SA23. (continued)

| | Fiscal years | | | | | | Totals, 1968–76 | |
| Borrower | 1974 | | 1975 | | 1976 | | | |
	Amount	Percent	Amount	Percent	Amount	Percent	Amount	Percent
Number of loans								
Papua New Guineans	1,529.0	92.4	2,182.0	90.8	1,751.0	94.5	13,074.0	90.6
General	1,526.0	92.3	n.a.	n.a.	n.a.	n.a.	n.a.	n.a.
Land settlement schemes	3.0	0.2	n.a.	n.a.	n.a.	n.a.	n.a.	n.a.
Expatriates	108.0	6.5	187.0	7.8	78.0	4.2	1,153.0	8.0
Joint enterprises	17.0	1.0	34.0	1.4	27.0	1.5	195.0	1.3
Total approved	1,654.0	100.0	2,403.0	100.0	1,853.0	100.0	14,422.0	100.0
Value of loans (thousands of kina)								
Papua New Guineans	3,164.5	37.0	5,818.4	57.1	7,206.3	66.1	28,741.1	48.0
General	3,161.6	37.0	n.a.	n.a.	n.a.	n.a.	n.a.	n.a.
Land settlement schemes	2.9	0.03	n.a.	n.a.	n.a.	n.a.	n.a.	n.a.
Expatriates	2,531.3	29.6	3,518.6	34.5	1,912.0	17.5	21,361.7	35.7
Joint enterprises	2,851.4	33.4	853.0	8.4	1,779.7	16.3	9,747.0	16.3
Total approved	8,547.2	100.0	10,190.0	100.0	10,898.0	100.0	59,849.8	100.0
Average loan value (kina)								
Papua New Guineans	2,070.0		2,666.0		4,115.0		2,198.0	
General	2,072.0		n.a.		n.a.		n.a.	
Land settlement schemes	967.0		n.a.		n.a.		n.a.	
Expatriates	23,437.0		18,816.0		24,513.0		18,527.0	
Joint enterprises	167,729.0		25,088.0		65,915.0		49,985.0	

n.a. Not available.
Source: Papua New Guinea Development Bank, *Annual Report and Financial Statements, 1975–76.*

Table SA24. Number and Value of Loan Approvals by the Papua New Guinea
Development Bank, by Industry of Borrower, Fiscal Years 1971–76 and Nine-
Year Total

	Fiscal years			
	1971		1972	
Industry	Number	Thousands of kina	Number	Thousands of kina
Amounts				
Commercial	554.0	1,464.9	592.0	2,803.6
Transport	349.0	627.6	350.0	962.4
Shipping and boats	32.0	89.8	26.0	138.4
Retail trade	115.0	305.8	133.0	267.3
Wholesale trade	18.0	8.4	24.0	292.3
Hotels and property development	8.0	263.0	13.0	544.0
Service industries and garages	17.0	79.1	20.0	332.2
Finance and professions	...	...	10.0	33.5
Other commercial	15.0	91.2	16.0	233.5
Industrial	47.0	617.6	108.0	2,070.3
Building and construction	28.0	319.4	54.0	544.8
Ship and boat building	3.0	6.1	...	...
Light and heavy engineering	2.0	5.0	8.0	10.9
Timber milling	4.0	10.1	14.0	1,021.1
Mining and quarrying	1.0	0.2	9.0	61.8
Printing and handicrafts	4.0	4.9	3.0	0.4
Bakeries	2.0	180.3	3.0	23.1
Other industrial	3.0	91.6	17.0	408.2
Agricultural	1,398.0	2,069.0	1,695.0	3,155.2
Cattle	394.0	622.6	522.0	1,391.0
Pigs and poultry	90.0	104.4	156.0	27.6
Fishing	69.0	93.9	179.0	88.8
Processing	183.0	106.9	117.0	50.4
Oil palm	304.0	473.3	339.0	985.3
Cocoa	80.0	88.6	26.0	36.5
Rubber	27.0	14.4	53.0	35.5
Copra	221.0	157.8	185.0	158.7
Coffee	20.0	24.3	19.0	72.9
Other crops	43.0	101.6	53.0	192.9
Other agricultural	12.0	281.2	16.0	115.6
Composition of loans (percent)				
Commercial	27.7	35.3	24.7	34.9
Industrial	2.3	14.9	4.5	25.8
Rural	69.9	49.8	70.8	39.3

... Zero.

Source: Papua New Guinea Development Bank, *Annual Report and Financial Statements,*
1975–76.

(*Table continues on following page.*)

Table SA24. (continued)

Industry	Fiscal years			
	1973		1974	
	Number	Thousands of kina	Number	Thousands of kina
Amounts				
Commercial	404.0	1,689.9	548.0	3,315.9
Transport	223.0	767.5	331.0	1,266.4
Shipping and boats	24.0	132.1	30.0	159.5
Retail trade	120.0	239.8	93.0	458.2
Wholesale trade	7.0	8.1	35.0	15.0
Hotels and property development	11.0	409.5	8.0	813.2
Service industries and garages	9.0	20.9	16.0	185.6
Finance and professions	4.0	101.7	11.0	6.3
Other commercial	6.0	10.3	24.0	411.7
Industrial	107.0	930.8	110.0	3,370.1
Building and construction	74.0	534.8	56.0	548.3
Ship and boat building	. . .	. . .	3.0	74.7
Light and heavy engineering	3.0	61.0	5.0	39.9
Timber milling	8.0	163.0	19.0	2,391.8
Mining and quarrying	3.0	3.2	. . .	. . .
Printing and handicrafts	5.0	16.7	3.0	21.0
Bakeries	1.0	60.0	1.0	0.7
Other industrial	13.0	92.1	23.0	293.7
Agricultural	988.0	3,160.5	996.0	1,861.2
Cattle	468.0	1,333.1	512.0	1,215.5
Pigs and poultry	113.0	51.9	121.0	106.1
Fishing	144.0	47.7	137.0	43.9
Processing	55.0	1,171.8	109.0	117.9
Oil palm	5.0	244.9	9.0	100.2
Cocoa	20.0	13.0	14.0	9.4
Rubber	48.0	19.8	6.0	2.3
Copra	64.0	32.8	50.0	26.0
Coffee	7.0	43.9	8.0	70.0
Other crops	46.0	103.8	18.0	22.0
Other agricultural	18.0	97.8	12.0	147.9
Composition of loans (percent)				
Commercial		26.9	29.2	33.1	38.8
Industrial		7.1	16.1	6.6	39.4
Rural		65.9	54.7	60.2	21.8

. . . Zero.

Source: Papua New Guinea Development Bank, *Annual Report and Financial Statements,* 1975–76.

Table SA24. (continued)

| | Fiscal years | | | |
| | 1975 | | 1976 | |
Industry	Number	Thousands of kina	Number	Thousands of kina
Amounts				
Commercial	901.0	4,630.4	861.0	6,294.6
Transport	661.0	3,493.4	616.0	3,483.5
Shipping and boats	33.0	74.2	35.0	122.5
Retail trade	139.0	449.2	132.0	1,020.6
Wholesale trade	14.0	15.4	30.0	224.0
Hotels and property development	8.0	204.3	16.0	315.2
Service industries and garages	9.0	47.2	8.0	125.8
Finance and professions	10.0	7.8	3.0	28.7
Other commercial	27.0	338.9	21.0	947.3
Industrial	224.0	3,580.6	69.0	1,772.1
Building and construction	62.0	727.0	17.0	236.1
Ship and boat building	1.0	4.6	4.0	16.2
Light and heavy engineering	8.0	68.9	10.0	484.0
Timber milling	10.0	294.9	14.0	433.2
Mining and quarrying	4.0	14.0	2.0	8.2
Printing and handicrafts	10.0	160.8	5.0	107.5
Bakeries	4.0	2.8	1.0	0.1
Other industrial	125.0	2,307.6	16.0	486.8
Agricultural	1,278.0	1,979.9	923.0	2,831.3
Cattle	431.0	1,205.0	312.0	875.9
Pigs and poultry	115.0	134.6	94.0	446.0
Fishing	237.0	93.4	98.0	35.5
Processing	137.0	95.9	67.0	72.0
Oil palm	101.0	232.4	112.0	216.4
Cocoa	16.0	7.4	14.0	16.1
Rubber	141.0	53.8	119.0	47.1
Copra	28.0	10.3	28.0	14.3
Coffee	3.0	13.7	8.0	374.8
Other crops	28.0	13.7	30.0	111.5
Other agricultural	41.0	119.6	41.0	621.7
Composition of loans (percent)				
Commercial	37.5	45.4	46.5	57.8
Industrial	9.3	35.1	3.7	16.3
Rural	53.2	19.4	49.8	26.0

Source: Papua New Guinea Development Bank, *Annual Report and Financial Statements,*
1975–76.

(Table continues on following page.)

Table SA24. (continued)

| | Fiscal years | |
| | Total, 1968–76 | |
Industry	Number	Thousands of kina
Amounts		
Commercial	4,473.0	25,785.6
Transport	3,006.0	13,546.8
Shipping and boats	180.0	716.5
Retail trade	814.0	3,333.8
Wholesale trade	128.0	563.3
Hotels and property development	93.0	4,308.6
Service industries and garages	87.0	934.9
Finance and professions	38.0	178.0
Other commercial	127.0	2,203.7
Industrial	771.0	13,907.7
Building and construction	338.0	3,366.6
Ship and boat building	15.0	179.5
Light and heavy engineering	51.0	1,038.5
Timber milling	90.0	4,850.1
Mining and quarrying	19.0	87.4
Printing and handicrafts	30.0	311.3
Bakeries	12.0	267.0
Other industrial	216.0	3,807.3
Agricultural	9,178.0	20,156.5
Cattle	2,892.0	8,022.3
Pigs and poultry	750.0	1,178.4
Fishing	922.0	524.0
Processing	720.0	1,727.1
Oil palm	1,800.0	3,995.0
Cocoa	305.0	460.0
Rubber	428.0	258.5
Copra	866.0	722.8
Coffee	78.0	725.9
Other crops	245.0	1,066.9
Other agricultural	172.0	1,475.5
Composition of loans (percent)		
Commercial	31.0	43.1
Industrial	5.3	23.2
Rural	63.6	33.7

Source: Papua New Guinea Development Bank, *Annual Report and Financial Statements, 1975–76.*

Table SA25. Expenditure on Rural Improvement Program, by Provinces, Fiscal Year 1975

Province	Number of projects	Grants (thousands of kina)			Local contribution (thousands of kina)			Ratios (percent)			Population, 1973 (thousands)	Per capita grant (kina)	
		Projects	Untied	Total	Cash	Kind	Total	Local cash to projects grant	Total local to projects grant	Total local to total grant		Projects	Total
Western	112	389.9	56.5	446.4	79.2	146.5	225.7	0.20	0.58	0.51	68.9	5.74	6.57
Gulf	43	270.5	33.5	305.2	9.5	71.9	81.4	0.04	0.30	0.27	72.1	3.75	4.22
Central	54	195.0	24.5	219.5	43.7	35.3	79.0	0.22	0.41	0.36	196.3	0.99	1.12
Milne Bay	73	253.7	25.5	279.2	74.3	106.7	181.0	0.29	0.71	0.65	114.6	2.21	2.44
Northern	64	236.7	21.5	258.2	23.0	98.1	121.2	0.10	0.51	0.47	63.0	3.75	4.10
Southern Highlands	98	331.0	24.0	355.0	57.0	18.2	75.2	0.17	0.23	0.21	207.4	1.60	1.71
Morobe	133	446.9	33.5	480.4	77.1	295.6	372.7	0.17	0.83	0.78	253.7	1.76	1.89
Madang	24	336.2	27.0	363.2	77.0	121.3	208.3	0.23	0.80	0.72	189.8	1.38	1.52
East Sepik	34	262.9	28.0	290.9	48.4	182.6	231.0	0.18	0.88	0.79	206.9	1.27	1.41
West Sepik	54	240.2	36.5	376.7	54.8	262.4	317.2	0.16	0.93	0.84	106.2	3.20	3.55
Eastern Highlands	60	232.4	24.5	256.9	139.4	13.8	153.2	0.60	0.66	0.60	239.8	0.97	1.07
Chimbu	65	204.1	22.0	226.1	103.1	75.7	178.8	0.51	0.88	0.79	194.1	1.05	1.16
Western Highlands	79	259.2	21.5	280.7	126.2	75.8	202.0	0.49	0.78	0.72	203.1	1.28	1.38
Manus	9	112.5	33.0	145.5	25.0	7.2	32.2	0.22	0.29	0.22	22.4	5.02	6.50
New Ireland	87	185.9	20.0	205.9	73.8	106.4	180.2	0.40	0.97	0.88	56.5	3.35	3.71
East New Britain	40	217.8	22.0	239.8	41.5	47.6	89.1	0.19	0.41	0.37	102.8	2.12	2.33
West New Britain	60	169.8	19.0	188.8	32.0	75.8	107.8	0.19	0.64	0.57	63.3	2.68	2.98
Enga	58	277.7	27.5	305.2	67.5	97.6	165.1	0.24	0.59	0.54	147.7	1.88	2.07
Total	1,147	4,622.4	500.0	5,122.4	1,152.5	1,838.5	2,991.0	0.25	0.65	0.58	2,508.6	1.84	2.04

Note: Figures are rounded.
Source: Area Authority, Goroka.

Table SA26. Characteristics of Foreign Enterprises, Fiscal Year 1974

Characteristic	Value of turnover (thousands of kina)	Number of persons employed	Number of enterprises
Major industries			
Agriculture, hunting, forestry, and fishing	66	30,000	
Mining and quarrying	5	1,000	
Manufacturing	148	13,000	
Electricity, gas, and water	...	...	
Construction	48	7,000	
Wholesale and retail trade, restaurants, and hotels	454	24,000	
Transport, storage, and communication	46	5,000	
Financing, insurance, real estate, and business services	76	4,000	
Community, social, and personal services	17	4,000	
Foreign enterprises			
Number in operation on June 12, 1974			4,422
Annual turnover in excess of K10,000,000			12
Annual turnover less than K50,000			2,853
Employing more than 1,000 persons			7
Employing less than five persons			2,861
Active in only one major industry group			2,937
Active in seven or more major industry groups			121

... Zero.

Note: It was necessary to allocate turnover and employment figures among activities for firms engaged in more than one major industry division. For this reason the figures should be regarded as only approximate.

Source: Papua New Guinea National Investment and Development Authority, *PNG: A Handbook for Industrialists,* pp. IV.5–6.

Table SA27. Value of New Buildings Commenced Fiscal Years 1970–76, by Ownership, Fiscal Years 1973–76, and by Type of Building (Thousands of kina)

Building type				1973		1974		1975		1976	
	1970	1971	1972	Total	Government	Total	Government	Total	Government	Total	Government
Houses and flats	12,604	11,925	8,005	8,494	4,466	6,633	4,686	9,926	7,360	8,676	7,157
Houses	9,498	8,584	5,658	7,318	4,303	6,416	4,555	8,091	7,303	8,169	7,023
Flats	3,106	3,341	2,347	1,176	163	217	131	1,835	57	507	134
Other buildings	21,750	22,423	17,256	24,104	9,396	13,618	10,245	15,518	11,318	25,276	21,674
Hostels, hotels, etc.	4,139	2,410	910	4,200	66	307	248	471	130	217	176
Shops	801	1,059	691	957	66	781	...	75	59	328	131
Offices	1,497	919	1,296	4,117	1,313	3,847	3,586	1,758	1,072	11,866	10,964
Other business premises	2,458	1,960	2,055	2,306	211	390	176	2,812	2,374	3,460	2,536
Factories	2,799	1,302	1,168	2,426	345	1,250	624	2,239	520	1,133	111
Educational	2,638	3,693	3,685	3,536	3,406	3,585	2,911	4,679	4,541	4,175	4,166
Religious	115	428	83	348	...	247	...	265	...	368	...
Health	629	2,643	3,288	990	989	390	390	988	988	860	860
Recreational	190	662	454	696	...	404	254	99	15	110	...
Indigenous staff quarters	3,010	2,109	1,397	1,078	936	77	...	74	20	40	39
Miscellaneous	3,464	5,238	2,229	3,454	2,065	2,338	2,056	2,058	1,599	2,719	2,695
Total	34,354	34,348	25,261	32,598	13,862	20,251	14,931	25,444	18,678	33,952	28,831

... Zero.

Note: The value of buildings commenced during the year is the estimated value of the buildings when complete. Figures relate to buildings in urban areas which meet the standards of various building boards and where the minimum value of work for each job is K1,000 and over. From July 1, 1968, alterations or additions of K10,000 and over are included as new buildings.

Source: Papua New Guinea Bureau of Statistics, *Building Statistics Bulletin,* various issues.

Table SA28. Number, Value, and Ownership of New Houses, Flats, and Other New Buildings, Fiscal Years 1968–75

Building type	Fiscal years							
	1968	1969	1970	1971	1972	1973	1974	1975
Commenced during period								
New houses and flats								
Number	1,664	1,824	2,128	1,684	1,336	1,273	1,732	1,928
Government	987	1,008	1,467	671	915	878		
Private	677	816	661	1,013	421	395		
Value (thousands of kina)	13,380	11,076	12,604	11,925	8,004	8,494	6,634	9,926
Government	8,131	5,343	6,965	3,914	4,565	4,466	4,686	7,360
Private	5,250	5,732	5,640	8,011	3,441	4,028	1,948	2,566
Other new buildings								
Value (thousands of kina)	13,648	19,214	21,751	22,423	17,256	24,104	13,618	15,518
Government	6,695	10,548	10,847	8,594	11,955	9,397	10,245	11,318
Private	6,954	8,665	10,905	13,829	5,303	14,709	3,370	4,200
Total, all new buildings								
Value (thousands of kina)	27,028	30,289	34,354	34,348	25,261	32,600	20,251	25,444
Government	14,825	15,890	17,811	12,509	16,519	13,863	14,931	18,678
Private	12,204	14,398	16,545	21,839	8,742	18,737	5,318	6,766
Completed during period								
New houses and flats								
Number	1,799	1,558	1,857	1,850	1,621	1,313	1,486	1,897
Value (thousands of kina)	15,250	11,237	11,613	11,610	9,636	8,474	5,802	10,123
Value of other new buildings (thousands of kina)	21,633	19,215	18,710	19,271	17,675	25,399	15,395	20,947
Value of all new buildings (thousands of kina)	36,882	30,453	30,324	30,879	27,311	33,874	21,197	31,070
Under construction at end of period								
New houses and flats								
Number	617	883	1,154	988	703	633	909	940
Value (thousands of kina)	5,095	4,946	6,073	6,396	4,832	4,892	5,751	5,547
Value of other new buildings (thousands of kina)	11,685	12,149	15,744	19,154	18,984	18,335	16,627	11,203
Value of all new buildings (thousands of kina)	16,780	17,095	21,818	25,550	23,816	23,227	22,378	16,750

Note: Figures relate to buildings in urban areas that meet the standards of various building boards and where the minimum value of work for each job is K1,000 and over. From July 1, 1968, alterations or additions of K10,000 and over are included with new buildings. The value of buildings in each category is the estimated value of the buildings when complete.

Source: Papua New Guinea Bureau of Statistics, *Building Statistics Bulletin*, various issues.

| Year | Cars[a] | Commercial motor vehicles[a] | | | | | | | Motorcycles | Tractors | Total | Registered as public motor vehicles |
		Station wagons	Light–open	Light–closed	Trucks	Other truck types	Omnibuses	Total				
1963	4,930	872	2,835	135	1,599	56	117	4,742	558	430	11,532	n.a.
1964	5,517	1,127	3,073	139	1,812	56	119	5,199	684	523	13,050	n.a.
1965	6,072	1,460	3,673	171	2,261	54	127	6,286	896	598	15,312	n.a.
1966	6,888	1,650	3,879	177	2,611	66	155	6,888	1,136	699	17,261	n.a.
1967	8,377	2,155	4,346	205	2,877	78	148	7,654	1,520	990	20,696	n.a.
1968	10,123	2,812	5,482	239	3,412	82	163	9,378	2,035	1,111	25,459	n.a.
1969	11,543	2,969	6,635	342	3,810	36	260	11,083	2,231	1,410	29,236	1,465
1970	14,634	2,880	7,410	418	4,385	78	288	12,579	2,857	1,717	34,667	1,681
	(3,085)	(791)	(2,290)	(106)	(1,377)	(27)	(102)	(3,902)	(1,197)	(533)	(9,508)	(936)
1971	14,917	4,048	8,526	436	4,959	146	388	14,455	2,994	1,749	38,163	1,515
	(3,048)	(813)	(2,355)	(133)	(1,373)	(23)	(99)	(3,983)	(1,114)	(387)	(9,345)	(596)
1972	15,673	4,384	8,345	585	5,095	204	444	14,673	3,047	1,921	39,698	1,331
	(2,709)	(732)	(1,903)	(153)	(1,336)	(46)	(136)	(3,574)	(1,099)	(404)	(8,518)	(449)
1973	14,813	4,227	8,666	648	5,137	97	529	15,077	2,949	1,940	39,006	1,601
	(1,662)	(649)	(1,921)	(126)	(921)	(10)	(172)	(3,150)	(1,073)	(314)	(6,848)	(692)
1974	13,396	3,914	9,402	662	5,582	52	700	16,395	3,395	1,863	38,966	1,852
	(1,730)	(714)	(2,660)	(134)	(1,544)	(3)	(266)	(4,607)	(1,570)	(353)	(8,974)	(753)
1975	13,908	4,015	10,608	584	5,775	54	885	17,906	3,815	1,786	41,430	2,187
	(2,056)	(806)	(2,752)	(105)	(1,455)	(2)	(275)	(4,589)	(1,712)	(410)	(9,573)	(863)
1976	(1,854)	(931)	(3,253)	(130)	(1,655)	(10)	(359)	(5,407)	(1,476)	(438)	(10,106)	(718)

n.a. Not available.

Note: Numbers in parentheses are for 1970 and after are new registrations.

a. Includes public motor vehicles.

Sources: Papua New Guinea National Investment and Development Authority, *PNG: A Handbook for Industrialists*, pp. A 2.18, A 2.19; and Papua New Guinea Bureau of Statistics, Papua New Guinea Statistical Bulletin, *Registered Motor Vehicles at 31 December 1975*, November 1976; and *Summary of New Motor Vehicles Registered – 1976*, September 1977.

Table SA30. Comparison of Consumer Price Index with Those of Selected Countries, 1971–77
(1970 = 100)

Country	1971	1972	1973	1974	1975	1976	1977	(With latest period)
Australia	106.1	112.4	122.9	141.5	162.8	184.9	205.6	(Second quarter)
Indonesia	104.0	111.0	146.0	205.0	244.0	292.0	319.0	(Second quarter)
Korea	112.1	125.5	129.3	160.0	202.0	233.1	253.7	(Second quarter)
Malaysia	101.6	104.8	115.9	136.0	142.2	145.9	150.9	(First quarter)
New Zealand	110.1	118.0	127.7	141.8	162.6	190.2	214.1	(Second quarter)
Philippines	114.6	126.3	140.3	188.4	203.4	216.0	228.9	(Second quarter)
Thailand	102.0	106.0	118.4	146.0	152.0	158.1	171.3	(Second quarter)
Papua New Guinea	105.9	112.4	121.7	150.0	165.7	178.4	183.9	(Second quarter)

Note: The official Papua New Guinea consumer price index was first issued in 1971; an index based on 1970 = 100 was constructed from the official index and data contained in *National Accounts Statistics*, 1960/61–1973/74.

Source: International Monetary Fund, *International Financial Statistics*, October 1977.

Bibliography of Recent References

Apthorpe, R. *Social Planning Indicators and Social Reporting for Papua New Guinea.* Port Moresby: Government Printer, 1975.

Clunies Ross, A., and J. Langmore, eds. *Alternative Strategies for Papua New Guinea.* Melbourne: Oxford University Press, 1973.

Conroy, J. D. *Education, Employment and Migration in Papua New Guinea.* Canberra: Development Studies Centre Publications, Australian National University, 1976.

Institute of Applied Social and Economic Research. New Guinea Research Bulletins. Various numbers. Canberra: Institute of Applied Social and Economic Research.

International Bank for Reconstruction and Development. *The Economic Development of the Territory of Papua and New Guinea.* Baltimore: Johns Hopkins Press, 1965.

Isaac, J. E. *The Structure of Unskilled Wages in Papua New Guinea.* Port Moresby: Government Printer, September 1970.

May, R. J., ed. *Research Needs and Priorities in Papua New Guinea.* Proceedings of a seminar sponsored by the Institute of Applied Social and Economic Research, March 1–3, 1976. Canberra: Institute of Applied Social and Economic Research, 1976.

Mench, P. *The Role of the Papua New Guinea Defence Force.* Canberra: Development Studies Centre Publications, Australian National University, 1976.

Mikesell, R. F. *Foreign Investment in Copper Mining.* Baltimore: Johns Hopkins University Press, 1975.

Overseas Development Group (University of East Anglia). *A Report on Development Strategies for Papua New Guinea.* February 1973.

Parker, M. L. *Papua New Guinea: An Inter-Industry Study.* Canberra: Research School of Pacific Studies, Department of Economics, Australian National University, 1973.

Sack, P. J., ed. *The Problem of Choices; Land in PNG's Future.* Canberra: Australian National University, 1974.

Smith, D. W. *Labour and the Law in Papua New Guinea.* Canberra: Development Studies Centre Publications, Australian National University, 1975.

Sturton, M. *Input/Output Model Building in Papua New Guinea.* Suva, Fiji: United Nations Development Advisory Team, April 1976.

Takeuchi, K. *Tropical Hardwood Trade in the Asia-Pacific Region.* World Bank Staff Occasional Papers no. 17. Baltimore and London: Johns Hopkins University Press, 1974.

White, K. J. *Constraints on the Development of Forest Industries in Papua New Guinea.* Port Moresby: Bureau of Statistics, February 1974.

Wilson, R. K. and W. P. Irlan, eds. *Import Analysis and Prospective Industries Study: Papua New Guinea.* Canberra: Australian Government Publishing Service, March 1972.

Papua New Guinea Official Publications

Bureau of Statistics. *Catalogue of Statistical Information on Papua New Guinea.* Port Moresby: Bureau of Statistics, February 1974.

———. *Papua New Guinea National Accounts Statistics, 1960/ 61–1973/74.* Port Moresby: Government Printer, November 1974.

Central Planning Office. *National Development Strategy.* Port Moresby: Government Printer, October 27, 1976.

———. *Programmes and Performance, 1976–77.* Port Moresby: Government Printer, August 1976.

———. *Strategy for Nationhood: Policies and Issues.* Port Moresby: Government Printer, 1974.

Department of Forests. *Annual Report 1972–73.* Port Moresby, Government Printer, 1973.

———. "Facts and Information." Paper compiled by Economics Branch, Department of Forests, Port Moresby, December 1975.

———. *New Horizons, Forestry in Papua New Guinea.* Brisbane: Jacaranda Press Pty. Ltd., 1973.

Department of Labor. *Income and Expenditure Survey of Local Public Servants, July 1970.* Vol. 1. Port Moresby: Government Printer, February 1971.

Housing Commission. *National Housing Plan.* Part One. Port Moresby: Government Printer, October 1975.

Interdepartmental Committee. *Incomes, Wages and Prices Policy.* Port Moresby: Government Printer, February 1974.

Ministry of Labor, Commerce and Industry. *National Investment Strategy.* Port Moresby: Government Printer, November 1976.

National Investment and Development Authority. *Framework for Industrial Development in Papua New Guinea.* Port Moresby: Government Printer, September 1975.

————. *Papua New Guinea: A Handbook for Industrialists.* Port Moresby: Government Printer, December 1975.

————. *Papua New Guinea Second National Investment Priorities Schedule.* Port Moresby: Government Printer, December 1975.

Papua New Guinea Government. *Statement on Petroleum Policy and Legislation.* Port Moresby: Government Printer, March 1976.

0